To Angela.
I hope you enjoy

Jeremy Aaben.

John Porter.

Legendary Trainer and his Legacy,

Newbury Racecourse.

Compiled and Written

by

Jeremy Barber.

Dedication.

This book is dedicated to my wife, Margarete, whose gift of the letters became the catalyst for it being written. Her support and enthusiasm for the project has been boundless.

Acknowledgements.

Very many people have helped me with the production of this book and I thank them all.
Rebecca, Nick, Helena,Tim and Charles for their differing inputs.
Lorraine for taking my handwritten scripts and turning them into readable computerised print.
Michael Frost for his photography.
Tim Cox, Trustee of The National Horse Racing Museum.
Julian Thick and Claire Ricketts from Newbury Racecourse Limited.
Brough Scott from The Injured Jockeys Fund.
Jonathan Pease.
Nick Smith for his cover design.
Keith and Amanda of Thumbnail Media.

Author's Notes.

The original Archive of letters will be donated to The National Horse Racing Museum at Palace House, Newmarket for safekeeping and availability for possible future reference or research.

Proceeds from sales of the book will be donated to The Injured Jockeys Fund in recognition of the support, care and rehabilitation given to Tim Sprake, who, as a claiming apprentice rode our first horse to win his first race on 28th April 1992. Sadly Tim's career was to be ended some years later as a result of an accident.

Another Book on Horse Racing!

For many years the followers of horse racing have been offered books on the subject. These commenced with the Racing Calendar and as racing became more accessible to the public at large, the variety of publications has grown to cover biographies and autobiographies of owners, trainers, jockeys and horses, histories of race courses and much else. The growth of writing and interest has expanded proportionately with the changes in ownership formerly dominated by a relatively small number of wealthy, or sometimes not so wealthy, private owners.

As of today, with the expansion of owner syndication, the growth of the betting industry, televised racing and the changes in the attitude of racecourse owners, with their Ladies Days and other themed attractions, the public attendance at meetings has grown and with it the market for books. The concept for this one, commenced with a pile of loose papers purchased by my wife from a second hand bookseller, allegedly having connection and reference to John Porter, the legendary Kingsclere trainer. In total there were nearly four hundred documents.

As a start and to get some semblance of order, it was necessary to try and identify who had written them – either from the addresses or signatures, the latter not always being readily identifiable, for as is so to this day, some peoples handwriting leaves much to be desired. However, it became evident that this "pile of loose papers" was a veritable archive, on the one hand covering Royal connections, peers of the realm and leading members of society – some clearly owners of horses trained by Porter, others, with whom he became friends through his interest in matters other than racing, agriculture and horticulture. A separate collection of letters in the main are from military personnel, relating to patronage of early meetings at Newbury – the course designed and built under Porter's guidance following his retirement from training. A third collection are letters within the family, which give a deeper insight of the family than anything in either of Porter's two autobiographies.

As a result of reading through these papers many times, the idea grew that other people might find their content equally fascinating and that they could be the basis for a quite different book on racing. My hope is that once read - you the reader will agree.

I am indebted to the original writers and to their families who will not be aware of the existence of these letters.

The format of the book does not always follow in chronological order, but is made up of four separate sections:
1   John Porter
2   Owners, friends and acquaintances
3   Newbury Racecourse
4   The Porter family

John Porter – quote from the Hon. George Lambton's book:
"Porter trained more winners of the Derby than any other man. Besides the Duke of Westminster, he at one time trained for King Edward, the Prince of Wales, Lord Alington, Sir Frederick Johnstone, Baron Hirsch, Mr Gretton and others. Year after year great winners came from Kingsclere. He was the most unassuming of men, practically never betted, a great believer in hard work for men and horses, and when a horse trained by him came to the front in a race, a quarter mile from home, it was a rare thing for him to be beaten.

He gave up training, greatly to the regret of all racing people, but he did not give up work, for he put his energy into the construction and management of Newbury Race Course, the success of which is notable".
From "Men and Horses I have known" by the Hon. George Lambton 1924

SECTION ONE

John Porter

John Porter was born on 2nd March 1838 at Rugeley in Staffordshire. Nearby was Cannock Chase, which provided excellent gallops for the racehorses trained at Hednesford.

The Porter family had lived in the area for over a century. His father John was a tailor by trade, his mother a dressmaker. Amongst his father's friends were trainers located at Hednesford. Saunders was an especially close friend, but Walters (who was one of John Porter's godfathers) was another. His second godfather was Charles Marlow, the jockey who rode The Flying Dutchman to victory in the 1849 Derby.

Walters was trainer to William Taylor Copeland, an alderman, Lord Mayor and MP. The latter gave commissions to John Frederick Herring Sr. to paint his racehorses and also offered him a house on his Essex estate.

A good school friend of John Porter at this time was Tom Ashmall who went on to be a jockey, winning the Two Thousand Guineas on The Wizard in 1861. John Porter spent a good deal of time with Tom at his home, Fairwell Hall. Sometimes they went to Tom's uncle, Tom Carr, who trained at Hednesford. Stays of 2 to 3 days were not uncommon and it was here that John Porter started his lifelong relationship with horses. Coinciding with these visits, John Porter frequently came in to contact with his father's good friend Saunders, who was related to the Ashmalls.

The importance of being with these people, was that John Porter became familiar with thoroughbreds, the regime of racing stables and the way that they were run. It was the catalyst for his future career.

Around 1848, his father's business took the whole family to London, but fortunately in 1850 they returned to Rugeley. Aged 14, John Porter left school – his father wanting him to become a lawyer. However, before this course of training was arranged, John Porter was allowed a holiday which he spent with his father's friend Saunders, at his stables. Days turned into weeks and weeks into months. John Porter grew more and more interested in the horses that Saunders trained. Amongst the owners were Mr James Merry and William Palmer, who was the Porters family doctor, but who later gained notoriety as "Palmer the Poisoner" and was hanged for murder.

With this extended holiday and the increasing appeal of open air life, the idea of an office bound career became less and less appealing to Porter.

He met at this time Robert Denman, one of Saunders nephews, who was to become a lifelong friend and later pursued a very successful training career in France as private trainer to Mr Edmond Blanc.

In 1853 at the behest of Porter's mother, his father made clear his current lifestyle could not continue. Porter's response was to reply to an advertisement for a light weight jockey at the stables of John Day, who trained at Michel Grove, near Worthing for Mr Padwick. In response he received a letter asking him to go to Michel Grove at once for an interview. The interview was a success and John Day agreed to a three year apprenticeship

It is not unreasonable to surmise that this positive response was very much the result of his having learnt a great deal from Walters, Carr and Saunders, which John Porter was able to demonstrate in his interview.

An early indication of Porter's attention to detail and having things done correctly was that at aged 15, he drew up his indentures himself and presented them to John Day for his signature. A trait of character that was to serve him so well in his later career.

Porter was fortunate that John Day had gained a fine reputation, including the nomenclature "Honest John" and he was greatly admired by most prominent men in the world of racing. John Porter certainly considered himself fortunate to work for him. They evidently got on very well, even to the extent of sitting together in church and for all his life John Porter was associated closely to his local churches. Porter learnt much from him – not only the need for early rising, the welfare for others – discipline in the yard – no swearing or smoking but above all be "respectful to the peer as courteous to the peasant".

Porter's weight was a mere 4st 10lbs. John Day tutored him well in the saddle and his riding improved. He also learnt much from watching the senior jockeys. In 1855 he rode his first winner at Brighton, beating both George Fordham, a top rider at the time, and also his old school friend Tom Ashinall. In 1856 he had but two rides, both unsuccessful. He did not race again until 1858 when he rode an unconsidered outsider in the Derby, which broke down at Tattenham Corner. He did not race ride again. Well before this he had decided not to pursue a career as a jockey.

During his years with John Day, John Porter handled and observed many horses, the most notable of which he records in his autobiography. It also brought him into contact with a variety of owners and afforded him the opportunity to see the interaction of owners and trainers. The most impressive of which was the rupture between Mr Padwick and John Day and John's son William with his owner Mr Merry.

Shortly before the rupture with Mr Padwick, John Day had moved from Michel Grove to Findon – currently the base of Nick Gifford who succeeded his father Josh Gifford, who in turn had taken over from Capt. Ryan Price – all trainers of steeplechasers. Reference is made to steeplechasers being trained there in John Porter's autobiography in 1914.

John Day died in 1860 but prior to this John Porter had not only continued with his work as an apprentice in a training stable, he had also assisted John Day in the keeping of his books and other clerical tasks.

On the personal side of his life, it was in Findon that he met and married his first wife – Miss Moodie. He was also able to indulge his horticultural interests – which intensified in following years. But above all he was able to further his learning of the details of the trainers' art.

At this time Mr Padwick appointed William Goater as his private trainer, and John Day joined his son, William, at Woodyates. After John Day's departure, John Porter's duties increased and he acted officially not only as secretary of the stables – but as manager. This, despite being just seventeen years old. With John Day's departure – John Porter's apprenticeship ended.
John Porter was clearly an outstanding employee for his age and very well thought of by Mr Padwick who was content to lodge money, for the running of the stables, at the bank in John Porter's name. John Porter paid all the bills and wages and kept the books. In addition to this secretarial work John Porter acted as head man to Goater, being responsible for the feeding of the horses, looking after the other lads and their welfare and medicating the horses when necessary. In short, everything other than the training of the horses – which Goater did. John Porter did however 'do' one horse. He would also involve himself in the 'breaking in' of yearlings.

There is no question that this dedication and passion for all the aspects of his work was noticed by owners and visitors to the stables and John Porter acknowledges that this largely contributed to the advancement of his career in the following years.

Mr Padwick owned a house in Findon run by a caretaker. In this, John Porter had rooms and instead of rent, paid for the schooling of the caretaker's son. John Porter also rented a garden near the house, at which he indulged his horticultural interests. The excess fruit and vegetables he distributed among the villagers.

Mr Padwick was a solicitor, who lived in Horsham. His racing interests were run as a business and John Porter was expected to be able to show him, from the books, exactly how he stood.

William Goater was one of three brothers who had worked for John Day's son, William, at Woodyates. William Goater's brothers had both ridden, William had not. John Porter considered William Goater a good trainer and a first- rate stableman, who was very conscientious. John Porter and William had an excellent working relationship and William never showed any resentment at the younger John Porter being placed over him. John Porter acknowledges that he believed William Goater was relieved that he did not have to be bothered with all the work he did.

During the second half of the 1870's Mr Padwick severed his connections with the Findon Stables and died in 1879. John Porter and William Goater remained at Findon – the stable now becoming a 'public' one. John Porter continued doing all the work that he had undertaken in Mr Padwick's time and William Goater provided the money. Everything continued to run smoothly as a result of the successful way in which the stable had been conducted after John Day's retirement, this ensured continuous patronage.

Amongst the owners was Lord Westmoreland who joined the stable in 1861, aged 26. He became a very good friend to John Porter, there being just a three year age gap between them.

1863 was an important year. John Porter was in charge of Mr Saville's horse – The Ranger. Although finishing unplaced in the Derby, he took it to Paris and won the first running of the Grand Prix de Paris. The Ranger was a bad mover and when looked at by Lord Strathmore before the race in which his own horse Saccharometer was also to run, Lord Strathmore said to John Porter "Why, the beggar cannot even trot" to which Porter replied, having found out that Saccharometer was not eating up, "Never mind that my Lord – he can eat". The next day The Ranger won, ridden by Jim Goater, William Goater's brother. The prize for this first running of the race was £5240 in addition to a cup, donated by the Emperor Napoleon. After the race John Porter was presented to the Emperor and Empress. Mr Saville's health was drunk that evening out of the cup.

It was during this time that Porter met George Fordham, the jockey, as he was used by some of Findon's owners. In later years Porter and Fordham became close friends. Up until the late 1890's in Porter's view good English jockeys, like Fordham, were plentiful with a few standing out by reason of their superlative abilities. From the late 1890's to the second decade of the twentieth century Porter deplored the fact that owners had to go to America and Australia for the best jockeys. The reason for this Porter believed was that apprentice jockeys were not given sufficient encouragement nor were they given the riding opportunities they required.

Porter very strongly believed that it was essential for a jockey to 'know' a horse in order to get the best out of it. Horses, like humans, he felt, differ in temperament and disposition. In Porter's career he picks out 3 jockeys whom he credited as 'geniuses'. George Fordham, Fred Archer and Tom Sloan. All three had different riding styles and techniques, but in their different ways, were able to get the best from their mounts.

John Porter was well liked in Findon and was always a welcome visitor in any house. He was a religious man and got on well with the vicar, Dr Cholmondeley who prepared him for confirmation and also conducted his marriage. Findon had been a good time for Porter and he had honed his skills in all facets of the work involved in taking control of a racing stable.

Around the end of 1862, now aged 24 and recently married, Porter considered he was suitably equipped to take full control of a training establishment in his own right. He had gained a wealth of knowledge during his years with John Day and William Goater, which added to his own attributes of hard work and attention to detail, as well as his ability to get on with people from all levels of society, augured well for his future career.

It came to his notice that Mr Saville, a patron of the Findon stables, might be looking for a private trainer. In that they already knew one another Porter felt that any approach he made to Saville might be agreeably received. However he decided, before so doing, to have a word with Lord Westmoreland with whom he had struck up a good relationship. Westmoreland advised him against approaching Saville, assuring Porter that he would be able to find him a post, presumably at a higher level than working for Saville. Porter took his advice and was content to wait. Westmoreland was as good as his word and effected an introduction to Sir Joseph Hawley in July 1863.

Westmoreland had been aware that Hawley's private trainer George Manning, was suffering long term illness. Manning's stables were at Cannon Heath, near Kingsclere. John Porter was asked to visit Hawley at his London residence, 34 Eaton Place. This he did en route to Liverpool with horses that were entered there. On being ushered in to Hawley's presence, he presented him with a letter from Westmoreland. Hawley after reading its content, looked at Porter with incredulity and asked if he was indeed the John Porter referred to. Porter confirmed that he was and asked to be given the chance to manage the horses. It should be noted that Porter himself thought he looked only about eighteen, although he was just 25 and a married man. Despite his apparent incredulity, Hawley asked him to call and see him again on his way back from Liverpool. This Porter did, and to his great happiness found that Hawley had virtually decided to give him a chance.

Arrangements were made for Porter to accompany Hawley on a visit to Cannon Heath to view the stables. Porter was horrified by what they found. The buildings were full of cobwebs, the yards overgrown with weeds and anywhere he looked there was untidiness and neglect. "Come back in a fortnight Sir Joseph and I will show you a difference" Porter said.

The head lad at Cannon Heath was much older than Porter and was resentful of his appointment. Porter had him ride out with him initially so that he could learn the geography of his new surroundings. On the fourth day, Porter informed him that rather than have him ride out, he wanted him to stay at the yard to clear all the cobwebs and remove all the weeds in the yard. The head lad did not take kindly to this instruction and told Porter he did not think he would suit him. Porter replied that if he felt cobwebs and weeds had a place in a yard, he certainly would not be suitable. However, if he was prepared to work with him and follow his requirements, there would be no reason why they should not get on well. Porter also told him that there was only going to be one master and that was Porter. The head lad accepted the situation and became a good worker. Porter had made his requirements quite plain. When Sir Joseph Hawley made his next visit, he noted the changes and told Porter "all right, you will do". This signalled the end of Porter's association with the stables at Findon where he had been since 1859.

Now, aged 25 and married he found himself the private trainer to Sir Joseph Hawley and launched on a more or less independent career. Prior to Porter's becoming his private trainer, Sir Joseph Hawley had accomplished a great deal on the turf. Initially he struck Porter as being stern and someone he could find difficult to please. As they became closer and worked together the more Porter came to like him.

When Porter took control at Cannon Heath at the end of July 1863, there were just twelve horses in the yard. For some years Sir Joseph had been breeding all or nearly all of the horses he raced.

His stud was at Leybourne Grange, Leybourne, between West Malling and Aylesford in Kent He stabled about twelve broad mares. There were several excellent paddocks and the whole enterprise was maintained in excellent order by his stud groom, Tweed. Porter made it a routine to visit the stud to review the foals and yearlings at least once a year. During Sir Joseph's life he could not remember ever receiving more than six yearlings in a season and Sir Joseph in that time rarely bought in horses.

September 1863 saw Porter's first attendance at a race meeting as a trainer. He won two races with Sir Joseph's home bred horses. One of them was ridden by Wells, a jockey that Sir Joseph retained at a fee of £100 per annum. Coincidentally £100 per annum was Porter's salary. Luckily for both, Sir Joseph was very liberal with his gifts. Porter was pleased to have the services of Wells as they were old friends and he trusted him without question.

At the end of September, Porter had another winner which is illustrative of his understanding of horses. St Alexis had been considered as too difficult to have any further value as a racehorse, so he had used him as a hack, which relaxed the horse. As Porter records he humoured the horse as much as possible, allowing him to stand around on the training ground watching the other horses do their work. Relaxed, St Alexis quietened down. Sir Joseph was delighted when he ran at Newmarket and won. The commerciality of the situation was that having won, he became saleable, which Sir Joseph arranged. For his new owner he won 3 races the following year.

Unhappily for Porter, he had joined Sir Joseph at a time when Sir Joseph's turf fortunes were at a low ebb. The three winners of the Autumn of 1863 brought prize money of £2180. The three succeeding years brought in £2485, £3360 and £1425.

Sir Joseph was a very patient man in this regard and recognised also that the horses coming from his Leybourne stud were moderate. The fates were however to change for the better.

In 1863, Sir Joseph had purchased a half share in a colt named Bedminster. Aged two, he showed considerable promise but disappointed with an unplaced run in the Champagne Stakes. The following month at Newmarket he won two races in two days and Porter felt he had classic potential. This feeling was further strengthened when he won his first race as a three year old, the following spring. He ran in the 2000 Guineas, but was unplaced. Hope springs eternal in racing and Porter and Sir Joseph hoped he would make amends in the Derby, but prior to that being run he broke down during a trial at Cannon Heath. Porter did everything he could to get the horse right for the Derby, sadly he broke down again during the race. As the figures above show, 1864 was not to be a good year.

For Porter it became worse. In September at the Doncaster meeting, he suffered a severe attack of typhoid fever. For a number of days he admits to being very ill indeed, but thanks to the nursing care of his wife and the presence of a very good doctor, he made a complete recovery.

At the start of his illness, Porter's wife was at Cannon Heath. Sir Joseph had written to her, assuring her that her husband was in good hands. She travelled to Doncaster none the less. She kept in close touch with Sir Joseph who strongly recommended that as soon as Porter was well enough, his wife should take him to the seaside for a few days rather than go home. As soon as Porter was well enough, he wrote to Sir Joseph and got the following reply:-

"I am delighted to see your handwriting again, as that proves to me how much better you are. I am going to Dover's tomorrow and to Cannon Heath on Friday. I saw from the first your illness must be tedious and that made me send some of the horses to Dover as I thought it would be too much of a charge for Harry… I shall write again on Saturday.

Do not fret about the horses' and I shall do nothing to the back yard till your return. Now take my advice – the moment you can move from Doncaster, go to the seaside somewhere. You will regain your strength there ten times as quickly as you would at Cannon Heath.   Ask the doctor if I am not right. Write to me if you want money and tell me where you are going".

This letter emphasises the good heartedness that Porter always felt was a trait of Sir Joseph and which appealed to him so strongly.

Kingsclere.

Prior to Porter's illness, Sir Joseph had decided to build new stables at Kingsclere – within a mile or two of Cannon Heath. The land had previously been purchased, but no plans had been prepared. Porter was very keen that the architect should incorporate the ideas that he had formed as a result of his involvement with Michel Grove, Findon and Cannon Heath, also from his engagement with the stables prior to his apprenticeship. Porter whilst he was convalescing obtained a drawing board, T square, pencils and paper and prepared a set of plans. The stables when constructed were very similar to his plans. Whereas many stables including Cannon Heath were conversions from farm buildings, Kingsclere provided purpose built racing stables.

Porter, having taken Sir Joseph's advice, went to the seaside once he was well enough to leave Doncaster. He returned to Cannon Heath at Christmas – there were no horses. They were at Ilsley with Jim Dover and remained there until March, when he felt fully fit. He was out of training for six months. 1865 and 1866 were quiet years.

In 1867 and whilst still at Cannon Heath, the new stables at Kingsclere not yet completed, saw a resurgence for Porter in the quality of horses. Blue Gown, Rosicrucian and Green Sleeves had arrived. All three were home bred at Leybourne by Sir Joseph and all sired by his Derby winner Beadsman.

Blue Gown won the Champagne Stakes, the most prestigious race for 2 year olds, but was disqualified as the jockey Wells, when weighing out, had had the tip of one foot on the ground, which gave an incorrect reading of the scale. He could not do the same when weighing in after the race. Sir Joseph refused to speak to Wells after the race - he had lost £4000 by the disqualification. He ordered Wells to see him the following morning, adding that his services would not be required again that week. For Porter this whole saga was a huge disappointment, as he had always had implicit trust in Wells. Wells did not ride again for Sir Joseph until October, when he rode an excellent race to win a Match at Newmarket. Sir Joseph forgave him his stupidity at Doncaster and his relationship with Sir Joseph was rekindled.

Porter's horses had a very successful Autumn – taking eight horses to Newmarket including the 2-year olds, Blue Gown, Rosicrucian and Green Sleeves, who between them won 5 races. Sir Joseph was anxious about travelling the horses, particularly the 2-year olds. They all travelled to Waterloo and were then walked across London to Bishopsgate Street. Sir Joseph headed the procession in his brougham. Porter was at the tail end, on his hack. Vans and cabs were constantly passing and it opened Sir Joseph's eyes to the risks that Porter, his staff and horses ran when travelling to the race meetings. Porter ran both Green Sleeves and Rosicrucian in the Middle Park Stakes and they finished first and second.

Rosicrucian was ridden by Huxtable, who thought he had won, but Green Sleeves was adjudged the winner – deceived by the finish line across the width of the track at Newmarket.

Following this successful meeting, Porter and entourage returned direct to Kingsclere having finally vacated the stables at Cannon Heath. The plans which he had drawn up during his convalescence in 1864 -1865 had become bricks and mortar. Park House, Kingsclere had come into being and was to remain his home for all the time he trained – that is to say until 1905. This is from 1867 to 1905 – a period of 38 years. In 1867 Park House was a mere cottage for Porter and his family and there were just 14 boxes for the horses. By 1905 it had been much extended.

Sir Joseph died in 1875, some eight years after the move to Kingsclere. In his will he stipulated that Porter was to be given the option to purchase Park House for just £4000 – approximately half of what it had cost. He exercised the option and as the stables developed had spent a further £20,000 on improvements by the time he sold up in 1905.

Porter was a religious man and the Church of St Mary's at the centre of the village held many precious and personal memories for him. He helped to add suitably to it and its ancient history by assisting the vicar, a good friend, including stained glass windows in the North transept. The surprisingly large church for a village charmed him by its simplicity, imposing tower and the magnificent views from the top of the tower.

One of the tombstones in the church yard is that of the jockey John Wells, who had been such a good and generally reliable rider for Porter and Sir Joseph Hawley.

In retrospect the move from Cannon Hall to Kingsclere had possibly been made too hastily. The consequence was that the horses suffered badly from a series of influenza, coughs and colds. Porter felt the cause to be dampness of the new boxes, where walls sweated badly as there had not been time enough for them to properly dry out.

Early in 1868, Mannington, the Brighton vet, was called in and he inserted setons in the throats of Rosicrucian and Green Sleeves, which were removed only three weeks prior to their runs in the 2000 Guineas. Blue Gown was also to run, but because of an error, did not. Mr George Henning, who at that time worked Sir Joseph's commissions, had, due to a misunderstanding laid heavily against Blue Gown and the horse was withdrawn because Sir Joseph did not want his agent to be placed in an awkward situation. George Henning sometimes visited Kingsclere and was godfather to Porter's second daughter. In later life, he became a very wealthy man, making much of his fortune in the City, where he was an associate of Baron von Hirsch.

Because of their ill health over the winter, neither Rosicrucian nor Green Sleeves ran well in the 2000 Guineas and Blue Gown had been beaten at the Craven Meeting because his plates had been put on too tight.

Porter and Sir Joseph planned a trial on the Downs. To avoid the touts getting knowledge of this, Sir Joseph travelled to Whitchurch rather than Overton or Newbury, his normal routes to Kingsclere and which were watched by reporters. A trap met him at Whitchurch and took him straight to the downs. At Kingsclere there were other problems as the touts had learnt that the trial was to be on the morning of May 12th. Unfortunately for them, but happily for Porter and Sir Joseph, they had taken possession of an old toll-house on the Overton Road for the night of May 11th. Unknown to them, one of Porter's staff had knowledge of this and knew that there was a chain and staple on the toll-house door. He fastened it with a padlock. By taking a diversionary route to the Downs on the morning of May 12th, they arrived there without disturbing the touts. The trial was held, with Rosicrucian beating Blue Gown – a neck, over one and a quarter miles. Sir Joseph in general did not object to the touts/reporters and felt it was good they had interest in his horses and their trades, but on this occasion he enjoyed the joke played at their expense.

Blue Gown won the Derby by half a length. Porter admits to being euphoric – this his first classic win. It was a great day for Kingsclere. That autumn at Doncaster, the Marquis of Hastings asked Porter if he would train the best two of his horses – Lady Elizabeth and the Earl. He replied that he could not give him an answer until he had consulted with Sir Joseph. Hawley said that his preference was that he should not train for the Marquis.

Porter was aware that many younger members of the aristocracy, like the Marquis, wished to outdo one another by gambling. Many were ruined. Porter's comment on this was that he had never countenanced gambling. He firmly believed that horse racing could very well be enjoyed without betting.

That year Blue Gown went on to win other races, including the Ascot Cup and the Cambridgeshire. One commentator noted "Blue Gown's running makes him out the best horse we have seen for a great number of years".

There were at times criticism of 'race-starts'. Porter's thoughts on this were that flag starts had well been stopped. The 'gate start' he felt was less favourable to a big horse, as he felt such animals needed longer to get into stride than smaller ones, when at a standing start. He thought that 'walk up' starts should have been given a fairer trial.

In the three years 1867 – 1868 – 1869 the horses Porter trained for Sir Joseph Hawley won stakes worth £52,697. A number of lean years followed and it was not until 1878 that Kingsclere achieved another five figure value in stakes won. Sir Joseph had died in 1875.

In the years following 1869, Sir Joseph's wealth went into decline, as did his interest in his own horses, though not in racing itself.

In 1869 and 1870 Sir Joseph became an advocate of Turf Reform. These proposals brought him into direct conflict with Admiral Rous, amongst others, amongst Sir Joseph's supporters was Mr Henry Chaplin. One of Sir Joseph's proposals was that 2 year olds should not be allowed to race before September 1st. Porter's view was that small horses could run in May, larger horses not until September. To run them any earlier would undoubtedly necessitate training them during frosted ground followed by heavy ground as the frost breaks down. Porter considered galloping young horses on heavy ground, most injurious. He preferred not to run two - year olds before June, in part because the Kingsclere gallops generally would not allow horses to be ready before then. The rule enacted in 1869 that stopped two year olds running before 1st May was abolished in 1873.

Due to Sir Joseph's ill health, Kingsclere was reduced to very small numbers in 1871 and the following year his connection with the Turf practically ceased. In 1873 nearly all Sir Joseph's horses in training, brood mares, yearlings and foals were sold. Sir Joseph clearly understood, as did his friends that his life was ebbing away. Following his last visit to Kingsclere, Porter found the stump of a cigar on the mantelpiece which he carefully stored and was still in his possession in 1919. Sir Joseph died in the Spring of 1875 and was buried at Leybourne.

Porter attended the funeral and felt that he was bidding goodbye to a really great man and to a man who had been a noble friend of him and his family. According to Porter, racing at that time had few supporters who can stand comparison with Sir Joseph, who had always had the highest interests of racing at heart. Though sometimes misunderstood, his critics were ready to forgive, as at the end of the day they understood he was driven by principles he believed to be right and fair.

At meetings of the Jockey Club, Porter recalls Sir Joseph was always 'Stern, straight and fearless'. He, more than most, recognised that Sir Joseph had a softer side, demonstrated from the early days with his interest in Porter's welfare when he had typhoid fever, right through to his visits to Kingsclere, when his first concern was for Porter and his family's wellbeing, in advance of the state of his horses. Sir Joseph was also a very generous man.

It was a matter of great satisfaction to Porter that many of Sir Joseph's greatest triumphs were associated with the enterprise at Kingsclere.

All the horses Porter won races with from when he went to Cannon Heath in 1863 up to 1873, were owned by Sir Joseph Hawley, with the exception of XI which was partly owned by Sir Frederick Johnstone.

The year 1873 was one of important change in patronage at Kingsclere. Porter took charge of horses belonging to Mr Frederick Gretton and Mr Thomas Eades Walker. The former having previously had his horses trained by Matt Dawson at Newmarket. The latter had horses trained by Captain Machell – also at Newmarket. Welcome as the patronage of these two was, in real terms it did not amount to much in the way of turf success. Kingsclere was from 1873 to 1875, not doing very well.

It was in 1875 that Porter took up the option to buy Park House and the land surrounding it, that had been given to him in Sir Joseph Hawley's Will.

From 1875, Porter became a public trainer. At the end of 1874 Mr Walker disposed of his horses. The stable had the horses of Mr Frederick Gretton only, plus two of Frederick's younger brother John Gretton as his patrons from 1875 to 1878. Fortunately Mr Frederick had enlarged his racing stud. The two most noteworthy that Porter trained were Pageant and Isonomy – neither bred by their owner. Porter comments that they were two of the few good horses he trained that were not bred by his patrons.

In the Summer of 1876, Porter visited the Yardley Stud near Birmingham to view the yearlings. This stud was run by two brothers George and Tony Graham and their sister, who was very active in the management. The two brothers were corn merchants by trade and supplied the Bass Brewery with barley. Mr Fred Gretton was not only one of Porter's owners, but also a director of the Brewery. Amongst the twenty yearlings, Porter was particularly drawn to the smallest – a bay colt, but a late foal being born in May. Having had this preliminary look, he was determined to purchase the colt at the forthcoming Doncaster sales. During the return journey to Birmingham with the Grahams, it was decided the colt should be named Isonomy, which translates as 'an equal distribution of rights and privileges'. It suited well, as though small, the colt showed he felt equal to the other horses.

At the Doncaster sales, Isonomy was purchased on behalf of Mr Gretton for 360 guineas. He never grew to more than 15.2 hands, but displayed the qualities of resolution and grit allied to a very hardy constitution. Porter brought Isonomy along with care and he did not race until August of 1877. As a two year old, he ran only three times. As a three- year old he ran only once as Mr Gretton did not want him to run in the Classics, that was in the Cambridgeshire which he won readily in a field of 38. It is recorded that he backed him to win £40,000.00. A goodly reward for the patience shown in his training.

Isonomy was foaled in May and was always small – it was Mr Gretton's wish that he was given time to mature – a policy that paid off. The owners patience was rewarded and it backed up   Porter's belief that many numbers of horses are ruined by being unduly forced to run as two - year olds and even as three- year olds. He believed that though some were unharmed by being run every horse is a law to itself and each should be treated accordingly. Isonomy showed this attitude to be so right, winning six of the eight races he ran as a four year old. As a five year old she ran twice, winning both – the Manchester Cup and the Ascot Cup. It was that year that Porter comments on the practice of owners rewarding the jockey, whilst overlooking their trainer. It came to a head when Porter was requested to tell Tom Cannon the jockey for the Manchester Cup that he was on £1000 to nothing if he won. No indication was made to Porter that he might be similarly rewarded, especially as he had saddled many good winners for Fred Gretton in the past, but had not even received a 'thank you'.

Porter admits to being very upset at what he considered was indifference to the services he gave. He decided that he must confront Fred Gretton on the matter and informed Gretton's factotum, John Princep of the facts, telling him that if he was not equally treated, Gretton could remove all his horses from Kingsclere the following Monday, also telling Princep that he would call on Fred Gretton at his hotel the following day. That Porter did act before having the chance to speak, brought an assurance from Gretton that he was to be treated equally with Cannon.

Porter always maintained that it was grossly unfair of owners to treat their jockeys more liberally than their trainers. If a trainer is able to present a horse at the post thoroughly fit then the credit for success belongs mainly to him. A jockey can and often does, undo in a minute the work of many weeks.

Porter remarks that if he had been dependant after his retirement on the money he made as a trainer, he would have been poor.

The agreement he had with Sir Joseph Hawley gave him a salary of £100 per annum plus a house, at commencement. The salary was raised and he was the beneficiary of handsome presents when big races were won. As he relates, he had to work hard. The assured income being modest, whilst he had a wife and family to provide for.

In 1881 Isonomy started at stud. Fred Gretton died two years later in 1883 and Isonomy was sold at Tattersalls to Mr Stirling Crawford, husband of the Duchess of Montrose. Isonomy's record at stud was splendid – he bred 254 winners that won £205,000 in prize money. In Porter's view, he was one of the best horses with which he was involved and he thought the world of him.

Porter trained two horses for Fred Gretton that were entered in the Liverpool Autumn Cup – Fernandez and Prestonpans. Both being prepared for the race, the former having the better form. Gretton placed a lot of money on Prestonpans to win leaving the declaration of which horse was to run until the last minute. Fernandez did not run. Following the race, the public showed animosity to the winner and connections en route to the unsaddling enclosure. Porter found this a totally disagreeable experience and was deeply upset by the whole episode. He took the decision to sever all connection with Mr Fred Gretton and asked him to remove all his horses from Kingsclere.

It was a big setback for Porter to lose so many horses, but he felt deeply that he could not afford a repetition of such manouvering. He did not entirely blame Fred Gretton, but felt it was the people around him that bore the responsibility, as Porter believed they acted in their own interests, rather than in Gretton's.

1881 saw the start of an extremely prosperous period at Kingsclere. Porter was entrusted with Lord Stamford's horses and also those of Lord Alington and Sir Frederick Johnstone. In the late Autumn, Porter was asked by the Duke of Westminster to take over the yearlings and the horses that had previously been trained by Robert Peck at Russley. Porter was able to direct the stables attention to Classic races rather than handicaps, also the important weight for age races. As he put it – 'The Hawley touch' had returned. Lord Stamford's patronage was to be short lived – he died in 1882. However, in 1881, Porter had purchased the filly Geheimniss on behalf of Lord Stamford from Tom Cannon. Following her purchase in the spring of 1881, she won four races for Lord Stamford, worth £3414. In 1882, Geheimniss won the Oaks. Sadly by the end of 1882, Lord Stamford had died. He was a generous man to Porter when his horses won, and gave him instructions that when his horses won – every lad at the stable was to receive a sovereign.

Following Lord Stamford's passing – Geheimniss was leased to Lord Alington and Sir Frederick Johnstone. As a four year old she won four races for them from eight starts. In total she ran in 31 races, winning 20 of them, a remarkable record.
Lord Alington and Sir Frederick Johnstone became known as 'The Old Firm' because of the length and durability of their partnership. They joined Kingsclere during 1881, Sir Frederick having previously been associated with it through his partnership with Sir Joseph Hawley in the horse XI.

Previously their horses had been trained near Lord Alington's home, Crichel, by Percy at Pimperne near Dorchester

At the close of the 1881 season, Robert Peck of Russley retired as a trainer and it was then that the Duke of Westminster sent his horses to Porter at Kingsclere. Amongst them was a magnificent but underdeveloped filly – Shotover, her dam by coincidence was Stray Shirt, one of the last animals bred by Sir Joseph Hawley. Porter notes that at first sight the Duke did not like the look of Shotover and it was agreed that Robert Peck would take her over at the price he had paid for her. Some time later the Duke changed his mind and repurchased her from Peck. To ascertain whether she might win the 2000 and 1000 Guineas, she was given a trial, in which she finished a close up third. In the 2000 Guinea she ran well and won – two days later, she ran again in 1000 Guineas, but the earlier race had taken too much out of her and she finished a close second. A month later she ran in the Derby, ridden by Tom Cannon and won by three quarters of a length. The Duke was delighted to win the Derby for the second time having won it in 1880 with Bend Or.

It was a matter of great good fortune that in the first batch of horses the Duke had sent to Porter, was this classic winner.

Following the filly's failure in 1000 Guineas – it coming too soon after her win in the 2000 Guineas, Porter and the Duke decided not run her in the Oaks. The stable was instead represented by Geheimniss, belonging to Lord Stamford, who won.

The Kingsclere stables celebrated the three Classic wins with a great picnic on the downs. Porter records that everybody in the village and from the neighbouring hamlets were entertained. There was a generous meal served in two large marquees, followed by other festivities. Balloons in the colours of the Duke of Westminster and Lord Stamford were released, followed at dusk with a firework display. The cost of these entertainments was shared in equal measure by the Duke of Westminster, Lord Stamford and Porter.

When Lord Alington and Sir Frederick Johnstone brought their horses to Kingsclere they were already a formidable partnership. Lord Alington, who had been given his peerage in 1876 was some 16 years older than Sir Frederick Johnstone. Previously their horses had been with William Day at Woodyates. Although Lord Alington was the more active partner, the horses generally ran in Sir Frederick Johnstone's colours of chocolate with yellow sleeves. Porter got on well with them and the management of the horses was very much left in his hands. Lord Alington and Sir Frederick Johnstone were at times known to bet heavily.

Porter considered them to be lucky as breeders and owners. Although rarely owning more than seven or eight brood mares at any one time, they did, whilst connected with Porter, produce some remarkably good horses – St Blaise, Common, Matchbox, Matchmaker, Friar's Balsam, Throstle, Michel Thrush and Plum Centre. In Porter's view there had been few studs able to record better results.

The Spring of 1883 was particularly wet and Porter was unable to give St Blaise sufficient preparation for the 2000 guineas, in which he was unplaced. Following that race, he improved rapidly and he gave him a trial on the downs a week before the Derby. The day was significant as it corresponded with the Prince of Wales (later King Edward VII) first visit to Kingsclere. He travelled to Overton Station then drove to the downs where he was met by Porter, Lord Alington and Sir Frederick Johnstone. Porter lent the Prince of Wales his grey cob Jack.

The trial proved very satisfactory – St Blaise was by two lengths with Shotover and Geheimniss finishing third and fourth. Porter had his expectations confirmed, St Blaise duly won the Derby, well ridden by Charles Wood. He next ran in the Grand Prix at Longchamps, losing by a short head to the French Derby winner, after a rough race in which he was ridden by Fred Archer. Porter wished to give St Blaise a rest and time for recuperation, however Lord Alington and Sir Frederick Johnstone desired he should run at Ascot at the end of the same week in the Ascot Derby. He ran poorly and finished third. As Porter put it 'this wretched exhibition was of course due to his not having had time to recover from the big effort in the Grand Prix three days previously'. On the subject of trials, in which Porter was a firm believer, he had during his training career four horses that he could have confidence in, to give trial results. Two were owned by the Duke of Westminster – Whipper In and Incendiary, of which the former was the best of the few.

The other two were XI and Lictor. These were in Porter's view the most reliable horses to give him the truth of any trial.

The first and only racehorse owned by Lord Grosvenor was Reprieve, who came to Kingsclere in 1883. She won five races and was placed 2nd on two occasions. Sadly Lord Grosvenor died before the commencement of the next season. The Duke of Westmister had a two-year old in 1883 called Cambusmore. He was a big overgrown colt needing plenty of time to develop. This, Porter gave him, running him only once as a two-year old. At three, he won four races, including the St James Palace Stake at Ascot. As a four-year old he was sold to Lord Londonderry, at that time Viceroy of Ireland, for whom he won at the Curragh. His results again emphasise Porter's strong conviction that patience must be exercised with young horses, particularly two-year olds that have grown beyond their strength.

In 1884 Porter's list of patrons was further enlarged with the addition of Mr Brodrick Cloete who brought a modest number of horses to Kingsclere.

The horse that brought him into prominence at Kingsclere was Paradox, which had been bred by the Grahams at Yardley, as had Isonomy.

In the Summer of 1883, Porter accompanied by Captain Bowling, visited the Graham's Yardley Stud. Captain Bowling was a bachelor and had retired from the military having sustained a wound to his left arm in the Zulu War. Porter trained for him and through Porter he had met Fred Archer with whom he was to become very close, later seemingly becoming his manager. The acquaintance with Archer had commenced in 1882.

Following a visit to Yardley Stud, Porter subsequently purchased a colt which he at first shared 50:50 with the Captain. As Porter was not particularly anxious to own horses he sold his half to the Captain. The colt was named Paradox.

As a result of problems in training him, Paradox did not have a race before the autumn of 1884. Prior to that race he had caught the eye of the Duke of Westminster at Kingsclere. The Duke approached Captain Bowling and agreed a purchase price of £6000 – a handsome return on the 700 guineas originally paid. It was in the Duke's colours that Paradox finished third in the Middle Park Plate, having whipped round at the start, losing many lengths. Given that, it was nonetheless a creditable performance. The Duke, whom Porter considered ill advised, told him that if he could find a buyer, he would sell Paradox. Porter approached Mr Broderick Cloete who agreed to purchase the colt for £5000. Two weeks later Paradox won his first race, by an easy three lengths - the Dewhurst Plate. Porter was aware that the Duke was unhappy at having acted so quickly in selling the colt on.

In the spring of 1885 he was trialled for the 2000 Guineas, having wintered well. He won the Guineas by a head. Porter was condemnatory of the criticism that Fred Archer received 'of having ridden a poor race'. His view was that Paradox by nature did not like making the running in a race. He was in Porter's eyes – a lazy horse, doing just enough to win.

This was borne out in the Derby where Paradox, ridden by an unfamiliar jockey, was beaten a head by Melton, trained by Matt Dawson, but importantly ridden by Fred Archer, who was more aware than any other of the tactics needed to beat Paradox.

A few days after the Derby, Porter took Paradox to France for the Grand Prix in Paris. Ridden again by Archer, he won easily.

Paradox was not an entry for the St Leger, but was entered in the Cambridgeshire, for which some of the patrons of Kingsclere had backed the colt to win substantial sums. When the weights were announce, Mr Broderick Cloete was in Mexico on business. Whilst on his journey to England he stopped over in New York and read that Paradox had been given 8st 12lbs. On his arrival in London he went to the Weatherby office and withdrew the horse from the race without reference to Porter or any one associated with the stables. Having withdrawn the horse, he went to Kingsclere to advise Porter of what he had done. Porter was astonished. He advised Cloete that he had seriously damaged his own reputation and at the same time had done a great injustice to his fellow patrons of Kingsclere.

Porter pointed out to him that the way Kingsclere was run meant that all the horses were kept in common and that no secrets or jealousies were allowed amongst its patrons. Cloete's action had cut right through this idea of commune. Some of the patrons of Kingsclere were so incensed at this breach of etiquette that Mr Cloete's horses had to leave Kingsclere at the end of the season. Porter did not entirely find Mr Cloete at fault and they remained friends until Cloete's death, when a passenger on the Lusitania in the spring of 1915.

The year 1885 was a memorable one for Porter and Kingsclere – it was Ormonde's first racing appearance. The horse that he rated the greatest horse he ever knew. Ormonde had arrived at Kingsclere in the autumn of 1884 and at that early stage, Porter expressed this view to the Duke of Westminster that Ormonde was the best yearling he had so far received from the Duke. During the winter of 1884-1885 the horse suffered with splints under both knees which stopped him from being able to flex his knees properly. The application of Ossidine cured the problem, in time. It was however in the late summer of 1885 that Porter deemed it sensible to allow him careful exercise. As progression was satisfactory, in early October he was ridden in a trial with other horses over 6 furlings. Ormonde was second, beaten a length by Kendal, a colt also by Bend Or that the Duke of Westminster preferred. Porter was well satisfied with the trial result. Ormonde's first race was at Newmarket later that October. He beat Modwena, who had previously won eight of her races, by a length in very heavy ground.

The performance, following the trial result, confirmed to Porter that Ormonde was a good horse. He had a good temperament and the asset of immense propelling power behind the saddle. He also had great width of head behind his ears, the like of which Porter records he was never to see again in any other horse. He had a wonderful constitution and according to his lad would eat anything offered to him. When galloping he tended to keep his head low but covered a great amount of ground at each stride when extended.

Having won his race at the first October meeting, Ormonde returned to Kingsclere before once again going to Newmarket for the second October meeting, in the Houghton. This inconvenience was due to the Jockey Club imposition of the Heath Tax on horses visiting Newmarket and remaining there more than a week. Ormonde was in two races at the meeting, including the Dewhurst Plate. These wins concluded Ormonde's two year old career.

He wintered 1885/1886 well and developed a great deal of muscle, particularly around the quarters. Porter did not bother with a trial for him as he was satisfied with his wellbeing, so took him straight to Newmarket for the 2000 Guineas. Prior to the race, Porter had taken his horses to the Bury Hill gallops. Here he met Matt Dawson who had Minting entered in the 2000 Guineas. They compared their horses and although impressed by Ormonde, Dawson still stood by his horse as being the better.

The race resulted in a win for Ormonde with Minting finishing second – beaten two lengths. Ormonde gained superiority coming out of the Dip, just as Porter had predicted in his conversation with Matt Dawson on Bury Hill. Following the race, Porter records Matt Dawson as being 'terribly crestfallen' – leaving the course immediately. The public at large now knew Ormonde to be a great horse. Between the 2000 Guineas and the Derby, Porter did not consider it necessary to give Ormonde a trial as his progression had been as good as he could have wished for. His opinion being that horses are tried on the training ground too much. His belief being that once you have ascertained the class within which your horse falls you merely want to know that he is well and in good spirits. Many times have races been lost by giving a horse one too many gallops at home.

Ormonde duly won the Derby easily – by a length and a half. The judge declared afterwards that he had not seen a race won more easily. This race win confirmed to Porter that Ormonde was the best horse he had ever had in his care. He was a giant among giants.

At Ascot, Ormonde won the St James' Palace Stakes. He was withdrawn from two race entries at Goodwood because Porter wanted him to run and win in the St Leger and believed that to do so a horse should not run between Ascot and Doncaster. He believed that you cannot hope to keep a horse in top form without a break and that they need to be let down so that there is something to work on in months ahead. For an important race like the St Leger you need more than the five or six weeks between Goodwood and Doncaster. Porter was not alone in this belief. The trainer, John Scott, who trained so many winners of the St Leger, attributed his successes largely to the rests he gave his horses in the summer. Ormonde duly won the St Leger, very comfortably, by a four length margin.

The Duke of Westminster, following the race, told Porter that he would like to make him a present. The choice, £500 or the horse Kendal. Porter chose Kendal, who had beaten Ormonde in that first trial. He knew that Lord Wolverton was at that time forming a stud at Iwerne Minster near Blandford in Dorset and that he wanted a stallion. Lord Wolverton agreed to lease Kendal for three years at a fee of £300 per annum with an option to buy the stallion within that three year period for £1200. Sadly Lord Wolverton died within the lease period and Porter accepted the return of Kendal at Lady Wolverton's request, despite having no use for him. He then sold Kendal, to John Gubbins the Irishman, who went to stand at Knockany Stud in Co. Limerick.

At the Newmarket first October meeting and the Houghton Meeting of that year, Ormonde won further prestigious races, including a walkover in the Newmarket St Leger when gave him a lead on his grey hack – Jack, much to the amusement of onlookers. Shortly after the Houghton Meeting ended, Ormonde had a walkover for the Private Sweepstakes. This was to be the last occasion that Fred Archer sat on him. For a few weeks later Archer became seriously ill and shot himself in a fit of delirium.

All was not totally right with Ormonde. Shortly before he won the St Leger, Porter was on the gallops and as Ormonde passed he heard him make a whistling sound. He was distraught to find that this, his most brilliant and successful horse, had wind problems. The Duke of Westminster was immediately informed and was upset at the news. At that point the ailment was very slight but in the weeks following the St Leger win it became perceptibly worse. During the winter of 1886 -1887 he received electrical treatment, although Porter saw no improvement and had little belief in it – it was the only treatment then available, so he persevered with it.

By the spring of 1887 Ormonde had become a pronounced 'whistler', but Porter and the Duke of Westminster accepted the situation. They chose not to run him until the Ascot Meeting of that year. He ran in the Rous Memorial Stakes beating a horse trained by Captain Machell by a long six lengths, despite giving it 25lbs. Prior to the race, Captain Machell told Porter "the horse was never foaled that could give Kilwarlin 25lbs and beat him". Following the race Porter met up with Captain Machell "Well what do you think of it now?" asked Porter of the Captain, who replied "Ormonde is not a horse at all; he's a damned steam engine".

The following day Ormonde took his place in the Hardwick Stakes. Porter admits to having little confidence in Ormonde, due to his wind problems and the previous days' exertions. Again he was up against Minting whom he had beaten in the Derby a year earlier. Matt Dawson, Minting's trainer said to Porter – "You will be beaten today, John. No horse afflicted with Ormonde's infirmity can hope to beat Minting". Again, Ormonde proved the better, winning by a neck and despite having been interfered with for a large part of the race, due to G Barrett's riding of Phil which incurred damage down the side of Ormonde. Porter had given the ride on Ormonde to Tom Cannon, rather than to Barrett, who had ridden Ormonde in the Derby.

The Duke of Westminster and Porter were two of the happiest and proudest men and it took some time for Porter to reach Ormonde, so great was the crowd. According to Porter's records it was the greatest display of enthusiasm for a horse he had ever witnessed.

Porter did not see Matt Dawson again that day. The competition between him and Matt Dawson in the big races was always there and in terms of success, Porter believed them equal, but because Ormonde was so great, he believed that the achievements of other horses were comparatively less significant.

Ormonde ran his last race in July – the Imperial Gold Cup. Ormonde won, beating the second horse by two lengths and giving him 6lbs in weight. Ormonde returned to Kingsclere with his unbeaten record and remained there until the Autumn before returning to the Duke of Westminster's stud. Porter records that when Ormonde left Kingsclere he felt there was a great blank and he felt a deep regret that he had not previously experienced. At the same time there was a great feeling of relief, for the responsibility of the two previous seasons had caused Porter great anxiety, particularly with the wind problem occurring.

In all, Ormonde won fiteen races – two of them walkovers. One of them, the St Leger was over one and three quarter miles, three of them over one and a half miles, the rest were six or seven furlings, or a mile. This versatility is a rare phenomenon indeed. The record is undeniable affirmation of Porter's talent as a trainer whose first priority was to understand the horses' capabilities, the care of his horses' welfare and close connection with the horses' owners.

Queen Victoria's Jubilee year 1887 saw the Duke of Westminster hold a big reception at Grosvenor House in Park Lane. Among the guests were the Prince and Princess of Wales, together with Kings, Queens, other Princesses and Princes and a number of Indian potentates. Ormonde was the chief 'exhibit' having been trained up to London's Waterloo Station and from there walked through the metropolis to Mayfair, via St James Park and Green Park. Porter's son was in charge of this journey. Ormonde did not go directly to Grosvenor House but to the nearby stable of Lord Manvers where a very large box had been made available. During the afternoon reception, Ormonde stood on the lawn. Enjoying the attention and devouring any food, including sugar and flowers. He was also a great devourer of flowery button holes if he could snaffle them.

From 1887 to 1889 he stood at Eaton Stud. In 1889 he was leased to Lord Gerard and stood at the Moulton Paddocks. This arrangement being made because of the shortage of accommodation at Eaton Stud. The move to Newmarket was not satisfactory, Ormonde catching a chill and being unable to fulfil his stud duties During his time there, Porter went to inspect the horse at the request of the Duke of Westminster. He records his annoyance and disgust at finding Ormonde shut in an unventilated box, with both door and window firmly shut. He advised the attendant to let in some air, or else the horse would die. He ordered the attendant to open the top door and leave it open. Porter was always a believer in the virtues of fresh air and this can be seen in the stables he designed at Kingsclere.

Ormonde returned to Eaton Stud in the summer. Chapman, the Duke of Westminster's stud manager found him in a very weak state. Back home he soon picked up and improved rapidly. In 1890 Ormonde was sold to an Argentinian breeder for £12,000. The Duke of Westminster was widely criticised for allowing Ormonde to leave the country. He was however justified in so doing, because it has been well documented that the wind problem 'roaring' from which Ormonde had come to suffer is a hereditary complaint. The Duke of Westminster was concerned that many of the country's top mares would be sent to Eaton for covering by Ormonde, as a result of which the 'roaring' genes would be passed on and the Duke did not want to be accused of that. By selling Ormonde to go abroad, he felt he would protect the best thoroughbreds from inheriting the complaint. From the Duke's point of view it was a sacrifice in the short term to protect the English thoroughbred in the longer term. Seen in that light it was a laudable decision he made.

After changing hands a number of times, Ormonde was put down in 1904 in America. Some months later his body was exhumed. The skeleton was sent to the Natural History Museum in South Kensington.

It is thought that his illness in 1889 when at the Moulton Paddocks, seriously and permanently weakened his procreative powers.

For Porter it was a consoling thought that the greatest horse he had ever trained was brought back home to England, albeit in skeletal form.

In the Spring of 1886, Lord Alington advised Porter that the Prince of Wales was buying some horses which he wished him to train. Lord Alington, whose home was at Crichel Down in Dorset, was a long- term friend of the Prince, also a member of the Marlborough House 'set'.
1886 brought two moderate fillies to Kingsclere. Having won a Maiden Plate, Counterpane dropped dead in a race at Stockbridge when in the lead. The post mortem revealed she had a diseased heart. Lady Peggy ran twice – winning a Maiden Plate at the Houghton Meeting in October, but never again saw a racecourse.
Thereafter until the end of the 1892 season, Porter generally had up to a dozen boxes at Kingsclere occupied by horses belonging to the Prince of Wales. In 1886 the Prince of Wales informed Porter that it was his intention to start a breeding stud at Sandringham. He wanted advice on the layout for the paddocks. Plans were made and the project proceeded.
The Prince of Wales required a stud groom and Porter suggested Edmund Walker who at that time was employed by Fred Archer at Falmouth House, Newmarket. Fred Archer had died in November 1886 so Walker was looking for new employment. He was engaged by the Prince, and asked that about six broodmares should be purchased but the Prince did not want to pay stupid prices. Porter was charged with seeking out and purchasing the mares. The first, Perdita II was offered at £1000 but after consultation with the Prince, he managed to purchase her for £900. Sir Dighton Probyn, the Prince of Wales' treasurer told him that if he went on buying these thoroughbreds, he would ruin the Prince. Perdita II was owned by Mr David Falconer and Porter underlines that it was only with him that he dealt.
Perdita II proved to be a goldmine, much to the Prince of Wales satisfaction. Some years later after becoming King, he told him "when you purchased her, you as good as made me a present of a quarter million of money". Porter's calculation was that it meant the Prince of Wales had all his racing for nothing. The purchase of broodmares for the stud remained in his hands for all the years he trained horses for the Prince of Wales at Kingsclere. In total Perdita II's offspring won 26 races from 64 entries with prize of nearly £73,000 . In addition Porter calculates that three of them, Florizel 2, Persimmon and Diamond Jubilee would have earned about £150,000 in stud fees. A fourth offspring Sandringham, was sold for £30,000, which gives credence to the Prince of Wales's estimate of a quarter of a million. Not a bad return from a £900 mare.

The Prince took a keen interest in his racehorses and his visits to Kingsclere were regular and often accompanied by others including Lord Arthur Somerset, Master of the Horse. After the bracing air of the Downs the Prince used to develop a capacious appetite. He was always kind and considerate and very grateful for all that was done which added to his comfort and enjoyment of the visits.
The kindnesses he bestowed on Porter included being a guest, on numerous occasions on the Royal Yacht. Amongst these occasions was the great Naval Review as part of the 1887 Jubilee Festivities and again at the time of the Review at Spithead in honour of the German Emperor.

Admiral Sir Harry Keppel was usually a fellow guest and according to Porter "one of the most delightful men I have met". His home was near the New Forest and most years he was a visitor to Kingsclere.

Porter's association with King Edward was ongoing until the King's death in 1910. Annual visits to Sandringham were the norm, usually in November. Porter would tour the estate with the King after lunch on a Sunday.

A frequent visitor to Kingsclere in the time Porter had the Prince's horses, was Mr Justice Hawkins, later Lord Brampton. His visits, usually over the weekend, coincided with his attendance at Winchester Assizes. He used to relate stories of his time at the Bar. He believed there were two classes of criminal, some natural to whom he gave as much punishment as the law allowed, others criminals by circumstance, these received more lenient treatment. In Porter's view, he was a just and discriminatory judge. Another legal friend, following Lord Brampton was Sir Charles Russell, later known as Lord Russell of Killowen, Lord Chief Justice. Porter found him an extremely kind hearted and genial person. Whenever he had a big case in the making, he would come down to Kingsclere so that he might study his briefs in peace. He liked to ride out with Porter in the morning on the Downs – then return to Park House, when he would retire to his room and where he would stay until the evening. After dinner he liked to play whist with Porter, his wife and son-in-law, Mr Leader or anyone Porter could call up to make up a foursome.

Sir Charles lived at Tadworth Court near Epsom and Porter used to visit there during Epsom race weeks.

Sir Charles Matthews was another very good and long term friend from the legal profession, who used to visit Kingsclere when he was able to.

In 1886 Porter, together with Captain Bowling, purchased a two- year old colt – Carrasco. The Captain was a great friend of Fred Archer and it was through him that Porter had met the Captain. Bowling had been retired from the army, having been wounded in the arm, which he was unable to properly use.

Carrasco won a few races including the Payne Stakes at Newmarket, after which he finished second in the Ascot Cup. He was then sold for £3000. In 1887 the most notable horse was one bred and owned by Lord Alington – Friar's Balsam. He ran seven times, winning every race and won £8666. As a horse he would have achieved much more, but suffered from a delicate constitution. In 1888 he finished fifth in the 2000 Guineas having burst an unsuspected abcess in his mouth. Mr Williams, the London vet, eventually removed a piece of loose bone from his jaw. It was not until the Autumn of 1888 that he was fit enough to race again and having run poorly in the Lancashire Plate in September, he achieved a sensational win in the Champion Stakes at Newmarket in October. Having never fully recovered from his ailment, he ran his last race in 1889 but was unplaced. When the Prince of Wales brought his patronage to Kingsclere in 1886, he brought with him a long term friend Mr (afterwards Sir) James Mackenzie of Kintail. A keen racing man who owned one or two good horses. 1886 was of course the Jubilee year and shortly before the Goodwood Meeting, Porter had spent a few days on the Prince of Wales's yacht in the Solent. When paying that visit, Porter recalls "I travelled down to Portsmouth from London with the Prince. When we reached the vessel the Commander was surprised to see me. He had not been told I was coming. No arrangements had been made for my accommodation". Porter accepted the offer for that first night to sleep ashore in the Commander's private accommodation – two rooms over a hairdressing shop in Portsmouth. The following morning, Porter returned to the Royal yacht and found his quarters on board made ready. On leaving the Commander's accommodation, Porter gave the hairdresser – who had been very attentive, ten shillings. The hairdresser had discovered who his visitor had been and on Porter's leaving told him that he would invest this tip in some of his horses running at Goodwood.

The Commander and most of the officers in the Royal Yacht attended Goodwood on the Friday – the last day of the meeting. The Commander came to Porter and said "You have done a nice thing for my landlord, the hairdresser. He has turned the half sovereign you gave him into more than £100". During the first three days, Porter's horses had won four races at odds of 3-1 to 25-1. Porter regretted that on the Friday he was unsuccessful for his friends from the Royal Yacht.

In 1888 whilst the Duke of Westminster was staying at Kingsclere, Porter was running two of his horses, Ossory and Orbit in the Eclipse Stakes at Sandown ridden each by the Tom Cannons, father and son. After the horses had left Kingsclere for Sandown, he said to the Duke of Westminster "of course you are going to see your horses run, your Grace". The reply was "No they are both moderate and I am not interested". On his return from Sandown, he was met by the Duke who asked "Well how did you get on?" His reply was "You won your Grace, with Orbit". The Duke's response was "really? " with some surprise. "What came second?" "Yours was second, you got all the money" he responded. Obviously astonished at this result and very pleased, the Duke of Westminster said he would make Porter a present of £500. Porter was equally pleased with the result as he, like the Duke, felt the two horses were moderate, but also that the field for the Eclipse that year were a pretty moderate lot.

As a result of the race Porter was pleased to receive a letter from Henry Hawley Smart – a novelist, grandson of Sir Joseph Hawley and a good friend. (See letters under Henry Hawley Smart.)

Another patron to join Kingsclere in 1887 was Mr William Low, whose father a Scotsman, had made a big fortune in the United States. Porter considered him a handsome man and always full of fun. The horses Porter trained for him won some good races. Mr John Gretton of the Bass Brewery family was another patron at this time and Porter won some good races for him in 1888 and 1889. In Porter's view, he was a splendid man in every way – never had a bet, but raced his horses purely for the love of the sport – many of his horses being home bred. Porter's association with the Gretton family ran right through the years, even after he had retired as a trainer, he managed a few horses for Mr F Gretton, a son of John Gretton and a nephew of Mr Fred Gretton who owned Isonomy.

In 1888 Porter paid his annual visit to the sale of yearlings that had been reared at the Royal Paddocks at Hampton Court. He was particularly taken by a chestnut colt by Springfield out of Sanda. In conversation with Sir Robert Jardine later in the day, he was asked if he had seen anything he particularly liked and he responded that he had liked the Springfield colt. Sir Robert suggested that they should together have another look at it. Having seen it, Sir Robert said he would buy it. Porter was somewhat taken aback by this and explained that he had intended to buy it himself. Whereupon Sir Robert suggested they buy it together and Porter should take it back to Kingsclere on the train. When the horse came into the ring, Porter purchased it for 550 guineas and they called it Sainfoin. Even when fully grown he was small – only 15.2 hands. He was, as Porter put it, "cleverly made and blessed with a most amiable disposition."

Sainfoin's first race in August 1889 at Lewes was won very easily. Prior to the run Porter had written to Sir Robert Jardine advising him of the entry. Sir Robert afterwards expressed surprise as he had apparently forgotten that he had any interest in the horse. That was Sainfoin's only race course appearance that year. As previously confirmed, Porter did not like to over expose his horses, firmly believing that the benefits came through giving the horses time to grow and mature. Clearly a view he had formed over the years at Michel Down, Findon, Cannon Heath and Kingsclere. During the winter of 1889-1890, Sainfoin progressed satisfactorily.

He had his first race of 1890 in April and won the Esher Stakes at Sandown Park, in a canter by four lengths. This performance caught the eye, amongst others, of Sir James Miller, who accompanied by Mr John Davis, manager of Hurst Park, went down to Kingsclere to open negotiations to buy Sainfoin. Porter informed Sir Robert Jardine of this approach and was told to deal with it in the way he thought best.

By this time, the public had come to believe that Sainfoin was a reasonably strong candidate for the Derby – the only horse capable of beating him being Surefoot, who had won the 2000 Guineas. Trying to take an objective view, Porter decided that Sainfoin on all known evidence would not have the beating of Surefoot. On that basis, he took the responsibility to sell the colt to Sir James Miller. The price agreed was £6000 plus half the Derby Stakes if Sainfoin won. Porter advised Sir Robert Jardine of the deal, with which the latter was perfectly satisfied. Porter was also satisfied that he had struck a good deal. Events however were to prove his judgement in this instance – very wrong. Sainfoin was to stay at Kingsclere until September 1890. His first race under his new owner was at Chester where he won easily beating his sole opponent. His next was the Derby – Surefoot his main rival had won races at Epsom, Ascot and Goodwood - all courses with ups and downs, whereas Sainfoin had basically only run on flat tracks.

Derby Day came and it was a miserable one – raining all day, which was particularly heavy during the race itself. As well as Sainfoin, Porter ran one of the Duke of Westminsters colts of Bend Or – Orwell, which ran a fine race, leading until nearing the furlong pole. At this point Sainfoin took over to beat Le Nord into second place by ¾ length with Orwell a very respectable third and Surefoot fourth. Porter's view and that of many onlookers, was that Surefoot proved to be short of stamina. It could be seen as a vindication of Porter's careful handling that gave Sainfoin the edge on the day, in addition to the weather.

Naturally Porter's feelings after the race were very mixed – he had trained the Derby winner but had also sold the horse before the race thus depriving his co-owner Sir Robert Jardine of having a Derby winner. Fortunately Sir Robert took his disappointment in a very sportsmanlike manner. Before leaving Kingsclere in September for Newmarket, Sainfoin ran in two more races with Surefoot – the former winning by good margins in each. After leaving Kingsclere, Sainfoin never won another race. When Sir James Miller established the Hamilton Stud in Newmarket, Sainfoin was his number one stallion where he begat his only truly successful offspring – Rock Sand, who in 1903, won the Triple Crown of 2000 Guineas, Derby and St Leger.

Another winner in 1890 of the Kempton – Jubilee Stakes, The Imp, was owned by Sir   J T Mackenzie. Two weeks after this success, ownership was transferred to the Prince of Wales. In 1891 one of Sir Frederick Johnstone's horses,Common was entered for the 2000   Guineas. This was a horse who physically looked all wrong. In Porter's words, "Common was walking round the paddock like an old cow". Sir Frederick Johnstone brought Prince Dimitri Soltykoff, a member of the Jockey Club, to have a look at him. Sardonic in his comment, the Prince said "He seems to be well named" Another to comment on Common before the race was M. Edmond Blanc, who owned the favourite for the race. He was a big owner and breeder from France where his horses were trained by Porter's old friend from Rugeley days - Robert Denman. M. Blanc's comment after seeing Common in the paddock was "the horse I am most afraid of is Common". After the race Porter overheard Sir Frederick Johnstone ask Prince Soltykoff if he could suggest a better name for the horse. Common was made favourite for the Derby following his success in the Guineas and despite the weather again being dreadful on Derby Day, won by a comfortable two lengths. Again having M. Edmond Blanc's horse behind him, Common went on to win the St James' Palace Stakes at Ascot but was then beaten in the Eclipse at Sandown, a course which seemed not his liking. He, having followed up that defeat with a hard fought win in the St Leger, giving him the Triple Crown. Prior to the race Lord Alington and Sir Frederick Johnstone had been approached by a representative of the Austrian Government with an offer of £4000 guineas. Two days later, after the race, an offer of 15000 guineas was made by Sir Blundell Maple, which was accepted. It was the largest sum ever paid for a racehorse. The following Monday Sir Blundell received a telegram from Austria offering him 20,000 guineas. His telegram reply was "Thanks for the offer. The English Turf requires Common's services. Money will not tempt me" he wanted Common to stand as a sire at his Childwick Bury Stud built on his estate. Sir Blundell Maple had made a mistake, for as happens with horse breeding, Common was to be a disappointment as a stallion. Sir Blundell was criticised for wanting to start Common as a stallion, aged four. This was not entirely fair, as Sir Blundell Maple had wished to keep the horse in training at Kingsclere . Porter was not able to accept Sir Blundell Maple as a patron because he was already training for so many owners. Porter would have liked to take him on, as he believed Common would have made a very good Cup horse. Porter's misgivings were somewhat assuaged by a letter from Lord Alington that he received shortly after Common had won the St Leger.

"Porter I send you a cheque for a thousand, and thank you also very much for all your trouble, not to mention skill, you showed in giving such good advice as to not training him as a two year old. Also for the splendid condition that brought him to the three posts. I think you won the races for us, not the horse. You are by far the best trainer in England – your friend – Alington. P.S. I am engaged to be married."

This letter again underscores Porter's long held belief that horses should be given time to grow and mature as individuals. Also how he was happy to give such advice to his patrons. It is why he could afford not to take on new patrons as he was content with the numbers he had to whom he was able to give individual attention.

Baron Hirsch was introduced to Kingsclere by the Prince of Wales in 1889 and had his first winner in 1890. He had winnings in 1891, 1892 and 1893. The winnings of 1891 and 1892 amounting to some £42,000 he donated to various charities. The winnings of 1893 of £7500 he doubled up and again the money was donated to charity. As Porter records 'The Baron was a very amiable and generous man. He seemed fond of his horses and I always got on well with him'.

The Baron's name will, in the sport of racing, always be associated with La Fleche. The Baron together with the Prince of Wales, attended the Hampton Court Yearling Sale of 1890. The Prince along with many others, was very taken with La Fleche, a daughter of St Simon. A big price was expected. The Baron appeared a disinterested spectator, but had instructed Lord Marcus Beresford to bid on his behalf. She was purchased for 5500 guineas. When the hammer fell, the auctioneer, Mr Edmund Tattersall called for "three cheers for Baron Hirsch and success to the Royal Stud". The price paid set a new record for a yearling but La Fleche's subsequent career in racing and then as a broodmare, showed it to be a shrewd purchase. Kingsclere was flourishing and other yearlings arriving included the Duke of Westminster's Orme, Lord Alington and Sir Frederick Johnstone's Goldfinch and Baron Hirsch's Watercress which Porter had purchased as a foal from Lord Falmouth.

Goldfinch proved to be unsound and was sold to an American breeder as a three year old. He sired many useful horses in America.

It was not until July 1891, that La Fleche had her first race, at Newmarket. She won well, beating horses that had run previously and won. She had three more races that year winning them all. Already as a two year old La Fleche had won £3415.

The Duke of Westminster's Orme showed great promise as a yearling and Porter soon felt he had a great future. This was underlined by a trial he gave Orme which compared with one he had given La Fleche, put him within a length of her. He took Orme to Goodwood for his first race, with high expectation. The horse duly obliged, winning the Richmond Stakes on the first day of the meeting and then the Prince of Wales Stakes on the third day. Whilst failing to win his next race Orme took part in the Middle Park Plate, which he won comfortably. Two weeks later he won the Dewhurst Plate. As a two year old he ran six times, winning five of his races, on form, the best colt of his year.

Baron Hirsch's Watercress, as previously mentioned, was another two year old that Porter liked – he only allowed him one race however due to his size – he was one that he felt, needed time.

As a three year old, Orme was prepared for the 2000 Guineas having wintered well and matured. A few days prior to the race, Prince Adolphus of Teck, Lord Marcus Beresford (who managed the horses belonging to the Prince of Wales and Baron Hirsch) and Mr Portal visited Kingsclere. On arriving at Orme's box, Porter noticed saliva dripping from his muzzle. On further examination a swollen mouth was evident. Initially he thought it a tooth problem and summoned Loeffler, the horse dentist from Newmarket, who diagnosed a diseased tooth, which he removed. On examination, after extraction, Porter could find nothing wrong with it. Loeffler stuck by his diagnosis and he was not in agreement. Orme's situation grew worse and Porter called in Mr Williams, the veterinary professor, together with his son. They concluded that Orme had in fact been poisoned with all evidence pointing to mercurial poisoning. Orme became very ill and for some days it seemed he might die. The Duke of Westminster initiated the publication of a £1000 reward to anyone who could throw light on the perpetrator. Porter and the Duke of Westminster were unable to identify the culprit although Porter suspected one of his employees. Without proof all that he could do was to discharge the suspect from his employment.

Fortunately due to his robust constitution, Orme recovered. Just three months after the onset of his illness, Orme won the Eclipse Stakes at Sandown Park. This was testament to Porter's under-standing and handling of his horses . The Duke was overwhelmed by the public's ovation at this victory and many of his friends made it their business to congratulate Porter on the result. Orme followed this win with success in the Sussex stakes, albeit by a head from his stablemate, Watercress, owned by Baron Hirsch.

The Baron's La Fleche won the 1000 Guineas in 1892 and Porter then held her back for the Derby. Sadly, due to her jockey riding an incredibly bad race, La Fleche finished only second behind an outsider. Porter was furious with George Barrett, the jockey. Two days later La Fleche ran in and won the Oaks. But it was of little consolation to the Baron that she prevailed by a short head or that this time Barrett gave her an impeccable ride.

Porter then rested La Fleche for two months and she won the Nassau Stakes at Goodwood. Her next scheduled run was to be the St Leger and a race against Orme. The race for Orme was a disaster. He was again ridden by Barrett and there were rumours that he had been 'got at', having been warned by the Duke of Westminster that his riding would be closely monitored. As a result Barrett let the horse have his head, the result of which was that a furlong and half from the finish he was a beaten horse. From a stables point of view, La Fleche's win made up for her loss at the Derby. Porter came in for criticism for running Orme at Goodwood so soon after his hard race in the Eclipse. He had some empathy with this view for as related earlier, he liked (when given a free hand) to avoid running a horse between Ascot and Doncaster if he felt it likely to win the St Leger. In this instance, Porter was aware that Orme was not a natural stayer, so that St Leger proved a step too far. A mile and a mile and a quarter were his distances. Having said that – Orme went on to win four more races that year, all at Newmarket. La Fleche for her part won three more races. Her versatility was said that she won races over eight, nine, ten and twelve furlongs. Porter put it on record that Baron Hirsch allowed him total freedom in the matter of La Fleche's training. The result of which was shown in her great record.

It was at the end of the year 1892, that the Prince of Wales and Baron Hirsch removed their horses from Kingsclere to be trained by Dick Marsh at Newmarket. Porter was resolutely silent on the cause of this removal. Whatever the reason, Porter received assurances later from both the Prince and the Baron that they greatly regretted the necessity of the removal. It is possible that Lord Marcus Beresford was in some way involved. The frequent letters from the Baron to Porter clearly show the Baron taking advice from Lord Marcus which Porter may have grown to resent – hence his reluctance to expand comment on the issue of the horses leaving Kingsclere.

The decision to sever the horses links with Kingsclere clearly caused the Baron to have second thoughts, for twelve months later he asked Porter to train for him once again. Porter had to tell him that it was not possible because his stables were full with other patron's horses. The Baron out of the blue and much to Porter's astonishment told him, "if you are willing to sell, I will buy Kingsclere for £20,000, pay you £1000 a year to train for me and a further £100,000 will be placed in the bank, which shall be at your absolute disposal for the purchase of bloodstock and you will have the sole management of my horses. Any boxes I do not fill, you can use for horses belonging to the other owners."

He thanked the Baron for his offer, but was unable to consider it, because of his wish to act fairly to his older patrons. Porter recommended George Blackwell as a trainer. Blackwell had been head man to Matt Dawson. The Baron acted on Porter's recommendation but approximately twelve months later, the Baron died.

Orme ran four times as a four year old, but at the end of the season his legs began to give trouble and he was retired to the Eaton Stud.

With the start of 1892 the fortunes of Porter's patrons changed. The return of good fortune came to Lord Arlington and Sir Frederick Johnstone. Two good yearlings arrived from Crichel in the autumn, Matchbox and Throstle, both with excellent breeding credentials.

Matchbox's first run was disappointing and he was put away until the autumn. He then won three races in quick succession including the Dewhurst Plate. Porter had hoped with him that he might win a classic the following year, 1894. Running in the 2000 Guineas he came second to Lord Roseberry's Ladas, who had been unbeaten as a two year old. Their rivalry was renewed in the Derby which Ladas again won. It was generally a popular win for it was the first time that a Prime Minister led a Derby winner into the winners enclosure. At the time, connections were unaware that it would be Ladas's last victory.

A day or so after finishing second in the Derby, Matchbox was purchased by Baron Hirsch for £15,000 with the hope he might win the Grand Prix de Paris. Although the Baron's horses were being trained in Newmarket, he continued to have Porter train his new purchase at Kingsclere. Porter took his horse to France but it could finish only a close second by a neck. With a better ride from Morny Cannon, he would have won. Matchbox ran in the St Leger, but was beaten by stable companion Throstle – in this instance, given an impeccable ride by Morny Cannon. The Baron before the St Leger had resold Matchbox to the Hungarian Government and in retirement he stood at the Kisber Stud in Hungary. 1895, 1896, 1897 and 1899 were all uneventful years with nothing particularly outstanding.

No book about Porter's training career would be complete without a section on Flying Fox. The story of this remarkable horse starts in 1893, when the Duke of Westminster requested him to purchase a broodmare. He noted shortly after receiving this request that a four year old mare by Galopin out of Irony was entered in a forthcoming Newmarket sale. On hearing that a high reserve had been put on the mare, Porter did not attend the sale. That afternoon he met Lord Hindlip who thought he was there to buy the mare, but he said that as the reserve as so high, he had changed his mind. Lord Hindlip advised that the mare had not been sold. Porter thereupon entered into negotiations and secured the mare for 1000 guineas. On reaching Eaton Stud she was found to have a very spiteful attitude, one day injuring one of the stud employees. The Duke was minded to get rid of her, but Porter said if he did, he would take her. Whereupon the Duke of Westminster changed his mind.

Vampire was mated with Orme – which because of this close blood link was a risk. However, against all the odds – the mating produced a wonderful colt – Flying Fox.

Porter saw the colt for the first time at Eaton whilst he was a yearling. Even at that early time, he informed the Duke of Westminster that he felt the colt had a "Derby look" about him. At Kingsclere the colt quickly showed great promise although he was also inclined to be mulish – an inherited trait from his mother. On later reflection Porter felt that it was for the best that he was only in training for 3 years, as he convinced Porter that had he been kept longer, damage would have occurred. As a trade off for the inherited trait from his mother he had from his sire inherited a very strong constitution. Porter being quite clear that Flying Fox was one of the toughest horses ever to be in his care. The week before his first race he gave him a trial which he won by three lengths with a further six lengths between the second and third. Porter was satisfied from this trial result that Flying Fox was extremely good. He won his first race as a two year old by ¾ of a length beating the filly Musa who went on to win the Oaks the following year. His second race, in July, was won. His next race at Kempton Park was the valuable Imperial Produce Stakes where he had nine opponents. Flying Fox was beaten, a head, but Porter firmly believed he should have won as he was convinced that he was better than he was showing. A week later he was again second in the Middle Park Stakes to Caiman ridden by Tod Sloan, the American jockey who in his memoirs told how he felt he had been able to steal the race and that in his opinion Flying Fox was the best horse he had seen in England. One more race was run as a two year old which he won comfortably. He had run five races and won three. A good record but one that should have been better.

He wintered well and in mid-April, he was given a trial before the 2000 Guineas which he won comfortably. Porter was well satisfied as the opposition in the trial were good horses.

Flying Fox duly won the 2000 Guineas by two lengths, beating Caiman who as a two year old had bettered him in the Middle Park Stakes. His next race was the Derby – which again he won by two lengths. In July Flying Fox won the Princess of Wales Stakes from Lord Alington's, Royal Emblem by three lengths despite giving the second, 17 lbs. On the 14th July, the Eclipse Stakes was won from another of the Duke's horses - Frontier. Flying Fox won by a length but also gave the second 3lbs.

The St Leger followed and Flying Fox again won by three lengths with Caiman second. The two beatings of Caiman, underline the correctness of Tod Sloan's comments of the previous year. Three weeks after the St Leger, Flying Fox won the Jockey Club Stakes. The end of his racing career, for right at the end of 1899, the Duke of Westminster died.

Porter had trained his horses for eighteen seasons and he and the Duke always had a very good relationship. He was, Porter tells us "one of the kindest of men – a nobleman in every sense of the word". He missed him sorely, believing that Kingsclere never quite seemed the same following the Duke's death.

Flying Fox as a two and three year old had won £40,096 in prize money and as a three year old was unbeaten. Thursday March 8th 1900, was a notable day in Kingsclere history. It was there that Messrs Tattersall held the sale of the late Duke of Westminster's horses in training. In total the nineteen lots made 70,440 guineas. Flying Fox alone made 37,500 guineas (£39,375.00) and was purchased by M. Edmond Blanc from Monaco, whose horses in France were trained by Porter's friend from Rugeley days – Robert Denman. M. Edmond Blanc had purchased him to stand at his stud near Paris.

Flying Fox proved to be a great investment and up to the outbreak of war in 1914 had bred winners of races - in France alone, worth £203,369. A phenomenal return on the original investment made in 1900.

Porter had strongly advised M. Edmond Blanc to buy Flying Fox. On visiting the stud some years later, M. Edmond Blanc told Porter "This is one of the best investments I ever made. Everything you have recommended me to buy has turned out well". Flying Fox died at the Stud on March 2nd 1911.

The yearlings were auctioned two days after the "Horses in Training Sale" and the prices made were very satisfactory. Twelve lots making 43,300 guineas.

It was in the late autumn of 1898 that the Duke of Portland's horses, previously trained by George Dawson, at Newmarket, came to Kingsclere. Amongst the yearlings was a filly, La Roche, part owned by Lord Berkeley Paget. As a two year old she did not show what Porter would describe as classic form – although in one race her performance indicated she had an abundance of stamina. As a three year old she finished a creditable fourth in the 1000 Guineas, then went on to a comfortable three lengths win in the Oaks. Her next run, despite a 10lb penalty for winning the Oaks, was the Manchester Cup. Despite her penalty she won by six lengths. At a mile and a half she was a very classy animal. In August she won the Yorkshire Cup, giving 19lbs to the second horse, who earlier in the year over a mile, had beaten her at level weights. At the end of the season the Duke of Portland purchased Lord Berkeley Paget's share and she went to the stud at Welbeck.

William the Third came to Kingsclere as a yearling from the Duke of Portland's stud at Welbeck. On arrival Porter considered him weedy and weak and clearly needed time to grow and mature. As a two year old he grew well. To compare him with others, Porter gave him a trial at the end of June 1900. From the trial result it was as Porter put it, "abundantly evident that William the Third was not yet ready for racing". With time, he continued to impress, also giving indications that his prowess would be as a stayer.

In September he was given a trial with other horses which he won comfortably by a length with a further three lengths between second and third. The trial was run over a mile and Porter concluded that he would be shown at his best in races needing stamina.

He progressed steadily throughout that next winter and in his first public race the Wood Ditton Stakes, run over one mile, he smashed the opposition, winning by six lengths. In his next race, the Esher Stakes, run over nine furlongs he again smashed the opposition, winning by six lengths, yet again. He had not been entered for the 2000 Guineas, so instead ran in the Newmarket Stakes over 10 furlongs, winning again, beating a horse owned by Mr Leopold de Rothschild, who had finished second in the 2000 Guineas, two weeks previously. In the Derby he finished second and had no entry in the St Leger.

As a four year old William the Third was a very much improved horse. He had over the winter filled out really well and was a much stronger horse than he had been at three.

In 1902 he first ran in the Ascot cup, where he revealed his superlative stamina. He had ten rivals that day, all having won top grade races The race was over 2 ½ miles which William the Third, ridden by Morny Cannon won by a very comfortable five lengths with a further three lengths between the second and third horses. He literally trounced the opposition. His win brought fulsome praise from many admirers. Six furlongs out he had been last, three furlongs out he was in front, coasting to the winning line.

The next day in the Alexandra Plate over three miles and carrying a 10lb penalty for his cup win, he again showed his superiority by a convincing six lengths win. His next run – the Doncaster Cup was won by eight lengths. These performances again underscore Porter's ability to know a horse, to treat it as an individual and not to ask too much of it too early.

Due to suffering a split pastern while doing a canter prior to running in the following year's Ascot Cup, William the Third was not to be seen on a racecourse again.

Porter regarded him and Isonomy as two of the better horse over distances that he had known. Porter was mortified by the injury as a five year old, for he had been a quiet, kind horse and a real "doer" who, when racing gave his all. After a period at Kingsclere to recover from his injury he returned to Welbeck to stand at stud. As a sire he was a success.

In 1905, Porter was responsible for perhaps his best offspring – Willonyx, born in 1906, the year that Porter sold his property, Strattons, to go and live in Newbury. The mare Porter purchased in 1904 was Tribonyx, which he sold to M. Edmond Blanc in 1906, as his home in Newbury had no accommodation for broodmares He did well, having purchased the mare for 100 guineas, he sold her on for £1000. When offered for sale at Doncaster in 1907, Willonyx did not make his reserve and was afterwards sold privately to Mr C E Howard for whom he won ten races. As a foal Porter had received £900 for Willonyx.

In 1900-1901, new patrons joining Kingsclere included Mr Alexander and Mr George (later) Lord Faber and Mr Low. None of the Kingsclere horses distinguished themselves in 1903 and total prize money won that year was £4319. – the lowest annual figure since 1876. At the end of the season Mr Alexander's horses left to be trained at Burbage by Mr Braime.

The loss of Mr Alexander's patronage and that of others was due to a change in the establishment at Kingsclere. The entire property was taken over by a syndicate, comprising the Dukes of Portland and Westminster, Mr Frederick Gretton and John Porter. The change was at the suggestion of the two Dukes. A limited liability company was formed – registered as "Kingsclere Ltd". The members of the company as above, holding equal shares. The company purchased Kingsclere from Porter who undertook the management of the company and continued to act as trainer.

This change in status caused the horses of Mr George Faber, Mr Low and Mr Alexander to be removed. The few horses of Lord Alington and Sir Frederick Johnstone remained and a few months later it was agreed that two or three horses belonging to Lord Crewe would be taken care of. All other boxes in the yard were for use only by the syndicate members.

In 1904 the chief contributors to a prize money total of £19,942 were two horses of the Duke of Portland, two of the Duke of Westminster and one of Lord Crewe's.

At the end of 1905 John Porter retired as a trainer. It should be noted, as it was by Porter himself, that Sir Frederick Johnstone had joined Kingsclere at the very start with Sir Joseph Hawley and it was his horse, Plum Centre, jointly owned with Lord Alington, that produced winnings of £2025 out of a total of £5685 that Porter achieved in his final year. A remarkably long connection between owner and trainer.

Porter, towards the end of 1905 had decided it was time to shed himself of the anxieties arising from a trainer's life. He had after all, been in training for 42 years. Experience had proved to him that the income received as a trainer merely provided sufficient monies to live on. There was never any surplus to bank. All that he had been able to save came in the form of gifts from his patrons and as a result of successful speculation in the bloodstock market, betting had never had any appeal for him.

The Kingsclere syndicate as formed in 1903, was now broken up. Porter and Mr Gretton selling their shares to the two Dukes who appointed William Waugh as manager and trainer for Kingsclere Ltd.

Porter felt considerable sadness on leaving Park House whose inception and growth he had been so involved with. Also his connection with Kingsclere village and its people were very much part of his life. He moved only a mile or so out of the village to a property called Strattons where he had paddocks in which he was able to continue to have broodmares and these with other activities kept him busy.

An idea he had thought about over a long period of time was now able to be given the full attention it needed. That was the formation of an entirely new racecourse on the outskirts of Newbury. He had long viewed a level area of land south of the railway line and just a half mile from Newbury Station as being ideal for a new racetrack. Within a radius of just a few miles there were many established trainers who could supply the horses to use the track.

The land belonged to Mr Lloyd H. Baxendale whose family lived at Greenham and who along with his sister Constance had visited Kingsclere, so they were known to Porter. Lloyd Baxendale's father, of the same name, owned Pickfords, the haulage and removals firm. He was willing to sell the land to Porter. With this green light, Porter set about putting together an outline proposal for the scheme together with sketches of the course and its layout. This was to enable him to apply to the Jockey Club for a provisional licence to construct and build a new racecourse. His hopes were not fulfilled. The Jockey Club felt there were already enough race courses in England and they seemed unwilling to accept Porter's arguments to the contrary. He left the meeting without any clear answer. The meeting had taken place at the Jockey Club in Newmarket.

On leaving, Porter happened to meet King Edward outside. He enquired what had brought him to Newmarket. Porter told him of the proposal and the unsatisfactory outcome of the meeting. The King asked Porter to meet him the next morning and to bring all papers with him. The interest shown by the King cheered him up enormously. They met the next morning and he was able to explain fully his plans so far as he had them developed. By the end of the meeting Porter felt he had gained a powerful ally.   His next interview with the Jockey Club was very amicable and he was given the licence. He did not know what, if any leverage the King had used, but it was at a time when the Northampton Meeting was abandoned due to a lack of support.

Porter secured an option to buy the land and the terms of purchase were agreed.

A promoting syndicate was organised – this consisted of Porter and Mr Baxendale. A company was formed but the shares were privately placed rather than being offered to the public. Amongst those subscribing were the Duke of Westminster, Lord Howard de Walden, Sir Ernest Cassel (a protégé of Baron Von Hirsch), Mr J Masher, Mr Buchanan and other gentlemen. Everybody Porter approached was very supportive and soon the monies were in place to proceed.

To fully appreciate Porter's input to his venture the author reproduces in full an article written by him and published in CB Fry's magazine. This is followed by a sample of letters relating to patronage of race meetings and letters of congratulation on the completed project.

John Porter - what do we learn about him from his autobiography and the letters?

John Porter was an only child. There are no references to any siblings. The education he received was normal for that time – pretty basic. For Porter it was also interrupted when the family moved to London for approximately two years. His formal education ended aged 15. Up to this time, he had spent as much of his time as possible working and observing thoroughbreds at stables around Hednesford. Having left school, his father had wanted him to become a lawyer. Porter was allowed a holiday which lasted not just weeks but months – almost fully spent at Saunders stable in Hednesford. From schooldays he had made two friends – Ashmall who was to become a jockey and Robert Denman, who was to become a leading trainer in France.

Under pressure from his father to get a proper job at aged 16, Porter turned his back on becoming a lawyer – preferring the open air life. He applied for and became a light weight jockey to John Day, a leading trainer at Michel Grove, whose principal patron was Mr Henry Padwick – a solicitor and money lender who lived and practiced in Horsham. Prior to this new phase in his life, he had spent time at the trainer Walters – who was one of his godfathers. Walters was principal trainer to William Taylor Copeland and it was at this stables he had come into contact with and learnt to engage with what can be termed 'the gentry'. His second godfather was Charles Marlow, a top jockey who sadly died young and in poor circumstance due to alcohol addiction. It seems he kept in touch with Porter as Marlow's son was buried in Kingsclere Church – it is likely that Porter funded the burial and memorial stone.

Church was always important to Porter and we know when apprenticed to John Day he used to accompany his master to church. When at Park House he used to have the vicar come up to the stables to give the 'lads' confirmation classes. He was engaged in Kingsclere Church, his first wife was buried there and there is a Porter tomb in which Porter himself was interred. He paid for stain glass windows – still viewable today. He was undoubtedly a devout churchgoer all his life.

John Porter was also a designer/architect. He used his early experiences to learn what his horses and staff needed. When Sir Joseph Hawley built the new stables and Park House, it was based on designs that Porter drew up whilst recovering from typhoid fever. Good airy stabling for the horses and good accommodation and facilities for the stable staff. These early buildings exist at Park House today.

He was also something of an engineer designer – see ref to cycle/ambulance at Newbury – referred to in a letter from General Sir Horace Smith-Dorien, asking Porter to show it to Sir John French.

With his father being a tailor and his mother a dressmaker, it is little wonder that Porter was always very well dressed and clearly his appearance to others was of great importance. This attention to detail also showed up in the attention given to the clean stables, tidiness and upkeep of the yard, garden and house. In photos of the stable staff – they all look very clean, tidy and well presented. This overall attention to detail was clearly an influence on his career successes. It appealed to and pleased his patrons.

Porter observed and learnt very quickly. He surprised John Day with his knowledge at interview, also by the fact that he drew up his own indentures for Day to sign. This was also evidence, at the age of 15, that Porter liked matters of detail to be properly handled.

Throughout his time with Day he learnt a great deal, how to ride, how to train and prepare horses and taking care of their welfare. He learnt the discipline of early rising, the welfare for others, particularly stable staff, with no swearing or smoking in the yard. As Porter himself put it "to be respectful to the peer, as courteous to the peasant".

Porter considered himself very lucky to be employed by John Day, who had gained a fine reputation including the nomenclature "Honest John" and he was greatly admired by the most prominent people in racing. Porter throughout his life had close association with his local church and he used to sit with John Day on a Sunday. Religion was always to be of importance to him. John Day had also taught Porter the administration side of the trainers' life, showing him how to keep the books as well as the other clerical tasks. This ability to learn and absorb detail was clearly something that Porter had been born with. John Day recognised this and encouraged him.

Mr Padwick shortly before John Day's death had moved the training establishment from Michel Down to Findon and at that time Porter's apprenticeship officially ended. Padwick appointed William Goater as his private trainer. Following John Day's departure, Porter's duties increased. He acted officially, not only as secretary of the stables, but as Manager, despite being only 17 years old.

Henry Padwick considered Porter to be an outstanding and trustworthy employee and he happily lodged monies for the running of the stables at the bank, the account being in Porter's name. He was responsible for paying all the wages and bills and the upkeep of the yard accounts. In addition to his administration work he was also the head man to Goater, having responsibility for the feeding of the horses, looking after the yard and all the staff and their welfare.

Plate presented to Porter in 1903, on his retirement as a
Public Trainer.   Listing all his Classic winner

Derby Scarf 1886. Ormonde, Duke of Westminster, John Porter and Fred Archer.

Common Winner of the Triple Crown 1891.

Flying Fox Winner of the Triple Crown 1899.

Water Jug, hand painted presented to Porter by unknown owner.

Ormonde Fred Archer up. Triple Crown Winner 1886.

Ormonde J Porter at head, Fred Archer up 1886.

Ormonde, Fred Archer up 1886.

Section Two

Introduction to Part 2

Owners, Friends and Acquaintances.

This section of the book covers the diversity of people with whom John Porter came into contact from his early years as an apprentice, right through to his retirement from training. His ability, hard work, honesty and general demeanour enabled him to make long term friendships and relationships with the Prince of Wales, later Edward VII, peers of the realm, lawyers, military men, authors, landowners, people from the world of the theatre, jockeys and fellow trainers, as well as people from the world of finance and business.

Many were not only his friends, but also became friends of his two wives and children with many enjoying the hospitality on offer at Park House.

From being a private trainer to becoming a public trainer shows his ability to move with the times and some of these "friends and acquaintances" were indeed owners. Due to the moral outlook of the time, it was not always considered appropriate for people holding certain positions to be owners of racehorses and therefore a number of horses shown as being owned by Porter were in fact owned by others, but were run in his colours. Albeit with the blessing of Weatherby's and the Jockey Club.

The following scripts only cover owners whose horses won a race. There were, no doubt, some owners whose horses did not win.

There are included under John Porter's ownership 19 winning horses from 1879 to 1901. These won 34 races with prize money of £10,438.

Some of them were either in partnership or most likely fully owned by others – such as Lord Russell of Killowen – but who felt it inappropriate to run them under their own names, for whatever reason (see Lord Russell's letter on this topic).

Very few, if any, were solely owned by Porter.

Sir Joseph Hawley

1   Photo of letter from Henry Hawley (Sir Joseph's brother) re funeral arrangements from 34 Eaton Place – the address where Porter had his first interview with Sir Joseph.
2   Photos of letters from Lady Sara Hawley (wife of Sir Joseph)
         a) re flowers, garden and visit to Kingsclere.
         b) re her husband's illness.

Sir Joseph was a noted English thoroughbred race horse owner and breeder.

In his early career he trained privately at Fyfield in Wiltshire. Later he employed private trainers. Firstly, George Manning of Cannon Heath and following Manning's death, John Porter at Cannon Heath and Kingsclere. He funded the purchase of the land at Kingsclere and the construction of Park House and its stables. Later he made arrangements in his will for John Porter to buy Kingsclere and its facilities following his death in 1875.

He was a keen reformer of racing and had arguments about this with Admiral Rous. He was a member of the Jockey Club and his horses won the Derby four times. He also won all the other Classics at least once, thus being able to claim winning all five English Classics. He bred the winner of the Belmont Stakes in America in 1874.

He lived and had his stud at Leybourne Grange in Kent as well as his London house at 34 Eaton Place where he first met John Porter, with the Earl of Westmoreland's introduction.

His nephew was Henry Hawley Smart, who following considerable losses in the turf, turned to writing novels – some of which he based on racing – an early Dick Francis! He was a long term acquaintance of John Porter (see separate sheet and copies of letters including those used in Porter's books).

Sir Joseph funded the building of Park House and the stables at Kingsclere, based on John Porter's original designs, drawn up whilst Porter was recovering from typhoid fever in 1865/66.

Sir Joseph was a very thoughtful and kind employer – eg his handling in 1865/66 of Porter's illness and so early in his employment. As a result they had a long and fruitful connection.

Two quotes from John Porter sum up Sir Joseph:

"He was a fine judge of racing, the very best hand at putting horses together I ever met with, and one of the straightest I ever knew. He played the game – small blame to him – like a sportsman".

"I felt when I was at the graveside of Sir Joseph Hawley, that I had seen the last of a splendid pillar of the Turf and parted from one of the very best friends I had had in the whole course of my career".

Thank you very much Porter
for the lovely roses you sent us
by Sir Joseph — I wish you
could see them now I have arranged them in a Basket
& Dish — They look quite
beautiful, & smell so sweet.
Some of the darker rich kinds
I have never seen before —
I hope soon to invite you
to see the horses — and

your garden — but I have not
been at all well this
Spring — and could not ac-
company Miss Marion —
I hope your wife & children
are all well —
Faithfully yours
Sara Hawley.

Wednesday 3rd

Porter I am happy to say
Sir Joseph is going on as well
as possible, he now walks
about the room, and drives
out every day — and has very
good nights — Sir William
Gull forbids him tho' to
attend to any business,

or exert his memory more
than can be avoided —
he joins me here immediately
accompanied by Mr Hawley
Yours faithfully
Sara Hawley

I hope your family are all well.

34 Eaton Place
Saturday.

Porter,

If it would be any gratification to you to attend the funeral of Sir Joseph I shall be very glad for you to do so.

The sad ceremony is to take place next Tuesday at Leybourne

We leave the Snodland Station about 12 o'clock on that day. And there is a train from London (Charing Cross) at 9-55 by which myself and others, who are going to attend. Shall go down —

I thank you much for the sympathy expressed for us in your letter dear Huxley. I am sorry to say, is still far from well but she hopes to be present

in the Church on Tuesday —

I have been with my dear Brother so constantly the last eight months, a more patient invalid I never saw, and so thankful for all that was done for him; I shall miss him sadly, he was such a kind Brother, and we were so attached to each other. I am

Yours very faithfully
Henry Huxley

Thomas Eades Walker
1843-1899

One of John Porter's owners. Porter trained eight winning horses for him winning a total of sixteen races but the prize money was only £3,357. The foregoing covers race years 1873 – 1879.
Thomas Eades Walker was the son of Thomas Walker, an industrialist, who amongst other projects had been involved in the design of the Manchester Ship Canal. In 1863 he had purchased Studley Castle which he gave to his son Thomas Eades Walker.
His son, educated at Harrow and Christ Church, Oxford, was MP for East Worcestershire from 1874-1880. Unfortunately he was also a notorious gambler, who over time frittered his fortune away.
He was forced to sell up and Studley Castle was purchased by Daisy Greville, Countess of Warwick, also mistress to HRH Edward, Prince of Wales. She, there, founded Studley College as the first all-female, horticulture and agriculture college in the Country.

This interest in agriculture cross references to her letter to Porter concerning the Agricultural Board votes. Both Daisy and Porter shared a long standing interest in horticulture and agriculture.

Prior to moving his horses to Porter in 1873, they had been trained in Newmarket by Captain Machell.

Frederick Gretton.

A Porter owner from 1873 – 1882 at Kingsclere. Prior to 1873 his horses had been trained by Matt Dawson at Newmarket.

Fred Gretton's wealth came from owning a one eighth stake in Bass, Ratcliffe and Gretton which by 1877 had become the largest brewery in the world.

During the nine years that Porter trained for him, he had 57 winning horses, providing 145 races won, with total prize money of £37,670.

Fred Gretton was a shrewd owner – Porter had purchased, for him, Isonomy for 360 guineas. He won once from three appearances as a two year old. As he was a May foal, Frederick Gretton asked Porter not to run him in the Derby or St Leger as a three year old, but to prepare him for the Cambridgeshire, which he duly won comfortably and landed a £40,000 gamble for his owner. In today's money £3,200,000.

In 1873 he eloped to Paris with a sixteen year old dancer, having left his wife. They settled in Paris and although never marrying, "Mrs Gretton" as she became known in Parisian circles, became a fashionable beauty. Gretton showered her with gifts. When he suffered a stroke in 1882, she rushed back to London but he never recovered and died within weeks. In his will he left her a lifetime annuity of £6,000.

Whilst not directly connected with racing it is of interest to follow "Mrs Gretton's" life based on this handsome annuity.

Within a year of Gretton's death she married the eldest son of a baronet – Theodore Brinchman. They divorced in 1895.

In 1901 she remarried, to George Byron, 9th Baron Byron of Rochdale, they remained married until his death in 1917. During the marriage she campaigned as a suffragette and was appointed a Dame Commander, Order of the British Empire for her support of a home for nurses who had served in World War One.

Her third and final marriage, in 1924, was to Sir Robert Houston, a Conservative MP and Liverpool shipowner. Within 18 months of their marriage, he died, leaving her £5,500.00 – the equivalent today of roughly £300,000,000. She became at his death one of the richest women in Britain, with the title Lady Houston.

From 1913 – 1931, she had financially supported the British aviation team in the Schneider Trophy. An event to find the fastest seaplane over a specified course. Her financial backing had stimulated the advancement of engine technology that would eventually lead to the Spitfire fighter plane during World War Two.

Britain had won the Trophy in 1927 and 1929 overseen by the aeronautical engineer R J Mitchell who was the Chief Designer at the Supermarine Factory. However the British Government faced with economic depression controversially withdrew financial support to the team.

Lady Houston came to the rescue with a private donation of £100,000 (£5,000,000 in today's money). She actually wrote in a cable to Ramsay Macdonald, Prime Minister – "the supremacy of English airmen can only be upheld by their entrance for the Schneider Trophy and I consider this of supreme importance"

On September 13th 1931, nearly half a million people gathered on the shore of the Solent to witness Britain's attempt to land the trophy for a third and last time. Lady Houston was aboard her yacht "The Liberty!". Not only was the British Supermarine Seaplane victorious, but it also broke the world speed record.

The lessons learned in building these racing seaplanes helped Reginal Mitchell to develop the Supermarine Spitfire used by the R.A.F and other allied countries during World War II and it became the backbone of fighter command during the Battle of Britain.

Lady Houston 'Poppy', the dancer – who eloped with Fred Gretton aged 16, died in December 1936, months after the Spitfire's first flight.

Fred Gretton could hardly have realised how the annuity he left would be put to such good use for his country.

John Gretton

Brother of Fred Gretton. John being the older brother.

Became an owner with Porter in 1876. Between 1876 and 1899, Porter trained thirty one winning horses for him who won 55 races and total prize money of £11,698.00. The majority of his horses, though, were quite moderate.

John bred some of his own horses. One that was useless on the flat, named Roquefort, was a more than useful jumper and in 1885 won the Grand National.

On the flat, his best but unluckiest horse was Miguel, who in 1888 won one race. The following year he finished second in both the Derby and the St Leger, to Donovan. He also finished second in the Ascot Derby and the Hardwicke Stakes.

Porter found John Gretton a splendid man in every way. He never bet, but raced purely for the love of the sport. He bred most of his own horses firstly at Coton near Burton and then at Bladon Hall.

John Gretton's son, Mr F Gretton, nephew of 'the' Fred Gretton also had Porter manage some horses for him.

Sir Robert Jardine
1825 – 1905

Sir Robert Jardine was a Scottish businessman and Liberal politician. In 1865 he became head of Jardine Mattheson & Co – one of the largest Far East trading houses based in Hong Kong. He was an MP for various constituencies both English and Scottish.

In 1888 he jointly purchased and owned Sainfoin with Porter but they sold the horse to Sir J Miller prior to it winning the Derby. They had purchased the horse from the Royal Stables at Hampton Court.

Jardine had other horses including the 1869 Derby winner Pretender, which was trained by Tom Dawson at Middleham.

The joint purchase of Sainfoin came about because Porter and Jardine had independently seen the yearling and each had decided they wished to buy it. Prior to the sale they agreed to do so on 50% each share.

George Grey - 7th Earl of Stamford
1827 – 1883

George Grey was an English cricketer, landowner and peer, who sat on the Whig benches in the House of Lords.

He had horses trained by Porter from 1880 – 1882. He had thirteen winning horses in those two years, winning a total of 31 races and prize money of £11,962. The most successful horse being the filly Geheimniss who won the Oaks.

After the death of George Grey, Geheimniss continued to be trained by Porter as the executors leased the filly to two others of his owners – Lord Alington and Sir Frederick Johnstone, for whom she won twelve races.

Lord Stamford was President of the M.C.C in 1851. His playing career was undistinguished - between 1851 and 1858 he is recorded having made just 81 runs at an average of 7.36, with a highest score of 17.

He was a prominent patron of the Turf and whilst he did not have many notable successes on the Turf, he did win the 2000 Guineas in 1861 and the Oaks in 1882.

Lord Berkeley Paget

Lord Berkeley Paget was the sixth son of the first Marquess of Anglesey, Henry William Paget (1768 – 1854).

He is recorded as having only had one horse in training with Porter. In 1881, he won two races and prize money of £254. Later in 1899 he had a half share in one of the Duke of Portland's horses La Roche, but in late 1900, this half share was purchased back by the Duke of Portland.

Lord Berkeley Paget sat as a Member of Parliament for Anglesey and Milborne Port.

Through the extended family, a notable racehorse owner later emerged – Dorothy Paget, who was to prove more successful as an owner than her forbear.

Lord Alington
1825 – 1904

Lord Alington was an owner – very often in partnership with Sir Frederick Johnstone. They were known as 'the Old Firm'. Born Henry Gerald Sturt, he was a British peer and Conservative politician. He was created first Baron Alington of Crichel in 1876. He married twice. His first wife was a daughter of the third Earl of Lucan.

He was MP for Dorchester from 1847 to 1856 and then one of two MPs for Dorset from 1856 – 1876. He became a peer in 1876.

He was a Jockey Club member for over fifty years, having become a member in 1850. His most notable win on the racecourse was with St Blaise, who won the Derby in 1883. Between 1881 and 1904 his horses won 114 races. Lord Alington and Sir Frederick Johnstone became patrons of Park House in 1881.

Prior to joining up with Sir Frederick Johnstone in 1868, when both were patrons of William Day at Woodyeates, he had two or three racing partners. Sir Frederick was the junior partner, being some sixteen years younger than Lord Alington. However the partnership horses generally ran in Sir Frederick Johnstone's colours of 'chocolate with yellow sleeves'. In John Porter's experience it was Lord Alington who was the more active of the two. He always got on well with both of them and they did leave the management of their horses very much in his hands. At times they were both quite heavy betters.

Although they never owned more than seven or eight broodmares at any one time, they were extraordinarily fortunate as breeders and owners of racehorses.

According to Lord Lambton's recollections, both Lord Alington and Sir Frederick Johnstone" were full of fun and wit, but with the sharpness of a sword under it when racing matters were concerned".

Lord Alington was close to HRH Prince of Wales. On two occasions he was inadvertently involved with two of Prince Edward's flirtations. One being that with Edith Aylesford, the other with Lillie Langtry while at a royal house party held at Crichel, Dorset - Lord Alington's home, in January 1878.

Sir Frederick Johnstone
1841 – 1913

Sir Frederick Johnstone first became an owner in 1867 and remained with John Porter until 1905. His horses were always in partnership with others. His greatest partnership was with Lord Alington, but he also had partnerships with Sir Joseph Hawley and John Porter. His partnership with Lord Alington became known as 'the Old Firm' – that partnership began in 1881 and was to endure, successfully, for the next 24 years. They had two Derby winners – St Blaise in 1883 and Common in 1891. A letter in the archive concerns the Paradox Scandal, involving another of Porter's owners – Mr Cloete, following his scratching of Paradox from the Cambridgeshire. The result of which saw the withdrawal of Cloete's horse from Kingsclere. The tone of Johnstone's letter emphasises the divide between aristocracy and someone from 'trade' or 'business'. Cloete made his money operating in the border zones between Mexico and the United States. It was the divide between 'old money' and 'new money'.
Sir Frederick Johnstone became a friend of the Prince of Wales whilst at Christ Church, Oxford. Johnstone was exactly the type of "fast" young man, Prince Albert, was anxious that the Prince of Wales should avoid - a heavy drinking member of the Bullingdon Club, devoted to gambling, horseracing and womanising. It was Sir Frederick Johnstone who first led the Prince of Wales astray, opening his eyes to the possibilities of his position and helping him to rub off his harsh German accent.

The Harriett Mordaunt Scandal

Harriett Mordaunt was sure the father of her child was Lord Cole, but she confessed to sleeping with the Prince of Wales and Sir Frederick Johnstone (although at the time she was already pregnant). Sir Frederick Johnstone, she told the midwife, was a 'fearfully diseased man' having been told this by her husband. Sir Charles Mordaunt petitioned for divorce in April 1869 accusing Lord Cole, Sir Frederick Johnstone and another, (the Prince of Wales) of adultery with his wife. The jury threw out the petition as Harriett Mordaunt was considered to be in no mental state to answer her husband's petition.
In 1881 Sir Frederick Johnstone's friendship with the Prince of Wales ended. Sir Frederick was behaving badly in the billiard room at Sandringham. The Prince of Wales put his hand on Sir Frederick's shoulder and said "Freddy, Freddy, you are very drunk". Sir Frederick replied, pointing at the Prince of Wales' expanding girth and said "Tum, Tum, you are very fat". The Prince of Wales left the room, the friendship was terminated and Sir Frederick left Sandringham the next day.

Wednesday

Dear Mr Porter

I am excessively sorry
for you about all this
Paradox business & I confess
that unless Mr Goate can
give a satisfactory explanation
of his conduct I should
request him to remove
his horses. He may have
bet on horses but it
will require a great deal

of explanation to show
that he does not bet
against them — Can
he explain as a gentleman
& a man of honour why
Fry never stopped laying
against Paradox —
Ask him? Hoping to
see you on Saturday

In truly

F. Johnstone

Hugh Grosvenor - 1st Duke of Westminster
1825 – 1899

Landowner, MP and member of the House of Lords. He inherited the Eaton Hall Estate in Cheshire as well as land in Mayfair and Belgravia, London. Politics was not his main interest, but rather his estates, horse racing and country pursuits. He developed a successful stud at Eaton Hall, achieving racing successes, including winning the Derby four times. Aside from this, he was generous in his charitable works. At the time of his death he was considered to be the richest man in Britain.

It was in 1881, near the end of the season that he asked Porter to take over his yearlings and the horses which had been trained for him at Russley by Robert Peck. The intake of these horses of a higher calibre raised the tune of Kingsclere from focusing on handicaps to focusing on the classics and the important weight for age races. The 'Hawley touch' as Porter put it, was reignited.

Hugh Grosvenor was educated at Eton and went from there to Balliol College, Oxford. He left without taking a degree to become MP for Chester, a seat he only relinquished on the death of his father in 1869 and then moved to the House of Lords.

His major interest was in horse racing. He established a racing stable at Eaton, eventually employing thirty grooms and boys, together with two or three stallions and some twenty breeding mares. He did not regard this investment as an extravagance, but more as his aristocratic duty. He was never known to gamble or place bets on any of his horses. In 1880 his colt, Bend Or, won him his first Derby, ridden by Fred Archer. He won three more Derbies in 1882, 1886 and 1899. With his successes and the sale of horses, it is considered possible that this stable enterprise was in fact self-financing. During the years 1881 – 1899 John Porter trained 74 winning horses for him, winning 240 races with prize money of £246,944. Grosvenor was teetotal and a supporter of temperance. Evidence of this was the reduction of public houses in his, Mayfair, London, estate from forty seven to eight.

He married twice, having eight children from his first marriage and four from his second.

His eldest son, Victor Alexander, Lord Grosvenor 1853-1884) had one horse, trained by Porter, in 1883, called Reprieve. It was to be his first and only horse. Porter felt that the Duke was not entirely happy about this. The situation was however resolved with Victor's early death, the year following, at which time Reprieve had won five races and been placed second, twice. Reprieve was purchased by Lord Alington and Sir Frederick Johnstone for whom she won no races.

Letters – addressed from Cliveden

Contratulations to John Porter following 'Ormondes' Derby win in 1886. Mentions training other horses, but he has to go to Eaton.

Letter addressed from Grosvenor House

Tells Porter he has an offer for Cambusmore for £1000. The horse won seven races (1884 – 1886). The Duke of Westminster asks Porter if he should sell or wait for nearer the end of the season when he might get the same price. Refers to Paradox and Mr Cloete.

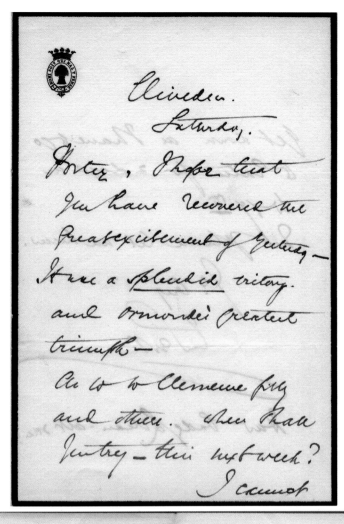

Cliveden.
Saturday,

My dear, I hope that
you have recovered the
great excitement of yesterday —
It was a splendid victory.
and Ormonde's greatest
triumph —
As to the Clemence fête
and others. When shall
I/you — this next week?
I cannot

get down as I have to go
to Eaton for 2 days on
the 19th
but please let me know.
...
...

Have lady Lilian — all well!

I should like to know
what engagements Ormonde
may undertake —
I hear he does not quite
like the last elections

53

and shall not be able
to [get] to [business] again
this week.

Next week, on Sunday,
I go to [Eton] and [Chester]
for [Germany] and return
15th of [Thursday].
[Yrs truly]

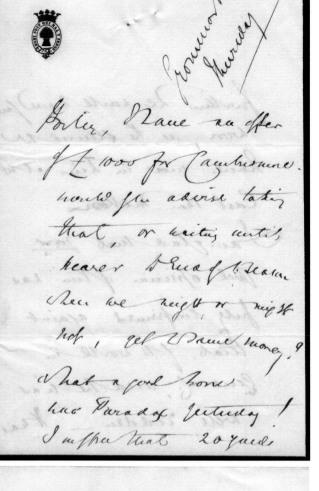

[Grosvenor] [Place]
Thursday

Porter, [have] an offer
of £1000 for [Cambresine].
would you advise taking
that, or waiting until
nearer to end of season
when we might or might
not, get the same money?
What a good horse
was Paradox yesterday!
I [suppose] that 20 yards

further he would have just
won, as he seemed to
have more in him at the
last than Melton.

I am glad that your
good opinion of him was
fully confirmed against
that of the world in
general, and he was
well ridden — It was

[Read] it and Robert [Deril]
over again — it is a pity
that he is not to be [kept]
but I suppose you will send
him over to Paris if
well meantime, and
none [worse] for the race —

My [Clare] might perhaps,
from what he said to me,
takes like the same
[Cambresine]? It was
not well yesterday [evening]

Captain Bayley
1823 – 1894

Owner of one winning horse - trained by Porter in 1883. The horse won just two races with prize money of £228.

No reference is made to this owner in either of John Porter's books.

It seems possible that Captain Bayley was Captain James Bayley who lived in Hobart, Tasmania, but had connections with the shipbuilder R J Bayley of Ipswich. It is recorded that he travelled from England to Tasmania with Elizabeth Bayley, daughter of RJ Bayley and his own daughter Harriett Louisa Bayley in 1872. He was then 49, his daughter was 12.

There is also record of him travelling to England in 1846 to see his family. He was a merchant navy captain travelling mainly in the Far East. He and his brother, Captain Charles Bayley, were two of the early day Tasmanian seamen.

His journey in 1872 lasted 11 days – one of the longest, due to adverse weather conditions.

Hugh Dawney - 8th Viscount Downe

Was a British Army General and President of the MCC.

Educated at Eton and Christ Church, Oxford.

He had just one recorded winning horse trained by John Porter. It won one race in 1884 with prize money of £989.

There is no reference to Viscount Downe in either of Porter's books, other than the record of his one winning horse.

Letter 12.10.83 from Wykeham Abbey

"Would like to visit on Saturday 20th to see the yearlings – might visit with Earl Spencer, if he is in London, I will try and bring him down. Please reply to Berkeley Square where I go on Monday.

Letter 06.08.91 from Cavalry Barracks-York

"Lord Marcus (Beresford) writes that neither he nor Porter had time to go and see the xxxx yearling at Dingley for another month. I am sorry etc – she is in the Oaks and others.

Should she not stay at Dingly for another month – she is growing fast and doing well. Let me know. I am here until the 18th, then to Dingley for a night before going to the Curragh"

Three letters from Cecilia, Viscountess Downe from Dublin where Viscount Downe was in command of the Cavalry Brigade at the Curragh in 1901.

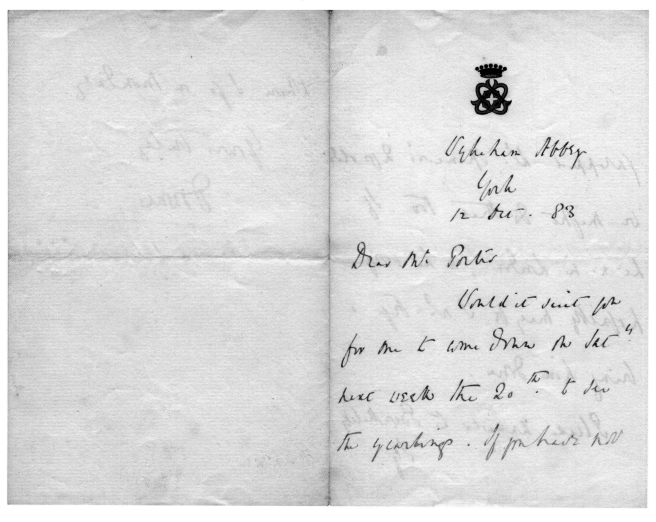

galloped Mr Spencer's 2 y olds
or might do that too. If
he is in London, he very
possibly may be & he keeps
bring him down.

Please answer to Berkeley
Sq.

When I go on Monday.

Yours truly

Drone

till 18th when I go to
Drigley for a night &
then to the Camargh.

Yours truly

Drone

Cavalry Barracks
York
6 May -91

Dear Mr Yates

Lord Marcus
writes that neither you nor
he have time to go & see
the Sanity yearling. I am
rather sorry, but still I

think you will be satisfied.
She is a [good] bit bigger
than Red Enamel. She is
in the Oaks & in 2
Races at Manchester,
one a big 10,000 one —
I have my book packed up

but you can look them out,
in time for [prefects]. The
Prince of Wales pays all
expenses & entries.
[Should] not she better stay
at [Drighly] for another
month. She is growing fast
& doing well. Let me
know this place. I am here

COOMBE COTTAGE,
KINGSTON, S.W.

Dear Mr. Parker. Will you
[house here] if you
have tried the [Andorian]
Colt this [week]? & if he
[runs] at all [at here]
or elsewhere. I [fear]
you [don't intend] [here]
[much good] do [you]?
I had hoped to have
[wanted to see] before
now

but have been permitted
but believe with certainty
ere one day —

Respectfully

[signature]

Cecilia Downe (wife)

18 Rutland Square
Dublin

Dear Mr. Porter – I think you asked me for my Votes for Incurable hospital – I can't remember the woman's name so send you the polling papers signed with your put 2. against her name & send it to Secretary

I have been

truly sorry for you in all this trouble about Bruce — it must have been most disagreeable & anxious work for you & wonderful that he has recovered as he seems to have done — I shd like how I shd like — Thanks Y⁰

Yrs truly Cecilia Orme

We have another colt by Weatherby this year — a ... How is Dorrie going on?

L⁴ Orme is away at Bath drinking the waters to get rid I hope of the last of that horrid typhoid heat ... came here this ... badly wanted

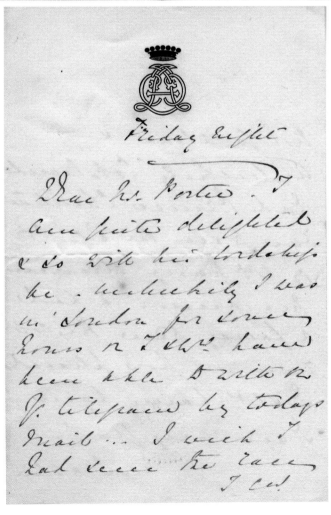

Friday night

Dear Mr. Porter — I am quite delighted to do with his lordship's he — Unluckily I was in London for some hours & I shd. have been able to write the I telegram by today's mail ... I wish I had seen the race I cd.

...to above —
unluckily [oh. Maude]
had Prince Christian
but I see he did.
& Mr. have drawn
her own... I had
a fancy to see her colour
... & how pleased
I should have been!
I am very glad
Mr. Chaplin

brought him... Now
I think you'll have
I find us another
St. Aliester has promised
I bring her over
I see you soon...
The Duke asked me
I come tomorrow but
is is so cold I am
afraid
Ever truly
Cecilia Downe

Martha Dowie
2 Votes given
My Lady
I am pleased to
inform your Ladyship
that Martha Dowie
was successful at
the last Election and
I beg to thank you for
your kind interest on
her behalf
I remain
Your Ladyship's
Dr. Stewart

Dublin
Feby 23.

Dear Mr. Porter
I will certainly vote
for the poor woman
I hope you have a
good winning year
before you — I wish
you'd tell me of
some early from
their ladyship —
Mr. Downe is back again
I am

thankful to say, but
he had a fearfully
long illness ..
We do not like Dublin
much . I am now
studying tonight for
England . & think
a change will do me
good . Yours
sincerely
Leila d'Arcé

Mr Brodrick Cloete

A winning owner of John Porter trained horses between 1884 – 1885. He had two horses – Cherry and Paradox, that won nine races between them with prize money of £19,190. Very successful.

Cloete did not fit into the image of the majority of Porter's other owners.

He was born in South Africa around 1851/1852, but was a British subject living in England. He worked in Mexico where he had extensive mining and plantation interests. His residence was listed as Hare Park in London's outskirts.

He was an established cricketer and played for the Surrey Club and from 1877-1893 he played for the MCC. He was a well known breeder and owner of racehorses.

Paradox had been owned jointly by Porter and Captain Bowling. Bowling then purchased Porter's share and some while later sold the horse to the Duke of Westminster. He in turn sold it to Brodrick Cloete, winning the Dewhurst as a two year old. At three he won the 2000 Guineas. In the Derby, without Archer to ride him, who knew his foibles, he was beaten. Shortly afterwards, Porter took him to France for the Grand Prix de Paris and reunited with Archer, he won.

In 1897 Cloete participated in the Klondike Gold Rush working on a development project for the Canadian Mining Company in Yukon.

In 1899 he edited and re-published the book which had been written by his Grandfather –
The History of the Great Boer Trek and the Origin of the South African Republic.

Mr and Mrs Cloete were on the Lusitania for Captain James Watt's last westbound crossing as commander of the ship on 31st October 1908.

In the late 1800s he founded a coal mining town in the Mexican state of Coahulia. Today the town is called Cloete, or San Jose de Cloete, which in 2005 had a population of 3,977.

The town adopted his name following his death in the sinking of the Lusitania in 1915. The ship having been torpedoed on 7th May 1915. Cloete's body was either not recovered or not identified. He left a widow, Violet, whom he had married in 1902.

Isaac Newton Wallop 5th Earl and
Newton Wallop 6th Earl of Portsmouth
1856 – 1917

One of John Porter's owners and a friend of Hawley-Smart. The soldier, turned writer, who is also one of Porter's friends and correspondents. Hawley-Smart's letters refer to Eggesford House and the Portsmouth family with whom he also stays.

Letter 11 December 1887 – Eggesford House

This is from the 5th Earl of Portsmouth – Isaac Newton Wallop as the 6th Earl succeeded to the title in 1891.

Letter concerns buying cheap stock – two stallions to be sent to Montana USA for his son's ranch.

Letter 7 January 1891 – Eggesford House

From the 5th Earl – Isaac Newton Wallop to Lord and Lady Lymington, title of 6th Earl pre his succession.

Letter refers to disastrous fire at Lymington's house and loss of all their possessions. Thanks to Porter for his letter of sympathy.

Letter 8th June 1890 from Gerald Wallop (Woodbridge)
Letter congratulating Porter on Sainfoin – Derby victory.

Letter 16th February 1889 from Gerald Wallop (Colonial office)
Pleased to hear you have made such improvement and are progressing so well. Ref to books he has sent him and will send some more.

This letter suggests it was to Porter's son following the loss of his leg.

Letter 17th July 1887 from Eggesford House
Terrier puppy weaned from bitch will send on Tuesday by first train reaching Overton about 2pm.
Details of puppy's parentage.
Yearling and filly going the right way
Suggest name for foal to be Union Jack
The weather will cause small fields at Goodwood
He, wife and children off to Switzerland but he will return in time for cubhunting.

Eggesford Manor
Wembworthy
N. Devon
July 17. 1887

My dear Sir

Your Terrier Puppy is weaned from the Bitch so it shall be sent to you on Tuesday by first train reaching Oveston about 2 pm.

D. By Bacchus out of Susan. The sire is a devil under ground and the dam a beauty & ready for fighting or Hunting at any time.

My Yearling grows the right way and so does the filly. The Colt promises to be a size larger than Gules and with more length & with better shoulders. My Standard foal out of Dart ought to be worth calling Union Jack.

It is a good one. I have not seen a better. It is time that I bred a winner again and saw him carry my jacket. This foal has such limbs with fine shoulders & great knees. This continued hard ground will stump up Horses and make fields small at Goodwood. I & my wife start with 2 of our children for Switzerland the latter part of next week for a short trip before I begin Cubhunting.

I remain
Y. Truly
Portsmouth

---

2. The big Yearl filly should improve with time. I trust she does not melt as she had very little green food last Summer and was not made up with mashes &c.

I remain
Y. Truly
Portsmouth

Eggesford Manor
Wembworthy
N. Devon
Dec. 11. 1887

My Dear Sir

I suppose you will go to Newmarket for the Sale this week. If you would kindly try to buy 2 stallions Bay or brown without much white, full sized, with bone and fair action, not under 3 y. (1887) sound in wind and eyes and Houghs, for me at prices not exceeding £ 200 for the 2 I should be very much

Eggesford House
Wembworthy
N. Devon
Jan'y 7. 1891

My Dear Sir
Thanks to you and other kind friends for sympathy in this terrible loss at Hurstbourne. It seems as if troubles would never end for me in Hampshire and now this worst of all. It is an awful blow to Lymington and to Lady Lymington too. They have lost all their personal treasures and their home. Although it can be rebuilt it must take time and it cannot be the same. Besides heirlooms are burnt that are irreparable. With kindest mems to Mrs Porter &c
Yrs truly
Portsmouth

obliged to you. I want them for my son Oliver who has a Horse Ranche in Montana America. I see there are a lot of animals to be sold and possibly between Horses that wont train or wont jump you might find me what I want. 2 cheap stallions to turn out with mares on a Ranche. Cripples are no use they cannot find their living and old Horses would not take to the climate. I see that

the Duke of Hamilton wants to sell a lot of mares of the Agnes and Music strain. I have only 2 mares in foal so I could do well with another mare. I should like a mare in foal to Trappist or Mask if you see a nice shaped mare going under £100. Hazeldean is in foal to Xenophon but Dart is barren. If you can help me to what I want I shall be greatly obliged to you. I hope my beasts are doing well. I shall be curious to know whether the Colt improves. I always liked him best of the

John Spencer – 5th Earl Spencer
1835 – 1910

Known as Viscount Althorp from 1845 – 1857. Also known as the Red Earl because of his distinctive long red beard. A Liberal party politician and a close friend of the Prime Minister, William Ewart Gladstone. He served two periods as Lord Lieutenant of Ireland from 1868 – 1874 and 1882 – 1885.

Porter trained only one winning horse for him – Cobbler in 1886 – winner of just one race value £102.00

His political life came before his racing interests.

See letters 1888 from Germany.

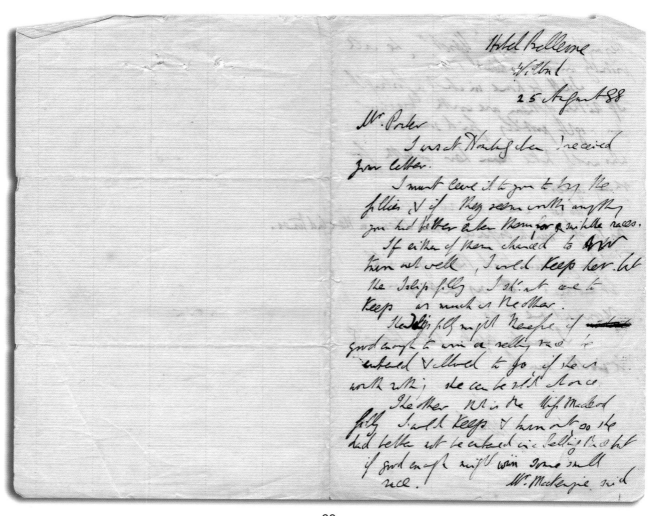

They might be tried with "Ysprot". He will probably write to you about that.

I shall be home in about a fortnight. If either of them are worth training you might probably find some one who will take them her or both for racing career.

I do not want to run the risk of much expence over them in these bad times.

When you have tried them you will let me know & I say what you recommend me to do.

I cannot expect that they will be worth much.

[signature]

N. Dale
Falkenham

7 Oct 88

Mr Parker

I daresay it is better to have got rid of the filly, for her bad legs might have been hereditary.

If she had been a few lbs better I sh'd have got well out of her.

I am sorry that I have had nothing better to send you.

The yearling colt own brother to the filly is a fine animal with very good legs. I sh'd like to get some one to take him for training career.

He looks as if he will make good country Stallion if he does not make a racer.

[signature]

69

HRH Prince of Wales - later King Edward VII
1841 – 1910

The eldest son of Queen Victoria and Prince Albert. Because of his Mother's longevity he served as her heir apparent and held the title Prince of Wales for longer than any of his predecessors. By his Mother's design he was largely excluded from political power and came to personify the fashionable, leisured elite. He enjoyed shooting, particularly, but was also interested in agriculture. He was always very interested in thoroughbreds and racing.

Between 1886 and 1892 Porter trained eleven winning horses for him, winning a total of 18 races and prize money of £6,768. He moved his horses from Kingsclere to Richard Marsh at Newmarket at the end of 1892 – the same time that Baron Von Hirsch also moved his horses. Nonetheless Porter remained on good terms with Prince Edward and by invitation made annual visits to Sandringham to view the stables, cattle etc. It was The Prince's influence that persuaded the Jockey Club to licence Porter's new racecourse at Newbury in 1905, having previously rejected it at least twice.

Prince Edwards's racing Manager, Lord Marcus Beresford, was in all probability responsible for the removal of his and Hirsch's horse from Kingsclere in 1892.

Prince Edward always had great popular following and when his horses won the Derby and the Grand National, the racing public was jubilant. He was a popular figure and over 400,000 members of the public filed past his coffin in the two days prior to his funeral.

Captain Bowling

A friend and owner of Porter's. Fred Archer had introduced them. Bowling was a very close friend of Archer and virtually acted as his agent/manager.

Bowling had been forced to leave the army, having been badly wounded which left him partially disabled.

Bowling's background is a matter of conjecture. According to Porter he was the son of a Pembrokshire rector. Fred Archer's sister Mrs Pratt, maintains he belonged to the firm of solicitors Bowling and Creagh.

The fact is that he was well off and was able to buy and race high class horses. His friendship with Archer really commenced in 1882, but grew closer and closer.

On the early death of Archer's wife, a daughter of John Dawson, Bowling his devoted friend never left his side, even sleeping in his room, as there was even then a fear he might take his own life.

The marriage took place at Newmarket on 31st January 1883. John Porter was among the congregation. The honeymoon was in Torquay, Devon and the couple received an invitation from Lord Courtenay, godfather of one of Porter's sons, to visit him at Powderham Castle. They did not accept.

That summer Porter and Bowling purchased a colt – Paradox, as it was later named from the Yardley Stud. It was purchased for £700. They did not run it until October 1884, in a trial. It ran well and they decided to run it in the Middle Park Plate. The Duke of Westminster's eyes had been caught by the colt and he asked Porter if Bowling would sell – he did so for the sum of £6000. The horse came third.

The Duke sold it to another of Porter's owners for £5000. Throughout this changing ownership Porter had been confident in the colt and he went on to win the Dewhurst Plate, beating a high class field.

Following the birth of Archer's second child, she suffered convulsions and died. Archer went into deep depression and Captain Bowling came to Newmarket to stay with him, as did Archer's sister – Mrs Coleman. The depression was so bad that the two of them decided on intervention to let Archer return to get on with his life. They suggested he went away for a complete break – the proposed location being America, where there would be no language difficulty and where there were existing connections. Archer agreed and at first wanted Herbert Mills, an old Cheltenham friend to travel with him. Mills was not free to do so and it was then that he asked Captain Bowling to accompany him. The trip started in New York, but took in also New Orleans, Washington, Niagra, Chicago, St Louis, Houston, Texas and Florida. Throughout, Bowling was there to support and look after his friend. A hack through Central Park on their return to New York was his sole contact with a horse, the entire trip.

They had left England on 15th November and did not return until 9th March 1885.

It left him little time to get fit for the new season as he had had no intention of giving up riding. The trip, suggested by Bowling and his sister had done him the world of good. Outwardly he looked much healthier, although his friends noticed lines of care etched on his face. The racing public gave him a hero's welcome back.

That year Archer rode a record 246 winners. They were the summit of his career but afforded him no happiness.

Beside him was the sombre figure of Bowling, devoted to his friend, doing his best to look after Archer's affairs and helping him with his business dealings and deal with the mass of correspondence - good and bad, that he received. As well as keeping at bay the hangers-on that were drawn to Archer.

At the start of the 1886 season Archer was not well. An accumulation of grief, physical strain, mental torment and wasting for the past thirteen years had taken its toll. He looked ghastly and his friends told him so. However, he kept riding . He was due to ride Secretband in the Derby, but it was scratched and John Porter booked him to ride Ormonde, owned by the Duke of Wesmtinster. Ormonde won. To ride in the Cambridgeshire, Archer had to reduce to 8st 6lbs, the one major race he had not won. He lost on St Moin by a head. His deprivation to make the weight had left him a weak, sick man – he had no strength left in a tight finish. He never recovered mentally or physically – despite a physical improvement his mental state remained very depressed.

Bowling and his sister engaged two nurses to help look after him. Despite this he kept telling the doctors and nurses he was going to die.

The morning of his death the doctor had been happy enough to leave the house at 9.30 am. The nurses stayed with him and Bowling and Archer's sister were in and out of the sick room. At 12.00 o'clock Bowling went out on an errand. This left Archer, his sister and a nurse in the room. Archer asked that the nurse leave as he had something private to discuss with his sister. Having looked out of the window, waiting for him to speak he said "Are they coming". On turning round she saw him half out of bed with a pistol in his hand. She went to him to try to remove it. They grappled but she could not stop him putting the pistol to his head and firing it. He was dead before help arrived.

Bowling identified the deceased at the inquest.

See letter from Ladysmith 10.07.1879.
Ref to arm injury – operation – prognosis
Also ref to Sir G Wolseley who was Commander in Chief of Zulu Wars in 1879.

officers Tent? I said half asleep
"yes" - Are you Capt Bowrij? An
"yes". Then I must see you =
This was our friend Mr. Archibald
Forbes who stopped in dead
beat having ridden about without
resting from Ulundi - He gave
me verbal account of all that
took place - He had despatch
for Sir. G. Wolseley and I sent
him on at once = He said
the Zulus were pluck to the
back bone - but that the
English soldiers stood like
rocks only wanting to
be at them with the
bayonet - The Lancers made
"great hay" of them when

they began to run - We all
hope now that the war is
near over in fact I have
applied to start home - I
wish I had never come - I
shall have to have my elbow
operated on as soon as I get
to England & I then fear I
shall have stiff arm for
life = I saw the account
of 2000 - 1000. Sely & Oxen
but my respected friend Mr. P
did not figure in either.
Major Wood 12 Lancers who
came out with Sir. G. Wolsly
told me Baron. R. had
a good haul over. Sir Garnet
How is Mr. P. tell
her Catchwayo wool
is not in the market as
yet & that there are no
feathers diamond or other

Sir James Mackenzie
1818 – 1890

A friend of H.R.H Prince of Wales and a self-made Scottish millionaire. He owned the Glenmuick Estate adjoining Balmoral.

Porter trained six winning horses for him between 1886 and 1891, winning a total of 13 races with prize money of £8401.

He died in August 1890 having received his Baronetage in March of that year.

According to Porter, he was a keen racing man.

It is on record that Prince Edward's court was in part subsidised by the self-made Scottish millionaire, James Mackenzie. The son of an Aberdeen stocking merchant who made one fortune in indigo in India and then another on Lombard Street. Mackenzie had purchased the Glenmuick estate (29,500 acres) bordering on Balmoral in 1869. Mackenzie's nickname given by Prince Edward was 'MacTavish' and he treated him as a cross between a factotum and a sugar daddy. Mackenzie also owned Sunningdale Park which Prince Edward used to borrow for Ascot Races. From at least 1884 Mackenzie lent him large amounts of money, secured against the title deed of Sandringham.

On Mackenzie's death his executors called in the loans – they were paid back by Baron Von Hirsch. The sum involved was approximately £250,000.

See letters 1888-1889 re Leyset, Pinehouse, Sunningdale Park etc.

Glen-Muick,
Ballater,
Aberdeenshire.
Sept. 5. 88.

Dear Sir,

I have got your telegram. Did not expect that Upset would win. I think it will be better for this racing season to keep him only for his own course 6 furlongs, after the racing is over we could try him for a mile and if he can stay, train him for that, next year.

As I did not know you had entered which for Derby I had entered him for the Portland Plate Doncaster, but as he has been running so much - unless he gets in at a very light weight I should not run him there but keep him for Epsom for some of the other 6 furlong courses.

I suppose the weights for Doncaster will be in the sheet Calendar on Thursday and will telegraph you about his racing on Saturday.

I hope the Kelpie may hull off the Nursery at Sandown. Telegraph me on receipt of this if you will be there as I want to back her both to win & for a place for the Prince & if you will not be there I will do so with Skel direct.

Yours faithfully
J G Mackenzie

I will get her in for some other Nurseries I will be at later on.

12, Carlton House Terrace.
S.W.

19 Oct: 1885

My dear Sir.

As I have bought Sunningdale Park which is not far from you & as I only keep about four race horses altogether I shall be very glad if you will take charge of them all — my racing is only done in a small way for something to do & I like breeding the horses

run. I only want to keep good ones — we will meet at the Hampton Meeting next week & settle it. I fancy the horses better remain with J. Dawson till the end of next month when the racing season is over —

Yours faithfully

J. W. Whe[...]

J. W. Porter

12 Carlton House Terrace
S.W.

Glen-Muick,
Ballater,
Aberdeenshire.

Aug. 2.89.

Dear Sir,

I hope you & Mrs Porter
will be able to get to Scotland
next week and if you
come at the end of the
week we shall be able
to put you up – but in
the early part of away
we shall be full.

Book through to Ballater
you will get through tickets
from Kings Cross leaving

at 8 o'clock in the evening
and reaching Ballater
at mid day next day;
with sleeping berths.

If you will be at
Ballater in the early
part of the week, write
to the Manager, Invercauld
Arms Hotel, Ballater for
a bedroom and come
up to us for the day

I see Upset got third; Mr Porter

he must have run un-
commonly well with
the heavy weight.

Yours faithfully,
J. W. Mackie

William Low/Mr Y.R. Graham

Low

Porter trained 27 winning horses for him between 1887 and 1903. Total races won was 67 with prize money £26,532. Left Kingsclere when the company, Kingsclere Racing Ltd was formed.

Y.R. Graham

Porter trained one winning horse for him in 1889 – races won 1. Prize money £112.00
A member of the Graham family who ran the Yardley Stud in Birmingham. Porter regularly visited to see what young horses they had. Three of which Porter purchased that were of note – Isonomy, Fernandez and Paradox.

Mr Marcus Daly
1841 – 1900

Porter trained one winning horse for him in 1890. It won two races with prize money of £595.00
Marcus Daly was an Irish born, American businessman known as one of the three "Copper Kings" of Butte, Montana, U.S.A.

Daly emigrated to the States as a young boy, arriving in New York. He sold newspapers but then worked his way to California and joined the Gold Rush that was to become Virginia City, Nevada and the fabulously rich silver diggings known as the Cornstock Lode in 1860. While working in Virginia City he met and became friendly with George Hearst (father of William Randolph Hearst) and Lloyd Trevis. In 1872 Daly recommended to the Hearst group that they buy the Ontario mine, near Park City, Utah. In ten years the mine produced $17 million, making many millions for Hearst. Their business friendship extended for many years and helped establish the Anaconda Copper Mine in Butte, Montana.

Daly originally came to Butte in 1876 to look at the Alice Mine as agent for Walker Brothers of Salt Lake City. They purchased the mine, made Daly superintendent and awarded him a share in the mine. Whilst working underground he found amongst the silver there were significant deposits of copper ore. He visited adjoining mines and came to the conclusion that the hill, of which the Alice mine was but one, held a body of ore several thousand feet deep. He urged his employers, the Walker Brothers, to purchase the Anaconda and when they refused, Daly purchased it. Lacking the money to properly develop it, he turned to Hearst, Haggin & Tevis with all of whom he had previous connection. The first couple of hundred feet were rich in silver and took a few years to exhaust. It was the same in surrounding mines. He closed his own mines and as prices of surrounding ones dropped, so he purchased them at knock down prices. He then reopened Anaconda and announced to the world that Butte was the "Richest Hill on Earth".

Thomas Edison had developed the light bulb and Daly had understood the market for copper that this development would need by way of electrification. Butte had copper, hundreds of thousands of tons of it, awaiting excavation. Daly built a smelter to handle the ore and by the late 1880s had become a millionaire, several times over and owned the Anaconda Mining and Reduction Company. He owned the Butte, Anaconda and Pacific Railway to transport the ore from mine to the smelter in Anaconda, the city he founded for his workers employed at the smelter. He also owned timber interests in the Bitteroot Valley, a mansion and special stables, south of Missoula.

In 1898 he sold out his mining interests to William Rockefellar and Henry Rogers of John D Rockefeller's Standard Oil of Ohio for 39 million dollars. He died in 1900.

Daly had invested some of his money in thoroughbred horse breeding at this Bitteroot Stock Farm. He had some success, winning the Belmont Stakes in 1897.

How he came to have one winning horse trained at Kingsclere is not known, with his wealth it is not surprising that he chose Porter as his trainer.

Sir James Percy Miller - 2nd Baronet
1864 – 1906

Educated Eton & Sandhurst
In 1890 he purchased Sainfoin from Sir Robert Jardine and John Porter.
Porter remained the trainer and won the Derby with Sainfoin in 1890.

Miller was a very wealthy young man and was a Captain in 14th Hussars from 1885- 1892.

In a letter of June 27th 1890, following the Derby win, he writes to Porter about keeping Sainfoin for the St Leger, so that he is not tired. He thanks Porter for training him to win the Derby. He goes on to say he will give Porter £1000 of the prize money should he win the St Leger – which he did not, finishing fourth. Sainfoin left Kingsclere to be trained at Newmarket, but he never won another race.

In a letter dated 17 September 1890, he commiserates with Porter over the St Leger result but goes on to profusely thank him – "I can hardly thank you sufficiently for having so kindly kept the horse so long for me and helping me to win the Derby". He then goes on to talk about arrangements to move the horse to Portslade where he keeps all his horses.

He says he will be encamped at Crookham the following week and asks Porter if it would be convenient for him and some fellow officers to visit Kingsclere on the Sunday afternoon.

14th Hussars
Uffington
Berks.

17-9-90

Dear Mr Porter

I was sorry not to see you after the race last week, to hear what you thought of it — I was very sorry that you were not lucky enough to [win] the horse, so I have no great object in picking up the £500 or so at Goodwood — but would be infinitely more pleased if the horse were to win the Leger —

I have therefore decided to give him every chance in my power, & would like you to train him especially for this race.

If he manages to win it I will gladly give you £1,000-0-0 out of the stake, the winning of which you may you will have greatly contributed to — if, on the other hand, there is a better horse in the race & he is beaten it can't be helped, and we will both have done our best for him — Neither will I have the horse

I expect we shall be encamped at Crookham next Saturday & Sunday, & if you have no objection, I think some of the Officers would like to have a look round the stable on Sunday afternoon — Please write to Crookham & tell me if convenient.

Early next week —

Again thanking you

Yrs truly
James Miller

Mr Francis Alexander

Was an owner with Porter from 1884 – 1903.
Porter trained fifteen winning horses for him winning a total of 33 races and prize money of £11,705.00
He left Kingsclere when Kingsclere Racing Company was formed in 1903, at which time he moved his horses to Braime at Burbage,where he lived nearby at Everleigh House.
No further information could be found on Mr Alexander.

Baron Von Hirsch
Maurice de Hirsch
1831 – 1896

A patron of Kingsclere from 1890 – 1894 during which time John Porter trained the winners of no less than 39 races for him, including three Classics with La Fleche.

Maurice von Hirsch was born in December 1931 in Munich. He grandfather, the first Jewish landowner in Bavaria, was ennobled with the title *"auf Gereuth"* in 1818; his father who was banker to the Bavarian King, was created a baron in 1869. For generations the family occupied a prominent position in the German Jewish community. At the age of 13, Maurice was sent to school in Brussels. At the age of seventeen he went into business. In 1855, aged 24, he became associated with the banking house of Bischoffsheim and Goldschmidt of Brussels, London and Paris. It was not only a business association, for the same year he married Clara Bischoffsheim. He accumulated a large fortune which he further increased by purchasing and working railway concessions in Austria, Turkey and the Balkans, additionally dealing in commodities such as sugar and copper. The highlight of his railway enterprises was the Chemins de fer Orientaux, - the Orient Express, linking Vienna to Istanbul. He lived in great splendour in Paris, London, Hungary and what is today, the Czech Republic.

Maurice died in Hungary in April 1896. During his lifetime he was amongst the top five richest individuals in Europe at that time.

He and his wife set up charitable foundations to promote Jewish education and improve the lot of oppressed European Jewry. He founded the Jewish Colonization Association which sponsored large-scale Jewish immigration to Argentina. Mention of this philanthropy is made in some of the letters to Porter. It is worth noting that the majority of these are in the hand of a secretary, although always signed by Maurice with the occasional addendum in his own hand.

There is clear evidence of his desire to ingratiate himself with the British Royal family, which was the least anti-Jewish court in Europe of the time. He was particularly keen to ingratiate himself with H.R.H Edward, Prince of Wales. In this he was helped by having his horses trained by Porter, who at that time was also training for the Prince. This gave him a common interest with the Prince and he was also able to use the services of Lord Marcus Beresford who was the Prince's racing manager.

It is on record that Maurice and the Prince became deeply involved financially. The Prince had borrowed large amounts of money from James Mackenzie who had the ownership of Glenmuick Estate, adjoining Balmoral. Also Sunningdale Park which the Prince used to borrow for Ascot. The loans from Mackenzie were secured against the title deeds of the Sandringham Estate. Mackenzie unexpectedly died in 1890, being owed a rumoured £250,000. Mackenzie's Trustees were obliged to call in the debt which caused considerable alarm at Marlborough House, especially as Queen Victoria had not been aware of either the loan or security given. Where was H.R.H. The Prince of Wales to find such a sum?

Maurice Hirsch seized the opportunity to ingratiate himself and paid off the outstanding loans. According to Lord Derby "Hirsch seized the opportunity to pay off the debt, make the Prince his debtor and so secure for himself a social position".

Throughout the 1890s Hirsch was very close to the Prince of Wales. According to Lord Derby "his influence over HRH was a puzzle to society, since he is neither a gentleman, nor reputed altogether honest". Derby's comments are harsh, but are probably mirroring the opinions of a certain strata of society.

The Queen herself was not entirely happy with her son's closeness to Maurice as she refused to invite him to a state concert and apparently was suspicious of him. The Prince of Wales was however happy to be entertained by Maurice at St. Johann, Hungary where Maurice had a vast shooting estate. The Prince being much impressed at its scale – employing 600 beaters, and shooting a total of 20,000 head of game in a mere ten days shooting.

'Daisy' Brooke, Countess of Warwick and a mistress of the Prince of Wales, wrote at the time "we resented the introducing of Jews into the social set of the Prince of Wales, not because we disliked them … but because they had brains and understood finance. As a class we did not like brains. As for money, our only understanding of it lay in the spending – not the making of it".

The Prince of Wales admitting Jews to the Court (Rothschilds and Hirsch) offended many, but it was his way of repaying their financing of his lifestyle and was unique in western countries.

Maurice who had become 'de facto' financial adviser to HRH Prince of Wales died suddenly in 1896, but had left in place his protégé, Ernest Cassel to take over his role. He had been well groomed by Maurice and was left instructions that all debts owed to Maurice's estate, which were estimated at well over £300,000 should be written off.

Cassel became the Prince of Wales's close adviser on investments and made himself indispensable to the Prince. When Cassel's daughter married, the Prince of Wales attended the ceremony.

Cassel purchased Brook House as his home in 1905 and had the vast mansion decorated with Italian marble. At the head of the staircase for all to see was a portrait of King Edward.

Maurice devoted much of his time to schemes for the relief of Jews in lands where they were persecuted and oppressed. This is referred to amongst his letters to Porter. He took a deep interest in the educational work of the Alliance Israelite Universelle, and on two occasions presented the society with gifts of a million francs. For some years, he regularly paid the deficits in the accounts of the Alliance, amounting to several thousand pounds a year. In 1889 he capitalized his donations and presented the society with securities producing an annual income of £16,000. On the occasion of the fortieth anniversary of the Emperor Francis Josephs accession to the Austrian throne, he gave £500,000 for the establishment of primary and technical schools in Galicia and Bukowina. Maurice donated all the prize money won by his string of race horses to charity, this included more than £35,000 won by his horse La Fleche between 1891 and 1894.

The greatest charitable exercise on which he embarked was in connection with the persecution of the Jews in Russia. He gave £10,000 to the funds raised for the repatriation of the refugees in 1882, but feeling that this was a very lame conclusion to the efforts made in Western Europe for the relief of the Russian Jews, he offered the Russian Government £2,000,000 for the endowment of a system of secular education to be established in the Jewish Pale of Settlement. The Russian Government was willing to accept the money, but declined to allow any foreigner to be concerned in its control or administration.

Maurice resolved to use that money for an emigration and colonization scheme which should allow the persecuted Jews opportunities to establish themselves in agricultural colonies outside Russia. To that end he founded the Jewish Colonization Association as an English society, with a capital of £2,000,000 and in 1892 he presented to it a further sum of £7,000,000. On the death of his wife in 1899 the capital was increased to £11,000,000 of which £1,250,000 went to the Treasury, after some litigation, in death duties. This enormous fund, which was in its time probably the greatest charitable trust in the world, was managed by delegates of certain Jewish societies, chiefly the Anglo-Jewish Association of London and the alliance Israelite Universelle of Paris, among whom the shares in the association had been divided.

The Association (J.C.A) which was prohibited from working for profit, possessed large agricultural colonies in Argentina, Canada and Palestine. In addition to its huge agricultural work it had a gigantic and complex machinery for dealing with the whole problem of Jewish persecution, including emigration and distributing agencies, technical schools, co-operative factories, savings and loan banks and model dwellings. It was also able to assist a large number of societies all over the world whose work was connected with the relief and rehabilitation of Jewish refugees.

Besides this great organisation, Maurice founded in 1881 a benevolent trust in the USA for the benefit of Jewish immigrants which he endowed with £493,000. He was involved in many minor charities and while residing in London distributed over £100,000 to local hospitals. Abroad he donated funds to the Biochemistry Building at the Pasteur Institute in Paris in 1900.

It was at the end of the 1892 and following La Fleche's splendid win in the Cambridgeshire that Maurice removed his horses to be trained at Newmarket by Dick Marsh. HRH the Prince of Wales did likewise.

Porter in his autobiography wrote "As I have no wish to reopen an old sore I shall not gratify the curiosity of inquisitive mortals by relating the inner history of this separation".

With the opportunity of seeing the letters from 1891 and 1892, although Porter had the horses in his care and saw them in their work every day, it seems that Maurice increasingly referred to the advice he was given by Lord Marcus Beresford as to what should or should not have been done. To Porter this must have been an ever increasing annoyance. It seems reasonable to suggest that this may certainly have been part of the cause of the separation and the reason that HRH the Prince of Wales' horses also left – being that Lord Marcus Beresford was the Prince's racing manager. It also could, be the reason for Porter keeping so many of the letters.

What was of comforting assurance for Porter was that both the Prince and Maurice came to express regret at the break in their association with Kingsclere.

It was just twelve months later than Maurice asked Porter to train for him again. It may have given Porter satisfaction to tell Maurice that he could not do so – for one very good reason, all his boxes in the stables were occupied.

Maurice was not happy with this and made Porter this offer "If you are willing to sell, I will buy Kingsclere for £20,000. As my trainer I will pay you a salary of £1000. Further, I will place £100,000 in the bank which shall be at your absolute disposal for the purchase of bloodstock and you shall have the sole management of my horses. Any box I do not fill you can use for horses belonging to other owners". Certainly an offer which could only be made by an extremely wealthy but contrite man who realised the mistake he had made a year previously.

Porter declined this offer in deference to all the other owners he had. He suggested another trainer to Maurice, but no sooner had his horses gone to Blackwell – Maurice died suddenly within the year.

It is an indication of Porter's ability to get on with people and of his generous nature that he summed up his feelings about Maurice with the following words "The Baron was a very amicable and generous man. He seemed fond of his horses, and I always got on well with him".

It seems probable that the majority of Hirsch's letters are in the' hand' of his long term secretary Martin Furth, who after Hirsch's death became Secretary to King Ferdinand of Saxe-Coburg – a long term friend of Hirsch.

Hirsch's taste for racing came through his son Lucien who owned a stud. Lucien however died young and Hirsch sold the stud and distributed the proceeds to charity. However he was persuaded by HRH the Prince of Wales to purchase through Lord Marcus Beresford, a yearling in 1890. Beresford was the Prince of Wales's racing manager. The yearling La Fleche was purchased for £5,500 guineas at the Royal Studs, Hampton Court sale – a record price.

28 September 1891.

My dear Porter,

I thank you for your letter of the 22nd inst. arrived in good time. Lord Marcus's previous letter said my decision of not running "Laflêche" any more this year was a capital mistake and gave me to understand that you were of the same opinion. Seeing that it was not the case I wired to him to leave "Laflêche" at rest till next spring, and there is an end of it.

I am very pleased with what you say of my yearlings; if they only will choose to distinguish themselves next year I shall be delighted.. Your news about "Fitz Hampton" are no good ones; how much do you think he would be worth if sold as a stallion?

You will not see me at the Newmarket Houghton meetings as I do not intend to leave Austria before late in November. I shall leave Eichhorn for St. Johann tomorrow or the day after. My address in St. Johann will be as follows:

St. Johann, par Hohenau, Basse Autriche.

Address for telegrams: "Morrasztjanos"

I have seen with great pleasure that you are taking interest in my great scheme for the emigration of the Jews in Russia.

Please remember me to Mrs. Porter.

yours sincerely

M W Hirsch

29 December 1891.

Dear Mr. Porter,

I regret very much that you missed me in London; I intended to pay you a visit at Kingsclear, but I was called back in haste to the continent on account of the funerals of one of my relatives.

I am delighted with the very good report you give me of my horses and should like very much to see you so as to talk

with

with you about different matters. I meant to go to England in a few weeks and shall not fail to go and see you in Kingsclear.

I shall then send you word beforehand in order not to miss you

yours very sincerely

My philanthropic scheme gives me a lot of trouble that I hope I will succeed

and I thank you very much for the interest you take in it

2. rue de l'Elysée.
Paris, 20 February 1892.

Dear Mr Porter,

I was in London this
week for two or three days but
could not manage to see you as
I was obliged to leave rather
suddenly on account of the illness
of one of my relatives.

I regret it all the more
that I very much wanted to go
to Kingsclere, to talk with you
and to see the horses. I hope all
this will take place when I next
return to London, but I wanted
you to be informed of the reason
why

---

why it has not been possible
this time.

I trust La flèche is well.

Yours sincerely

M M Hirsch

---

2. Rue de l'Elysée

Paris 12th May 1892.

Dear Mrs Porter,

I have your letter of the 10th
inst. but you need not apologize
as I have once for all told Mr.
Porter that he was to open all the
letters that would come for me in
Kingsclere.

Yours sincerely

M M Hirsch

Bath House
Piccadilly.

London, 18 May 1892.

Dear Mr. Porter,

I send you herewith a letter of
next mornings
Mr. Chaplin - which please return to me.
Should you agree with his views I would
gladly approve of a serious trial of the two
horses which should take place as soon as
possible. — I am leaving today for Paris
but shall return here next week.

Yours very sincerely

M M Hirsch

Until Wednesday next please to address to Paris.

2. Rue de l'Elysée

Paris, May 22ᵗ 1892.

Dear Mr. Porter.

Thanks for your letter concerning the trial of "Windgall" and "Watercress."

I have also your telegram of yesterday; I never doubted that the Sportsman had been wrongly informed, but being a little anxious nevertheless I thought there would be no harm in asking to make sure.

D₃

I am actually laid up with bronchitis but hope to be all right again for Epsom.

Kindest remembrances to Mrs. Porter

Yours very sincerely

M. Ephrussi

I am very glad to hear that La flèche is all right

---

2. Rue de l'Elysée

Paris, 29 may 1892.

My dear Mr. Porter,

Alas I shall not be able to be in Epsom on Wednesday; since my return from London I have been laid up with a serious attack of influenza and congestion of the lungs.

You may well imagine how very annoyed I am and nothing is left to me but to wish both of us good luck.

After you have had the

Ξ

---

horses tried, as suggested by Mr. Chaplin. you will oblige me by the sending of a telegram saying: "excellent." "middling." or "bad."; I will understand the rest.

Yours very sincerely

M. Ephrussi

If La flèche wins the Derby and I hope she will, I shall drink a glass of champagne at your health

Monday   2. Rue de l'Elysée

Dear Mr Weller

I just received a
telegram from
Lord Marcus
"Good"
I would have preferred
Excellent.
Do you think that

Wingall has a certain
Chance for the
Jubilee Stakes?
I would be very
Obliged if you
would send me
in one line your
opinion about it
Yours very truly
[signature]

2. Rue de l'Elysée
Paris, June 2. 1892.

Dear Mr. Porter,

I am certain you are very
much depressed on account of Lafleche's
failure: I feel so myself; but as I know
that everything has been done to make
her win, I feel it was only bad luck and
I hope for a better share another time.

I fear less the tremendous
exertions of yesterday should have considerably
diminished her chance of winning to
morrow, but I leave it to you to decide

with

with Lord Abarcus what is best to do.

Please let me know what is the mare's next engagement after the Oaks. I also will like to have your advice concerning Windgall and Watercress; do you think there is the slightest chance for them at the "Grand Prix". I hope anyhow that you are going to make a very serious trial and there is not much time to loose.

Yours very sincerely

M. Ming

I am preparing steadily

been cured at once —

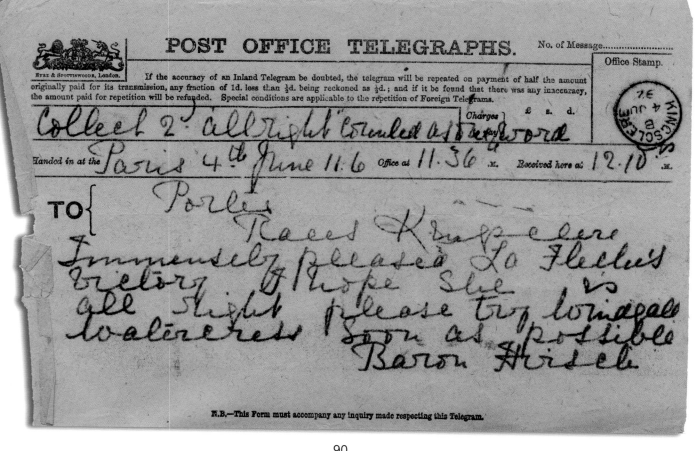

Collect 2° "all right" counted at Ingeword

Handed in at the Paris 4th June 11.6 Office at 11.36 M. Received here at 12.10 M.

TO { Porter
Races Knapclere
Immensely pleased La Fleche's victory I hope she is all right please try Windgall Watercress soon as possible
Baron Hisch

2. Rue de l'Elysée

Paris 5th June 1892.

Dear Mr. Porter,

I have received your letter of the 4th inst. and I cannot suffi-ciently tell you how pleased I was with the mare winning the Oaks. I think George Barrett did his best and that I owe him a good gratification; please do the necessary.

I see that Windgall is quite out of the question for the Grand Prix and that you are going to try Watercress with Vasistas.

Lord Marcus writes that the trial is to take place on Thursday next, it seems to me very late and I do not see the reason why it should not take place any sooner. — I fail to under-stand how Vasistas, should be run to-morrow at Kempton Park in a big race, is to be able to work in the trial on Thursday especially if, as I believe he has to run in Ascot. Have you no other horse to try Watercress with and could you not make the trial before Thursday.

I do not think Watercress good enough for the "Grand Prix"; however it is not impossible; but should the trial take place on Thursday the horse will be tired on Friday which is the last day for his leaving for Paris

in order to get seen if he is to run at all in the Grand Prix.

For all these reasons I do not understand why the trial is to be on Thursday and think that it ought to take place on Tuesday for the latest. I hope you will do the necessary for that purpose and I have wired to you accordingly this morning.

I send you a copy of this letter to Kingsclere, as a precaution.

I enclose a letter from Dublin; if you think one or the other of the horses offered to be a good purchase, please see to it.

Yours very sincerely,
M. Ephrussi

My best remembrances to Mrs Porter please tell her how much I was pleased to win the Oaks.

1) The enclosed I send to Kingsclere, with copy of this P.

Hotel 4 Towers.
Bad. Ems, 16 August 1892.

Dear Mr. Porter,

I must ask you to send me a photo. of La Flèche, if you have any; if not please have one made and sent it to me here at the above address (untill the end of this month) as I promised the Duc d'Aosta to let him have one.

I am very pleased to hear that all the horses are doing well.

Please give my kindest regards to Mrs. Porter.

Yours very sincerely

M de Hirsch

2. Rue de l'Elysée
Paris, 26th. August 1892.

Dear Mr. Porter,

Mr. Chaplin now in Carlsbad writes me that he would very much like to know what you think about La Flèche & Watercress and that he desires me to ask you to send him a line directly to Hotel Bristol, Carlsbad, Austria, telling him just what you think of their respective chances to win and how they both are.

If you find the time to do so, you would oblige me by referring to Mr.

Chaplin's request.

Yours very sincerely

M Menier

I am afraid I am not well enough to go to Doncaster, however my absence is not quite certain. My best remembrances to Mr Porter;

I forgot to tell you that I have backed in your favour both

Le fleut et Waterun, and I hope it will benefit us both well.

P.S. I may leave Paris for a certain time, but anyhow please direct your letters and messages, 2 Rue de l'Elysée, Paris " to be forwarded."

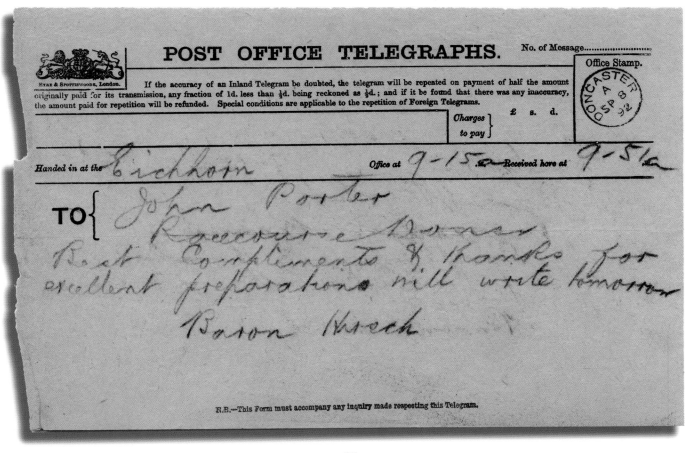

POST OFFICE TELEGRAPHS.

No. of Message..........

Office Stamp.

DONCASTER
A
SP 8
92

If the accuracy of an Inland Telegram be doubted, the telegram will be repeated on payment of half the amount originally paid for its transmission, any fraction of 1d. less than ½d. being reckoned as ½d.; and if it be found that there was any inaccuracy, the amount paid for repetition will be refunded.   Special conditions are applicable to the repetition of Foreign Telegrams.

Charges to pay   £ s. d.

Handed in at the Eichhorn   Office at 9-15   Received here at 9-51

TO { John Porter
Racecourse Doncaster

Best compliments & thanks for excellent preparations will write tomorrow

Baron Hirsch

N.B.—This Form must accompany any inquiry made respecting this Telegram.

Eichhorn
near Brünn
Austria

2 Rue de l'Elysée
Paris, 8 September 92

Dear Mr. Porter,

I hope you got my tele-
gram of yesterday relating to our
double success; you could not
have given a better proof of your
words to me before I left England,
"I will do my best that the best of
the three should win" and I again
thank you for the care you have taken
of my mare in preparing her for the
race.

Rot

Eichhorn
near Brünn
Austria

2 Rue de l'Elysée
Paris, 8 September 92

Dear Mr. Porter,

I hope you got my tele-
gram of yesterday relating to our
double success; you could not
have given a better proof of your
words to me before I left England,
"I will do my best that the best of
the three should win" and I again
thank you for the care you have taken
of my mare in preparing her for the
race.

Rot

Referring to my last letter I have
the pleasure to enclose a cheque
for £ 2000.——
With kindest regards to Mrs. Porter
Yours very sincerely

P.S. You would oblige me by
writing to me what are your ideas
about the further running of my
several horses from now to the
end of October.

EICHHORN
PAR BRÜNN
AUTRICHE

1. Oct. 92.

Dear Mr. Porter,

        I am
very glad that your prognostic
about La Flèche, Windgall and
Watercress was a right one,
and that they really won all
three. I am indeed in a good
run, and I hope that it
will continue. You ask me
when I intend to return to

England. I should of course like
very much to see my horses
running, but having the house
full with guests just now, I
could not think of leaving them. —

      Yours very truly,

      M. d'Hirsch

My best remembrances
to Mrs Porter, please don't
forget the Photographs
of La Flèche, those were
being

is plenty of time for her to forget all about
her being clipped.

    My best remembrances to Mrs Porter

    Yours very Sincerely

    M. d'Hirsch

St. Johann a.d. March.
16 October 1892.

Dear Mr. Porter

    I thank you for your letter of
the 4th inst. and your information concerning
Orme and the Champion stakes; I have exchanged
letters on the subject with Lord Marcus and I feel
particularly obliged to you for your straight-
forward explanations.

    I am anxious that you and every-
one should know that I never back my horses
for my own benefit; if I made up my
mind to run La Flèche in the Cambridgeshire
it is because Lord Marcus wrote me that the
public quite fancied her and that it would

                    b z

be most unpopular to have her scratched out. In fact I did back her for that race, only the bet is not meant in any way for my own benefit but to the purpose of giving satisfaction to several friends and to other persons as well for whom I never did anything in the way of betting and who keep bothering me with requests to lay out some money for them; I seized the opportunity of doing so, seing that I could not help running Laflèche in the Cambridgeshire. I deemed it necessary that you should know of all this as I do not wish the rumours to spread abroad that I bet on my own account; I keep race horses as a sport and to no other purpose whatever.

As regards clipping the mare, I understand to a certain extent your being anxious about it, but one ought to think that any horse which gets clipped on or about the 25th of October is certain to recover its coat before long during the winter; besides there is a way of clipping and singeing so as to shave only such parts that mostly need it so as to prevent a horse from perspiring. I trust Lord Marcus will proceed very carefully and arrange the matter with you in the best possible manner.

We also ought not to lose sight of the fact that the mare has after the Cambridge-shire no further engagement until next spring and that in consequence there is

TELEGRAMMADRESSE
MORVA St JANOS

St JOHANN A.D. MARCH
PER HOHENAU-NORDBAHN
NIEDEROESTERREICH

31 October 1892.

Dear Mr. Porter,

Once again I have to express to you the immense satisfaction that was given to me by Laflèche's victory of which the greater part is due, I know it, to your excellent preparation; let the gallant little mare now enjoy the rest and the peace which she has so richly deserved ...till next spring.

A good friend of mine has introduced to me Mr. Alfred Elias, a painter who wanted to ask leave to paint

portrait of the mare; I have complied
with his request provided he takes
your convenience as to the "sitting".
He will write to you, no doubt; please
to answer him accordingly.

My kindest regards to Mrs. Porter

Yours very sincerely

[signature]

7th November 1892.

Dear Mr. Porter.

Our letters crossed; I know
I ought to have sent you a telegram
but no doubt you have received my
letter in due course, conveying to you
my congratulations on LaflÈche's
gallant performance and my thanks
for your most excellent preparation
which I now reiterate. I wish you had
a share in the big profit made by Lord
Marcus if really the same is anything
near the figure you name, which seems
indeed

indeed enormous.

As I have granted Mr. Ilias's
request with regard to LaflÈche's painting, I cannot now alter it; ofcourse
if you wish to have one made by any
one else on your own account, I have
no objection whatever. Have you any
photos. of the mare? I hear some
had been taken; if so, please send
me one; I should like very much together.

I am going to England to stay for a few
days at the end of the month and hope to
see you then

Yours very sincerely

[signature]

P.S. I shall leave here in
about 10 days; so please
address your letters again to
Paris

2. rue de l'Elysée.

Paris, 17th November 1892

Dear Mr. Porter,

I thank you for your letter and I am happy to tell you that the person to whose illness the papers were alluding to is not the Baroness but some relation; however I am in mourning owing to the

death of the Baroness's Mother and this will prevent me from going over to England at the end of the month as I intended to do; my visit will have to be postponed till about the middle of December.

Yours very sincerely

M Deschnit

P. S. I was very glad to win the three races at Liverpool, and await Laflèche's photo.

My best remembrances to Mrs Porter I am sure she was also immensely pleased with the successes of my different horses

82, PICCADILLY,
W.

Janr 12th 1894.

Dear Mr. Porter.

I am very pleased to hear that Matchbox is in such good form. I hope to leave for Paris myself on Friday by the ten o'clock mail. It is an understood thing that you are to stay at my house in Paris de l'Elysée and if you bring your son over with you he will be welcome to stay there also.

Yours faithfully

M. V. Vinct

Vienna, 27th August 1894.

to better terms but I am certain you will ask for the best.

I shall be

Dear Mr. Porter,

I received but yesterday here your letter of the 20th, as I have been constantly travelling from one place to another. From Yorkshire, where I stayed for a week, grouse shooting, I had to come straight to Vienna to keep an appointment and thus was unable to pay you a visit at Kingsclere, which I would have liked very much. With regard to "Matchbox" and the Roger I must leave the whole matter to you: I know I could not trust it

---

99

[date] 1894.

Dear Mr. Porter,

I received both your telegram & your letter.
I have really no luck with "Matchbox" and
I am as disappointed as you are. I am sure
everything went as straight as possible and
I know that with regard to the training of
the horse you deserve but compliments as I
am told on all sides that "Matchbox" could
not have too Red fitter, than he did. It
seems he was beaten by the distance.

You know how I am [...] with

Stables and Himself it would be best if you
came to an understanding with Lord Marcus
to the effect that none of my horses in
Marsh's stable shall run in any race with
"Matchbox". Should you prefer me to give
orders direct to that effect and specially for
Master Minting not to be run with "Matchbox"
then please send me a wire.

Yours very truly
M. [signature]

to better hands and I am certain you
will act for the best.

I shall be glad to hear of you again
before the race; my address is:

For letters: Schloss Eichhorn bei Brünn
                Austria
and for telegrams: "Eichhorn . Austria"

Yours truly
M. [signature]

Could you take Lt. Tolan
(my two year old [...]) in
training, I think [...]
[...] letter in your [...]
[initial]

EICHHORN
PAR BRÜNN
AUTRICHE

23 September 1894.

Dear Mr. Porter,

I received your letter and just wired that after all I prefer not to run "Matchbox" in the Cesarewitch (as I hear it would not look well for me to do so) but in any other race you shall choose. Besides I should not like the horse to get beaten once more, for I think the distance is rather too much for him ... the circumstances ... will be better ... to run the Cesarewitch ... but for the ... leave it to you to do for the best and to run "Matchbox" [3]

"Matchbox" and that I have to deliver him to the Austrian Government at the end of the season. Therefore I should like to run him as much as I possibly can to give him the chance of winning one or two stakes. I cannot find out what race he is to run in at Newmarket the first October week, but I know he is engaged in the Champion Stakes. — As regards the Cesarewitch I find that "Matchbox" is much better handicapped than Lafleche and would much prefer Matchbox to run. But as the distance is the same as in the Leger I fear he might be beaten by Callistrate. — Toward [3]

a better judge in the matter than I am; what I wish is to make as much money as I can for the Hospitals; therefore do as you think best. Unluckily the day of the Cesarewitch is also the date of one of the greatest Jewish religious festivities and it is not custom for Jews, nor would it look the proper thing for me to do, to run a horse on that day. So I should like "Matchbox" for this reason, to run under Lord Alington's or Sir Frederick Johnstone's colours, should they not object to it. — Anyhow I have given orders that Lafleche should not run in the Cesarewitch. — I see that "Maid Marian" is engaged in the Champion [3]

in as many races as you can, according to what I wrote in my previous letter. Unfortunately I shall not go to Newmarket this autumn and cannot be in England before the end of November. I regret that it should be so, as I would like to speak with you on various subjects; but I had better wait until I come over.

Yours truly

My best compliments to Mrs Porter.

2. Rue de l'Elysée

Dear Mr Parker,

Many thanks for having informed me of the arrival in excellent condition of La flêche & Watercress.

I have send to George Barrell a present of £1000 (rather too much afte[r]

his riding at such rate, but received never an answer acknowledging the receipt of the money ... of my letter. Will you please ask him if he has received my money I hope you are all

right and that the Kingston Stakes will have a good and successful autumn.

My best remembrance to Mrs Parker
Yours very truly
W R Wood
Sunday Paris

Clara de Hirsch
June 1833 – April 1899

She married Maurice in 1855. Her nationality was Belgian. She had a very substantial fortune in her own right and was as great a business woman and philanthropist as her husband. She was fluent in French, German, English and Italian. When her husband was abroad she was her husband's able assistant.

In the archive of letters there is only one card definitely in her hand – referring to a meeting on a racecourse with a Mr Phipps.

Chemins de fer Orientaux or Orient Express

The railway was to run from Vienna to Istanbul. Maurice's interest commenced in 1869, construction began in 1870 and was completed in 1888.

Karaagac station built in 1873 but no longer used by the railway is now a fine museum.

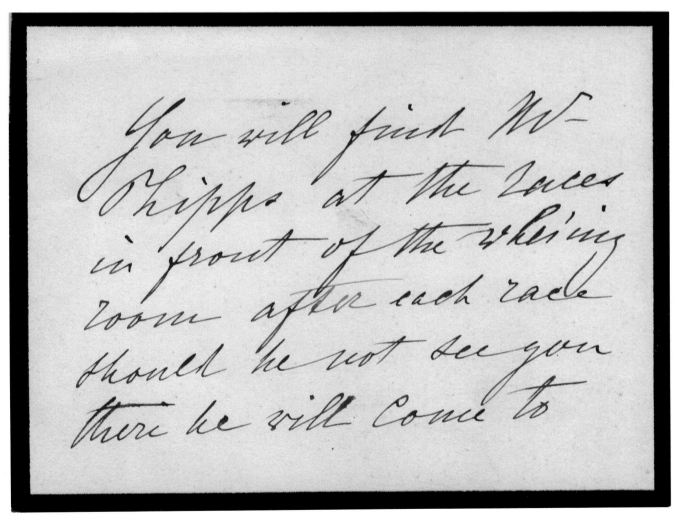

Bagatelle immediately
after the Races – 5 or 5.30
He is very anxious to see
you. The Baron is coming
this evening.

Baroness Hirsch

Lord William Beresford
1847-1900

Was awarded the Victoria Cross for gallantry.
1875 was appointed ADC to Lord Northbrook.   Whilst in India he did some racing and won the Corinthian Purse at a meeting attended by HRH Prince of Wales.
John Porter trained one winning horse for him in1892, winning £180.00
His racing in India did much to improve the quality of horses in India. His main competitor being a wealthy Calcutta merchant, Apcar Alexander Apcar, who had a stud of Australian horses.
Beresford won the Viceroy's Cup at the Calcutta Turf Club in 1881. In England he won the 1000 Guineas in 1899 and was second in the Oaks with Sibola.

He lived at Deepdene, Dorking and died there on 30th December 1900 from peritonitis, aged only 53.
See letter from Lord Marcus Beresford
Letter 2.6.1876
Sends Mrs Porter an Indian Chudder Shawl as thanks for visit to Kingsclere and hopes to visit again before returning to India. Going abroad tomorrow but hopes to be back for Goodwood.

Letter August 5 1892
Enquiring if Porter has Catarian's bridle. Could you send it before Monday next before he goes away to India, if bridle went with horse ok. Hopes Porter will have 1,2,3, in the St Leger.

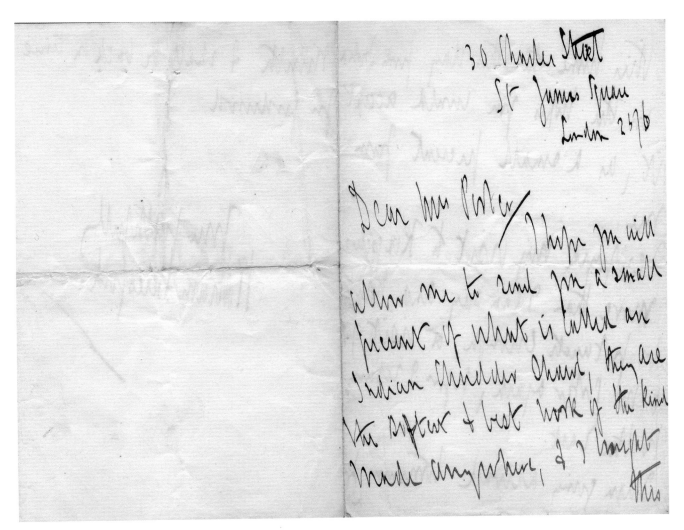

...his home the other day from India in the hopes you could accept it, as a small present from me.

I enjoyed my visit to Kinspeter more than I can say and hope to be fortunate enough to visit you at Mr Porter again, before I return to the East.

I am going abroad tomorrow for a

month & shall be back in time for Goodwood.

Yours faithfully
William Beresford.

Aug. 5/92.
30, CHARLES STREET,
ST. JAMES' SQUARE,
S.W.

Dear Mr Porter

Will you kindly let me have a line to say if you have got Catarina's bridle that Lord Marcus sent to you for her & if so could you have

it sent to me to the above address at your earliest convenience so that I get it before I start on Thursday next. If the bridle happened to go out with the mare, could you also let me know.

I am sorry to bother you so much good bye. I hope your stable will be no: 1. 2. 3 for the leger. Yours faithfully William Beresford

106

Colonel Paget
1849 – 1933

Porter trained one winning horse for him in 1892. It won one race valued at £136.00 in prize money.

A military career. Joined 7th Hussars, fought in the Sudan and Boer Wars
Had connections with 'Paget Horse' an elite equine detachment in the Army.
How he became associated with John Porter and Kingsclere is not recorded.

Lord Marcus Beresford
1848 – 1922

Porter trained one winning horse for Lord Marcus Beresford in 1892. It won one race, value £436.00

Younger brother of Lord William Beresford. Lord Marcus was an equerry and racing manager to HRH Prince of Wales.

He ran the stables of HRH Prince of Wales from 1890 on the Princes' succession to the throne in 1901 he was appointed an extra equerry and manager of his Majesty's Thoroughbred Stud – posts he held until the King's death in 1910.   King George V appointed him to the same position in 1910 and Lord Marcus remained in that post until his own death in 1922.

He was close also to Baron von Hirsch who relied on his advice, even when his horses were in training with Porter at Kingsclere. It is likely Lord Marcus was instrumental in Prince Edward's and Baron von Hirsch's horses being moved from Kingsclere in 1892, when they transferred to Newmarket.

See letters from Lord Marcus, also the reference to him in Hirsch's letters to Porter.

Letter Dec 20th 1900 to Porter

The Duchess (William's wife – previously Duchess of Marlborough) thanking Porter for sympathetic letter.   William is very seriously ill but holding his own. If his strength can be maintained, hopes he can pull through.

In fact William had peritonitis and died ten days later.

Robert Crewe-Milnes, First Marquess of Crewe
12.01.1858 – 20.06.1945

Was Lord President of the Council from 1905 to 1908 and from 1915 to 1916.
Was leader of the House of Lords 1908 to 1916.

Letter October 2nd 1898 from Crewe Hall
Thanks to Porter for sending him a copy of Kingsclere. Very pleased to accept as author's gift and a most handsome addition to his library.
Will be sending two yearling fillies - Duchesse de Berry and Atlanta to Kingsclere before the end of October. Mr McCrachan will inform you of the date. A smaller Rightaway filly will follow later.

Letter April 17th 1899 from Brook's Club St James.
Encloses 3 tickets for the Abbey (Westminster) for funeral of Farrer Herschell,

1st Baron Herschell. Come early for seats. Much enjoyed his visit to Kingsclere today (17th April).
Include in book indicative of position in society that Porter had achieved.

Letter dated 17th September 2003 from Crewe Hall.

Sending Lord & Lady Crewe's very best wishes on his marriage (to Isabel, 2nd wife)
Reference to Cyllene Colt – very hopeful
Reference to Lady Wishfort – not worth keeping in training another year.
This colt was named Polymelus.

Letter 28th March 1905

Tells Porter he will be selling all his mares and yearlings at 1st July meeting (Newmarket sales).
Will keep horses in training with Porter until end June when final decision can be made on what to do with them.
Decision to give up his racing interest he indicates to be partly connected with political work, at that time he was Lord President of the Council.
Speaks in glowing terms of their past relationship and wishes to keep this warm friendship and thanks for all the pleasurable visits to Kingsclere (His local geography was not good – Kingsclere is in Berkshire – not Hampshire!)

Porter trained six winning horses for him between 1899 and 1905. They won 16 races with total prize money of £11,139. Of the 16 races won 7 were won by Polymelus in 1904 – 1905 and five were won by Saint Lindi in 1899 – 1900.
He was very much a politician, holding a panoply of public offices over a span of sixty years, including Secretary of State for India, Lord President of the Council, President of the Board of Education, Minister for War, Secretary of State for the Colonies, Lord Privy Seal and Ambassador to France.
He married twice, but though losing both wives prematurely, did have children but they too died young. He was left without an heir and around 1931 – 32 sold Crewe Hall and its land to the Duchy of Lancaster.
The sadness of his private life and his involvement in politics clearly curtailed his racing interests. In 1931 he purchased a smaller estate, West Horsley Place, between Guildford and Leatherhead where he lived until his death in 1945. The estate passed to his daughter, the Duchess of Roxburghe who on her death in 2014 left it to a grand nephew, Bamber Gascoigne, the broadcaster and author. In 2015 he was instrumental in setting up the Mary Roxburghe Trust to preserve and maintain the Estate. Also to promote the performing and visual arts, opera, music, drama and ballet. Permission was given for the building of a 700 seat theatre and a 99 year lease was arranged with Grange Park Opera. The first performance took place in 2017.

CREWE HALL,
CREWE.

TELEGRAPHIC ADDRESS
"CRWA, CREWE."

Oct. 2. 98

Dear Sir

First let me thank
you sincerely for the beautifully
bound copy of "Kingsclere"
which I found awaiting me
on my arrival here yesterday.
I am very glad to possess
it as the author's gift, and
it will be a most handsome
addition to my library -
Nothing interests me more
than the account of the
byegone trials, with the

curious light they throw
on the different horses'
performances in public -
I found everything going
on well at the stud here!
the 2 yearling fillies
Duchesse de Berry and
Atlanta will come to
Kingsclere later this month,
Mr. McCracken will inform
you of the date - Both
have grown and are
looking well - The little

Rightaway filly will be
sent later -
I am yours sincerely
Crewe.

Mr. J. Porter.

110

April 17. 99

Dear Sir

I have pleasure
in enclosing 3 tickets
for the Abbey on the
20th. I hope you
may find it possible
to arrive in pretty
good time, as I am
told the earliest comers

will have considerable
advantage in getting
seats –

I much enjoyed
my visit to Kingsclere
today.

I am yours faithfully
Crewe

W. J. Porter.

(Crewe Hall
Crewe)

17 Sept. 03.

Dear Sir
First I must
send you Lady Crewe's
and my own best
wishes for your happiness
in your marriage:
we trust that you may
have a very pleasant
home, and every help
in the management of
affairs at Kingsclere.

I am glad you think the yearlings a useful lot: the Lyddord colt has always been my favourite, and he certainly was a remarkable mover in the paddock.

It would be advantageous if Lady Wishfort could get through a little race before she comes

home: but I apprehend there is no object in keeping her in training another year.

Yours faithfully
Crewe.

John Porter Esq.

Aboration's accident, and trust she is not seriously the worse. I shall be glad to hear if you think Polymelus is going on the right way, and if he keeps his action — I fear I shall hardly get to Liverpool, or should hope to see you there.

I am
yours very sincerely
Crewe

J. Porter Esq.

CREWE HALL,
CREWE.

28 March 05

Dear Sir
I must write to tell you, before you hear from elsewhere, that I have decided not to train any more horses for the present, and as I do not care about breeding for sale, I am going to send up the mares etc. as well as yearlings at the 1st July Meeting. My reasons are partly connected with political work, among others, and I have contemplated the possibility for some little

TELEGRAPHIC ADDRESS
"CRIWA, CREWE."

time before making up my
mind. As regards the horses
in training, we must of course
be guided by what they do
between now and July. If
any of them are not much
good, they can go up with
the stud; if on the other
hand any seem to have a
chance for a good engagement,
there need so hurry in
parting with these. By the
end of June, at any rate,
we shall have been able

to make up our minds.
I need not tell you how
sorry I shall be when the time
comes to close, at any rate
for a time, my association
with Kingsclere. You have
always made the whole concern
of racing, and my visits to
Hampshire, as pleasant as
possible. I shall always regard
you, and hope to be regarded,
with a warm feeling of
friendship.
Meanwhile it does not seem
as if this will involve any
difference in the way you
go on with the horses.
I was sorry to hear of

William Cavendish – Bentinck – 6th Duke of Portland
1857 – 1943
And Winifred Duchess of Portland
1863 - 1954

It was in the late Autumn of 1898 that the Duke's horses which had formerly been trained at Newmarket, came to Porter at Kingsclere. The Duke's stud was at Welbeck Abbey, the family seat.

It was late in Porter's career that this patron came but it was to prove a very close, indeed friendly arrangement. The intimacy in some of the letters was intriguing. The Duke, one of the wealthiest men in the Kingdom, clearly found in John Porter someone he could trust, not only to train his horses, but to work with as a colleague in business. At the end of the 1903 season when Porter had reduced his training activities and Kingsclere Ltd was formed, it was the Duke who became a founding member.

The Duke notably served as Master of the Horse for two periods 1886-1892 and 1895-1905 under both Queen Victoria and King Edward VII.

Letter December 11th 1887 – from Welbeck Abbey, invites Porter to a shooting party commencing 9th January 1888 and to look at the stud that week saying "and the longer you stay the better I shall be pleased" "Mr Turner will send your daughter some of St Simon's tail"

Letter Feb 22nd 1902
Offers help of a nurse for Mrs Porter, who is in very poor health and Portland has ordered some flowers to be sent to her"
A letter which would only pass between very close friends.

Letter May 23rd 1902
Following Mrs Porter's death, this letter shows the deep friendship and affection between the families.
Winifred, Duchess of Portland
Letter April 30th, 1900
Thanking Mrs Porter for plovers eggs
A letter of close friendship
Letter May 6th, 1900
Again referring to more plovers eggs, also of horses; again friend writing.
14th August 1900
A letter between friends who have come to stay and refers to children and sister Grace. Refers to birth of youngest child on 27th July.
Letter 1st August 1900 (from the Duke) to Mrs Porter. Refers to birth of Portland's youngest child Lord Francis Bentinck.
Letter August 29th 1900
Letter thanking for 'wonderful time' Pleasure having them stay at Langwell. Even so soon after giving birth. A letter of real friendship.
Letter from Grosvenor Square London 14th July 1901
To John Porter form Duchesse Winifred expressing sorrow and anxiety about Mrs Porter's illness. Visit of Sir William Watson Cheyne – surgeon and bacteriologist.
22nd May 1902
Letter of sympathy on death of Mrs Porter
The letters from the Duke and Duchess need to be carefully selected for book, as apart from the racing side, they reveal a very, very close friendship.
Letters from the Duke and Duchess' children
From Victoria Bentinck 30.08.1900 (Aged 10.)
Thanking Mr & Mrs Porter for books. Comment on her little (new born brother) "My little brother is very well and grows".
From Lord Titchfield 4th September 1900. (Aged 7.)

Thanking Mr & Mrs Porter for his book.
PS "I take my book to bed every night"

Dec: 11th 1887.

WELBECK ABBEY,
WORKSOP,
NOTTS.

Porter –

I am going to have
a shooting party here
during the week, commencing
Jan 9th and I shall
be very glad, if you
will come to have a
look at the place, anytime

during that week. and
the longer you stay the
better I shall be pleased.
I was at Newmarket
last week & Appleton has
made a great deal of
improvement so look and

your Balsam & will
learn to put them here
feet forward –
Mr Turner will send your
daughter some of
82 Sermons Tail

Yours truly

Portland

anxious indeed about it,
though there my brother was
well on Feb 12th.

With kind regards to
Mrs Porter & you

I am

Yours sincerely

Portland

My modest bid of 400 gs
for [Celerity] was also [in] vain.

I did so, to show you
that I had not then,
nor have I now, any objection
whatever to your doing so.
and I should like you to
do whatever you like with
regard to the matter.

When [my] old Falmouth Stud
was sold Sheet immediately
handed over Harvester to
Capt Machell though!

I believe he offered to
keep him till the 2000 gs
which was to be run for a
very short time. & I remember
he remarked to me that
it was much better so, as
it relieved him of all future
responsibility —

This was indeed a grand sale
[which] I [could] have [received]

[with] the [Duchess] was in
London & she expects her
[officials] to be there, in case
they are wanted —

Mr. Turner has written
me a most flourishing
account of the horses, &
I am going to see him this
afternoon.

[Sends they] would [return]
[Morphine]. [Yesterday]

Dec. 11th 1892

WELBECK ABBEY.
WORKSOP.
NOTTS.

Dear Sir —

Many thanks for
sending me the letter
you enclosed. Anything
relating to Ld. G. Bentinck's
racing career interests
me & I will ask Mr.
Braham to send me
the letter.

I need hardly say I
have now finished with

W. Day & I should
never have taken any
notice of him if he had
not so persistently
slandered a dead man
who could not defend
himself. & that to my
mind is the act of a
coward.

I saw Raeburn on
Thursday he is going on

very well. & I have great
hopes for next year..

I am.

Yours truly
Portland

thermans. Woodbine
Hockash: Honeysuckle &
so he breeding in good
enough for anything.

Gives place to the Lowrood
has well as Judi and Lord
Allington tells me he has
a small filly by Donovan.

& Isa

Yours Sincerely

Portland

Please of Hay bad I ga
to the race.

Langwell
BERRIEDALE. R.S.O.
CAITHNESS.

Aug 29th 9

Dear Sir.

I am much obliged
to you for saying you will
take Smear I have
heard from the Duke
Lord Allington & Dr Sutton
who all say give their consent
so I believe she far to
you tomorrow.

I have told George Dawson

---

how nicely you mentioned
her in the letter you wrote
to Mr Turner, and he
quite understand why I
have sent the filly to you.

If you can get her fit I
should like to run her this
autumn. — She has never
been a good mover but
her some form last year
which she apparently lost altogether

---

during the spring & summer.
She was nothing but skin
& bone when she came to
Welbeck after Ascot but
when I saw her there alone
three weeks ago I was
astonished at the improvement
she had made & thought
it advisable to give her
another trial — under
new auspices.

She is by Bluemerin
out of Muermerin by
Scottish Chief — Violet.

Dec. 26th 1897

WELBECK ABBEY,
WORKSOP.

Dear Sir.

Thank you very
much for the book and
the good wishes which
you so kindly send me.
I shall read the one
with interest and I
value the other because
I know they are meant.

I hope some day you
will train another horse
for me — & with all
good wishes to you &
yours

I am
Yours sincerely
Portland

I hope Mrs. Porter is better.

June 3rd 98 -

WELBECK ABBEY.
WORKSOP.

Dear Sir -

Mr. Turner has told me the result of her interview with you today & I am very glad to think my yearlings are going to Kingsclere - As I am personally very much attached to

George Dawson that you will not say anything about the proposed change as I should not like it to get to his ears until I tell him about it myself and I wish to help hurting his feelings as much as possible - I am afraid some disappointment

on his part is inevitable but I hope to be able to palliate his feelings and I am leaving some homes for him still to train for me.

I am writing to the Dorset master & Lord Alington to ask their permission to join your stable and their

they will grant it.

I am still a bit of an invalid but am making good progress. and with all good wishes I am

Yours sincerely

Portland

Jan 10th 98.

Dear Sir.

Many thanks for your letter. I am very glad I am to be made welcome to Rangeclere and I am sure it is very kind of you other patrons to want to have my horses under your care.

I have had a very nice

letter from G. D. and I must say it has caused me a considerable amount of pain to intimate to her the change on the future training of my race horses. I assured her that you had in no way acted behind her back and he expresses in his letter to me the kindest feeling towards you —

He has tendered his resignation as my trainer at the end of the season so I hope besides my yearlings you will be then able to take whatever horse are considered worth keeping in training for another year. I hope you will be able to pay a visit to Welbeck the week after Ascot and I hope to be able to go down with you. I like my yearlings very much, in fact

I think they are the best lot I ever produced. The Carbines are particularly promising having peat backs & quarters.

I hope to see you at Ascot next week —

Perhaps you could come over to Harewood Lodge some morning to talk over matters quietly

I am
yours truly
Portland

June 16th 98.

HAREWOOD LODGE,
SUNNINGHILL.

Dear Sir –

I saw the filly by Carbine out of Donna Fortuna & thought her rather a real little filly. As it would be rather annoying if she were to win for other people

for him – & his winning policy is such as I like –

I hoped to see you today, but the paddock at Ascot is rather too long for me at present.

Yours
Portland

Will you please bid for her for me up to 500gs.

I am very glad you can take on [Greens?] horses. he & I are such old friends that I should have been sorry to have separated

If you think the filly is worth 600, please do not lose her for the sake of £100 ?

She is a late foal. Her hocks are a little away from her.

123

Dec. 20th 1899.

3, GROSVENOR SQUARE,
W.

Sir

I have received the
enclosed for Lord Langford
& I have wired to Daly
to know if he will send
the horse to the Royal
Mews for Ld Kitchener's
approval — I will
let you know Daly's

answer.

Major Hamilton could
not come to the R. Mews
this morning but will
look at the horse for
the 10th Hussars as soon
as possible.

I go to Welbeck this afternoon

I hope you will find
some suitable horses.

Yours truly

Portland

124

in the Auc4 ... and ...
trained both horses, that
the Revnd might say disagreeable
things, which however
unanswered are always
unpleasant.

When I remarked to you
during my last visit to
Knightsden that I supposed
you would go on training
FF whoever bought him

March 11th 1900

WELBECK ABBEY,
WORKSOP.

Dear Sir.

Many thanks for
your letter, kind congratulations
& for consulting me about
the training of Flying Fox.
Let me say at once that
I should not like to stand
in your way for one moment
if you wish to do so as
I can imagine it to be quite

naturally the case
that you much regret
seeing him leave Knightsden,
but on the other hand
I do not think any one
can rightly say that you
are behaving at all
unfairly to Mr Blanc
if you decline to train
his horse for his future

engagements. I presume
you made no promise to
do so before the sale, &
as the horse was sold by
public auction, the buyer
must take all risks, including
the future training &
management of the horse —
It seems to me too that
if by the remotest possible
chance in the World
Manners beat Flying Fox

/o to Welbeck the Saturday
after Ascot. Can you
come —

June 8th 1900

TURF CLUB,
PICCADILLY.

Dear Sir.

Please accept the
silver tankard which
I have instructed Messrs
Lambert to send you
as a small memento
of La Roche's Oaks victory
The tankard is of the

Queen Anne period
dated 1706 and it has
evidently been used as
there is an inscription
on the bottom of it
I hope you are better
and with kind

regard.

I am

Yours sincerely

Portland

I have just heard La Roche
has won the [2n?] [?]
I am so pleased.

126

Aug 14th. 00.

BRAEMORE LODGE
DUNBEATH
CAITHNESS

Dear Sir –

I am very glad
to hear Mrs Porter and
you have arrived safely
at Langwell & I hope you
had a good journey &
will have a pleasant day
shooting – I want you

to come over here tomorrow
morning & shoot with me
returning to Langwell on Thursday.
So bring your things for the
night – We wear smoking
coats for dinner.

Ld Henry & I killed 156 brace
of grouse yesterday which is
the record bag for the season

& I hope to do as well today
but there is no breeze.
We shall I hope have a good
day tomorrow.

Yours try

Portland

Feb 22nd 1902

TELEGRAMS-
WELBECK, WORKSOP.

Cuckney House,
Mansfield,
Notts.

Dear Sir,

I need hardly tell you how sorry I am that Dr Watson Cheyne's report of your wife was so unfavourable & I sympathise most sincerely & deeply with you. I hope however he may be able to

do something to alleviate the suffering. If there is anything you can do & care to, please let me know. I have ordered some flowers to be sent to your wife.

I think the horse means immense

are satisfactory features & Belomolsky must be fine colts.

Many thanks for the 2 letters I stayed in for two days which I have not done for 20 years.

The yearling is looking splendid.

Yours sincerely
Portland

May 23rd 1902.

Cuckney House,
Mansfield,
Notts.

TELEGRAMS:—
WELBECK, WORKSOP.

Dear Sir—

I know letters & words can afford very poor consolation in such a deep & overwhelming grief such as you are at present undergoing still I feel I must once

poor consolation to you to know that your dear wife is now at rest & that her long & terrible sufferings have come to an end. The —

I know wrote to you yesterday so I do not

again intrude on you today how deeply and sincerely I feel for you & how I hope that time will assuage though I fear it can never heal your terrible wound — He cannot help being some

send any message from he & am

Yours most sincerely

Portland

I must on no account trouble about the horses unless you feel inclined to do so.

Would you like me to

Welbeck Abbey,
Worksop,
Notts.

30 December 1919.

Dear Sir,

Thank you very much indeed for
the kind gift of your book, which I
am sure that I shall find full of
interest.

I am glad that you keep well in
health, and with the very best wishes
that you may have a Happy New Year,

I am,

Yours sincerely,

Portland

*I wonder what the
future of Kingsclere
will be.*

13, GROSVENOR PLACE.
S.W.

Dear Sir

Can you meet me at
Tattersalls this
morning at 10.30?

Yours
truly

Henry Bentinck

130

TELEGRAPH
BERRIEDALE.
LANGWELL,
BERRIEDALE,
R.S.O. CAITHNESS.
STATION
HELMSDALE.

Aug 26th 1900.

Dear Mrs Porter.

Thank you very
much for your kind
letter. I am glad
to say everything passed
off very easily and well
and Mother soon an
progressing most favourably
I hope she will make

Aug 29th 1900.

Dear Mrs Porter

How kind of
you both to send
us such a
wonderful ham.
I have never
tasted one before,
but have always
heard how good
they are!

The Duke eats
ham at each
meal, so he
will indeed
appreciate a
new kind!
It was such
a pleasure
having you
here, a I hope
you

---

are none the
worse for the
long tiring journey.
Please tell Mr.
Porter how sorry
I was, I did not
see him too.
Yours truly
Winifred Sutherland

131

an excellent recovery in
this lovely air. I wonder
if you & your husband
are coming here next week.
I shall be so glad if you
do.
With all good wishes
I am
Yours sincerely
Portland

& sympathising much
with you now you
are not well —
Please remember me
to Mr Porter —
Yours truly
W Portland

Jul. 14th 1907.

3, GROSVENOR SQUARE.
W.

Dear Mrs Porter
The Duke tells
me you are still
very poorly, & I
must write you
one line to tell
you how sorry I
am — & how I
hope you will
soon get much
better —

132

Telegrams, Welbeck.

Feb 24th 1902

CUCKNEY HOUSE,
MANSFIELD,
NOTTS.

Dear Mrs Porter

I must send you one line of heartfelt sympathy with you in yr terrible anxiety about Mrs Porter. Nothing seems to be of any comfort, when ones greatest treasure is

I daresay you are very glad to get back to yr nice home again - one always longs to get back, especially if not feeling very well - I wish so much I had been able to go down to Kingsclere with the Duke yesterday, but I was rather knocked up with the

heat - I am sending you a little box of Malmaison Carnations from Welbeck - though I know you have so many lovely flowers of yr own. Please do not think of answering this letter - it is only to show you that I was thinking of you

133

in such dangers, I
know — & I fear she
is having   much
suffering   to contend
with —

I do trust that Mr.
Watson Cheque may
have given   her some
relief yesterday —
Sister Grace has been
telling me daily about
her —

I shall be so glad to
hear if you will
send me a line —
I have given orders
to send her a few
flowers — from me —
The Duke & I are
feeling with you
each day — &
sympathize so deeply —
Yours truly
W Portland

Welbeck
May 22nd 1902.

Dear Mr Porter
One line I
must send you
of the deepest &
tenderest sympathy
in your great
sorrow —
I know what you
were to each
other — & how
awful

134

LANGWELL,
BERRIEDALE,
R. S. O. CAITHNESS.

Aug 30th 1900

Dear Mrs Porter,

Thank you so
much for the nice books
you sent us, both Sonny
and I like them very much.
We think it very good of

you to have sent them.
My little brother is
very well and grows.

Yours Sincerely

Victoria Bentinck.

September 4th 1900

Dear Mrs Porter

I thank you
very much for the nice
book you sent me.
I like it very

much with the
beautiful butterflies
in it.

Yours sincerely,
Titchfield.

P.S. I take my book
to bed every night.

136

Mr George Faber (later Lord Faber)
1852 – 1931

Porter trained five winning horses for him from 1901 – 1903. They won ten races and prize money of £14,846. The most successful horse being Pietermaritzburg.

He was an MP for York 1900 – 1910

For Battersea & Clapham 1910 – 1918

Became 1st Baron Wittenham of Wallingford in 1918. Sat in the House of Lords until his death in 1931.

How he came to be an owner with Porter is unrecorded.

Hugh Grosvenor - 2nd Duke of Westminster

Was grandson of 1st Duke of Westminster

Porter trained 11 winning horses for him from 1901 to 1905. A total of 16 races were won with prize money of £9024.

As he was one of the world's wealthiest people, the prize money was not of the greatest importance.

Together with the 6th Duke of Portland, Porter and Mr F Gretton, he was a member of the Kingsclere Syndicate.

Charles Marlow – Jockey
One of Porter's Godfathers.

Was born at Hour Cross, near Newborough, Staffordshire in 1814. At an early age was sent to Captain Meynell, of Phantom College, where he received his equestrian education.

His first race was ridden at Houghton in 1828, when he rode as a featherweight.
He accepted a fixed engagement with Mr. Copeland in 1827 and at once showed his exceptional talent. Mr. Copeland owned the pottery of the same name.
Marlow won the Chester Cup on King Cole in spring 1828 – though the horse was considered unworthy of being mentioned in the betting.

In 1848 began an engagement with Lord Eglinton, which included the most conspicuous success of his career. Among the events of his first year was the Triennial at Ascot. In 1849 he won the Derby and the St Leger on the Flying Dutchman; and at Ascot the Emperors Plate on Van Tromp, beating fellow jockeys Flatman, Butler and Templeman, who were the best around. In 1850 Marlow again won the Emperor's Plate on the Flying Dutchman and in 1853, on Catherine Hayes, he won the Coronation Stakes at the same meeting. Ascot Heath was always a lucky course for him, and to the above successors must be added – the Hunt Cup, for Sir R. Bulkely on the Bishop of Rumford's Cob, and the Ascot Derby in 1851, on Phlegethlon. In 1855, riding into the gates, his mount Nettle, bolted and fell over the chains, breaking Marlow's leg. He returned to riding only in 1857.

In 1873 it is recorded that Admiral Rous while at York, subscribed to a fund that was being raised for a once famous jockey, Charles Marlow, then dependent on charity.
It was the twenty-second year after Marlow won the great match at York on the Flying Dutchman against Voltigeur.

Marlow possessed three admirable qualities, which normally would have made him a top class jockey 1. Inflexible honesty 2. Nerves of steel 3. Sheer physical strength. Sadly alongside these attributes he was a chronic alcoholic.

He had in 1844 married Mary Ann Saunders, a relative of John Porter's father's friend, Saunders from Rugeley had an early influence on John Porter herself. There was a son of the marriage who died young and possibly through John Porter's care was buried in the churchyard at Kingsclere.

Tom Ashmall (Jockey)
1838 -1875

Tom Ashmall's best friend at school was John Porter. Tom Ashmall was the nephew of Tom Carr, who trained at Hednesford. Tom and John Porter spent much of their time at Carr's stables where they both caught the racing bug.

Tom was apprenticed to Thomas Taylor, eventually marrying one of his daughters. Another apprentice who was to do likewise was John Wells who went on to be a Classic winning jockey. He also rode for John Porter. Tom rode three Classic winners for John Scott's stable, and a further two for the trainer T. Eskrett.

His career finished after a bizarre race when riding for the Marquis of Exeter. During the race he was torn from the saddle by another horse having been seized by the thigh and shaken like a doormat.

Tommy later trained for a while in France. He died in May 1875.

Robert Denman
Trainer in France.

Robert Denman was a lifelong friend of Porter from his school days. Despite Denman moving to France, they remained very much in touch.

Denman was private trainer to M. Edmond Blanc. Blanc was a great horse breeder as well as a politician. His father built the Casino and Marina in Monaco. M. Edmond Blanc built and owned Saint Cloud Racecourse as well as having stud farms in La Celle-Saint-Cloud, Heras Villebon and Haras Hardy. Porter and his son-in-law George Williams both visited the stud in Paris when meeting with Denman at the Haras de Jardy at Versailles, owned by Edmond Blanc. Sadly Michel Bouchet, the nonagenarian Chantilly turf historian died in August 2016 before contact could be made with him. Fortunately Jonathan Pease who trained in France for 40 years, has been able to provide the attached detail.

See letters from Denman and cross reference to Jonathan Pease email.
Robert Denman (letters)

Letter 8th August from La Fouilleuse

This was a training stable built by Edmond Blanc in 1902, alongside Saint Cloud racecourse which he had constructed in 1898. It was clearly being used by Robert Denman, Blondel's trainer.
The letter is in reply to a letter from Porter about the possible sale in England of Bayardo. Denman had received a letter from Blanc in Deauville saying he will buy Bayardo if the price is convenient to him and to write to Porter to that effect – so go ahead. Clearly nothing came of negotiations and Bayardo retired to the Red Post Stud. Initially he had health problems but once cleared up, he was a success.

Sadly his stud career came to an abrupt end when he contracted thrombosis and he had to be put down on 4th June 1917. He was only eleven years old.

Denman enclosed two proofs of photos of Porter and Denman together. 'Send them back and say if you have a preference and mark the same. Denman will have the same copies done and send to him'.

He hopes Mrs Porter and Porter are both well. In Saint Cloud the weather is warm and dry and he is busy breaking in the yearlings.
Commenting paragraph of the political situation, Germany and the Vichy – whom Denman obviously considers a bad lot.

Ps Miss Farmer wishes Denman to convey her fond remembrance to Porter and Mrs Porter.

Letter Wednesday 26th August 1914

Note the letter has black surround – normally associated with the writer being in mourning. No doubt from the content of the letter – Denman felt that way

"Pleased to receive Porter's letter and to learn he is feeling better and hopes for his continued improvement.

Racing here is completely finished for this year. The military have taken possession of all racecourses around Paris and Denman has put sheep and cattle all over the grounds of the racecourse and stables.

Denman has had billeted on him 700 soldiers and 400 horses – which I will not easily forget for some time.

Everything does look so sad over here – towns and villages look all so empty. The men folk have all gone to the war.

Only military trains have been running – no one could leave or go anywhere by train and we are obliged to carry a military passport about with us, even to go outside the gates, even then you get stopped every ¼ or ½ mile.

Monsieur Blanc cleared out directly the mobilization was proclaimed, down to Pau* in readiness to cross over to Spain in case of emergency – he left without saying a word.

I have all my yearlings broken in and ridden about – no one else has taken any yearlings up whatever – everything looks so very sad over here – hundreds of stable lads stranded.

Miss Farmer sends her very kind regards to Mrs Porter with my own.

*a town in the south west close to the Spanish border.Letter – 28th June 1916 – Hotel Maria-Christina, St Sebastian Spain from Robert Denman

"You will see from the above address I am in Spain – family ref's.

I am here with 29 horses for the June meeting of St Sebastian. This is a most lovely and delightful place – how happy everybody would be if we could only see the finish of this war within sight.

An emotional letter

Letter 3rd October 1919 Chamant par Senlis.

This letter written from Robert Denman's home. Chamant is a village near the town of Senlis which lies just to the west of the A1 Paris/Lille road and slightly to the east of Chantilly – both to the north of Paris.

This shows evident relief of hearing from Porter as Denman had been receiving mixed messages as to Porter's health. This war seems to have cut all friends apart. Robert Denman had been living in Chamant since 1st January 1915. At one time the Germans had been within 37 kilometers of them and the fright from the air bombs has been terrible. They never knew from one day to the next if he would lose his home and all it contained – either to the Germans or the French army.

Living in the army zone we were not allowed to remove our greater part of our things.

When he left to go racing in Spain on 5th June we were being bombed every night all around – the fires and destruction and the shock nearly sent us crazy. However Miss Farmer and my daughter-in-law stayed on. I had to leave for Spain and take all the horses I could with me, 36 in all. I was allowed a passport to leave with the horses and a special train right through to Spain, but felt a coward in doing so, to leave my people behind. But my home was saved through my daughter-in-law and Miss Farmer's courage by staying.

Since leaving Mr E Blanc, how I have wished for this horrid war to finish with the hopes of engaging some horses at Newbury (the course built and constructed by his friend – Porter) and to pay you a visit and see you both once again.

La Foucilleuse
par Rueil
S & O. 8 Aout 1913

My dear Mr Porter

In answer to your letter
Mr Blanc has written me from
Deauville to say he will Buy
Bayardo. if the price is
convenient to him: & to write
you to that effect, so go a head.

Enclosed is two proofs of the
of our Photograph taken together.
Send them back to me. & say if
you have a preference. & mark
the same. & then I will have
some done — & send to you.

Wednesday   26 Aug 1914

Dear Mr Porter
        I was pleased to receive a
few lines from you. & know you
are feeling better. & hope you will
still continue to improve.
    Racing here is completely finished
for this Year. The Military have
taken position of all Racecourses
around Paris. & have put Sheep &
Cattle. all over the Grounds. I
have had Bilited on me. 700.
Soldiers & 400 horses. which I shall
not easily forget for some time.
    Everything does look so sad over
here. Town & Villages looks all so
empty. the men folks have all
gone to the War.

Only Military Trains have been
running. no one could leave. or go
anywhere by Train. & we are obliged
to carry a Military passport. about
with us. even to go outside the gates.
even then get stopped every quarter of
a mile. or half mile.
    Mr Blanc cleared out. directly the
Mobilisation was proclaimed. down to
Pau. in readiness to cross over into Spain
in case of emergency. He left with
out saying a word;
    I have all my yearlings Broken in
& Ridden about, no one else has taken
any yearlings up whatever. everything
looks so very sad over here. Hundreds
of Stables Lads stranded
    Miss Farmer sends her Very kind
regards to Mrs Porter. with my own
Best Wishes & kind regards to you both,
    I remain
        yours Sincerely
            R Denman

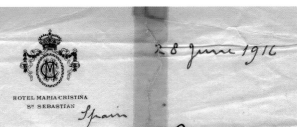

HOTEL MARIA CRISTINA
S? SEBASTIAN
Spain

28 June 1916

My dear Mr & Mrs Porter

You will see from the above address. I am here in Spain. & your letter has been sent on to me here. I will write to my Son in Law in America at once. where he has been. since the outbreak of the War – with my Daughter & her little Son. who I am longing to see once again: how I miss them – they are living at his Home in California. so at the same time. Johnnie Rief can send. his Brother Lister's signature at the same time I am glad to hear Mr Porter is keeping well. & hope he will do so –

I am here with 29 horses. for the New Meeting of St Sebastian.

This is a most Lovely & delightful place – how happy everybody would be. If we could only see the finish of this War – within sight?

With best Wishes and regards to you Both, also Mr Porter family

I remain. my dear Mr Porter

Yours Very Sincerely

R Denman

144

CHAMANT
PAR SENLIS (Oise)

31 October 1919

My dear friends
Mr & Mrs Porter

I was quite pleased to received your letter - with news about yourselves - I had heard so many different accounts about Mr Porter's illness - I had felt at times quite timed about writing you - and this terrible War seems to have cut all friends apart:

I have been living here since 1st of January 1915 - under terrible times - once the German Army was within 37 Kilometres of us. and the fright from the Air Bombs - has been terrible. We never knew one day from another if I should loose my home - and all it contained - either by the Germans - or the French Army of Soldiers -

Because living in the Army Zone we where not allowed to remove our greater part of our things - when I left here - to go Racing in Spain 5th of June - we where being Bombed every night all around - the fires & distruction - & the Shock - nearly sent us crazzy - however Miss Farmer & My Daughter in Law - stayed on - I had to leave for Spain & take all the horses - I could with me - 36 in all - & was allowed a Passport - to leave with the horses - & a special Train - right through to Spain - But felt a Coward in doing so - to leave my people behind - But my Home was saved - through My Daughter in Law

and Miss Farmer's courage by staying - Since leaving Mr E. Blanc - how I have wished for this horrid War to finish - with the hopes - of Engaging some horses at Newbury - and to Pay you a Visit & see you both once again -

I have had a fair good success for Captain Cohn - since I have trained for him - & won him in the Three years over £40.000 - & this year over £12.000:

I like My Home better than at La Fouilleuse - I would be Very happy if I could intertain you here for a while - If such an occasion would permit you both to come & see me again,

My Daughter - her Son & Husband are still in America - California - I am happy to tell you - They are all quite well - She is Very happy & contented in Life - and anticapate coming over this next year - if so I shall

be happy too -

Last Saturday was visited by Stables too - altho your return - was managing her Stable - & with what Splendid success - It has told in her favour - Yes I think I have a Stud Winner for next Year - But I have a good lot of Yearlings - which may win the Derby the coming Year - Which you will see in the coming Calendar.

Engagements made for them - Concluding with heart greetings - and best of Wishes for both your health and happiness -

I remain
Yours very Sincerely
Walter Farmer

PS always glad to hear from you.

Subj: **Robert Denman**
Date: 24/08/2016 12:47:22 GMT Daylight Time
From:
To:

Dear Jeremy,

I feel contrite that I have not replied to your nice card and the fascinating
Porter-Denman letters you enclosed;

My excuse is that I wanted to show them to Michel Bouchet, the nonagenarian
Chantilly Turf historian in August. Sadly, Michel keeled over after a good
dinner and I attend his funeral 2 weeks ago.

However, I have done some research (through internet, of course) to find
out that Denman was the Mathet/Fabre of his era.

He still holds the record number of wins in 4 current Group races:

The Prix Morny (8 wins 1896-1926); this was pointed out in Sunday's race card when the race was
run.

The Poule d'Essai des Poulains :11 wins (1901-1926)

The Prix la Rochette 10 wins (1901-1926) and the Grand Prix de Vichy
(4 wins).

I am sure he won countless other present Group 1s including the
Eclipse Stakes 1906 with Val D'or but my French racing books are still in storage.

For all the winners he must have had, Denman's greatest legacy to the
thoroughbred is that he trained 3 'chef de races' in Teddy (who raced in Saint
Sebastian in 1916 so presumably one of the horses referred to in his letter) and his 2 sons ,the full
brothers Sir Gallahad and Bulldog.
All 3 stallions attained huge success in the US and are present in most American
pedigrees today. Teddy is also the sire of La Troienne, the most influential
broodmare in the US studbook.

Like all Champion trainers, Denman needed a Croesus rich owner and he seemed to have one in
Edmund Blanc, who financed the building of Monaco
(marina and casino). Like Boussac, after him, he also owned Saint Cloud race-
course and the haras de Jardy at Versailles. Blanc built Saint Cloud in 1898 and   constucted a training
stable (La Fouilleuse mentioned in the Denman's letter) on the course in 1902. Presumably Denman was
his private trainer. Blanc also purchased Flying Fox to
stand at Jardy which may have established the connection between Porter and Denman. The Prix
Edmund Blanc is still run at Saint Cloud.

Blanc died in 1920 and seemed to be selling his horses (like Teddy)
anyway.Denman must have moved to Chantilly (or Chamant 10 kms away)
after the war. Denman's post war big client was an American, Jefferson Davis Cahn who purchased the
famous Haras de Bois Roussel.

Denman was Staffordshire (another connection with Porter?) born but
sadly Michel is not there to tell me more.

Do look us up next time you are over and best regards to you both from
us both

Jonathan

Francis Fane – 12th Earl of Westmoreland

The Earl, a military man until 1859, when his father died – retired from the Army in 1860. From that time he became a member of the Jockey Club and a racehorse owner. He never won any of the Classics, but was well known to place large bets.

He became a patron of the Findon stable which at the time was run by Porter and William Goater who had taken over from John Day. The Earl of Westmoreland was aged 36, and was to become a very good friend to Porter. He kept horses also with William Day at Woodyeates.

His interest in horseracing was costly and in 1866 he sold the family portraits of Mr Fane and Lord Berghersh by Joshua Reynolds.   Eventually his situation reached a point where he had to sell his horses. He then managed Lord Harlington's stable.

His greatest contribution to racing was suggesting to John Porter in 1863 that he should not approach Mr Savile concerning the vacancy that he had for a private trainer, but that he should wait for a better opportunity. Through his friendship with Sir Joseph Hawley the Earl of Westmoreland knew that Sir Joseph's then trainer was seriously unwell. The Earl gave Porter a letter of introduction and told him to call on Sir Joseph at his London home, which was en route to Liverpool, with some of the Earl's horses. Sir Joseph was to engage Porter and as a result his future lifestyle and that of Park House, Kingsclere, was established in the annals of racing history.

No owner saw more of the ways and work of John Porter than Lord Westmoreland during his sojourn at Findon. It was no doubt this that gave him the confidence to recommend Porter to Sir Joseph Hawley.

Henry Padwick

A solicitor and money lender based in Horsham. Porter first came into contact with Padwick when he became apprenticed to John Day at Michel Grove. Padwick was one of John Day's patrons. John Wells was the recognized stable jockey

Padwick and John Day had a falling out and Padwick engaged William Goater formerly head lad to John Day, to run his stable at Findon. Padwick made arrangements for Porter to move there as well, where he took up residence in Padwick's house and was given managerial responsibility in the stable, being responsible for feeding the horses, keeping the books, being paymaster and generally looking after everything bar the actual training, which suited William Goater, despite Porter's young years.

Many people found Padwick unpleasant to deal with, but John Porter always found him a kind and considerate employer, one of the least suspicious men and one whom he enjoyed serving.

In Porter's own words 'Findon in more than one respect proved the turning point of my career'. In the year of Blue Gown's Derby win, Padwick had been assigned most of the Marquis of Hasting's horses as security for a loan advanced to meet his most pressing debts. This is a measure of the type of money lending that Padwick was involved in.

Padwick was a wealthy man and became involved in the history of the development of Epsom Racecorse. In 1877, Edward Studd, Lord of Manor of Walton on the Hill, died. He instructed his trustees to sell the Walton estate to pay his debts and funeral expenses. Catalogues of Sale were prepared in 1878, but before the property (which included part of the land on which Epsom Racecourse stood) could be auctioned, it was sold to Henry Padwick of Horsham for £25,000. The Epsom Grand Stand Association who ran the racecourse, were incensed, but began negotiations with Padwick to buy not just the Walton Land that crossed a section of the racecourse, but the whole estate. Padwick, so the Committee thought, had agreed to sell for £30,000. They paid a deposit of £1000. The whole to be paid as £3,500 in cash, £4000 in promissory notes @ 5% and a mortgage of £22,500. In September 1879, Padwick announced that he required £30,000 within ten days or the deposit would be forfeit. The EGA's solicitor put this demand down to Padwick's severe illness and advised abandonment of the purchase. Indeed Padwick died within a few days of making his demand.

Two years following Padwick's wife's death in 1886, Padwick Junior sold to the Association, 205 acres of land including part of the racecourse, but at a cost of £20,000. It is fair to say that Padwick's influence on racing came in diverse contrasts.

Padwick was an associate of the Days in 1846 and tried to form a syndicate to buy Lord George Bentinck's stud for £10,000. His offer was rebuffed.

Amongst some members of the Turf fraternity – Henry Padwick's reputation was poor. Admiral Rous considered him a character of great danger to the public and attributed to him the demise of the Marquess of Hastings, although acknowledging he was capable of bringing about his own downfall.

Padwick was the son of a Horsham butcher, but had received a good education, a pleasing presence, plausible manner and great financial ability. He initially trained as a lawyer but then set himself up as a moneylender in London, firstly in Davies Street, then in Hill Street, Berkeley Square. He was an able moneylender and soon private banks and wealthy individuals would put at his disposal large sums of money at 10%. Gambling appealed to him but he had recognized that the turf was where he would most likely come across the young men who would become his clients. He helped to ruin a fair proportion of the young men who used his services.

The Marquis of Hastings being perhaps the most notable.

Henry Huxtable - Jockey

Henry Huxtable was born in 1845 and started as a jockey in 1860.

He won some good races before moving first to Germany in 1885 and then to Austria. He won the Austrian Derby and was rewarded with the gift of a small mansion in the Hungarian Training Centre at Alag.

He rode for John Porter and Sir Joseph Hawley. Most famously he rode Rosicrucian to 2nd Place in the Middle Park. Initially he thought he had won but was in fact beaten a head, by the other Hawley/Porter runner – Greensleaves. They finished the width of the track apart. Huxtable had been deceived by the camber of the track.

From Alag he wrote to Porter, sending his condolences in a letter dated 26th May 1892. He had reversed the 2nd and 3rd numbers – it was in a fact in 1902 that Mrs Porter dies. Nonetheless it shows how Porter seems to have kept a network of connection going at all levels. The very fact of the letter being written also indicates the affection and esteem in which John Porter was held.

Admiral Sir Henry (Harry) Kepell
1809 – 1904

Sir Harry, an Admiral, albeit only 5 feet tall, was very much a favourite at Marlborough House.

A career naval officer, Sir Henry completed his service as Admiral of the Fleet, his appointment being made in 1877. He retired from the navy in 1879 having been First and Principal Aide-de-Camp to Queen Victoria.

Having spent much of his service at sea on overseas appointments, he does not appear to have been one of Porter's owners, but he does seem to have had a very close relationship with him.

Letter re Porter's attendance at the Naval Review on the Royal Yacht. This was the 1887 Queen Victoria's Golden Jubilee Fleet Review, with a note asking for Porter's postal town.

Letter written on 8th September 1892 "Leger Day" from the Royal Yacht, Osborne, situated in Copenhagen. Porter had clearly invited Keppell and Admiral Stephenson to the St Leger, but because they had been "in the neighborhood of Copenhagen for the last fortnight" the invite had only just caught up with them. Keppell leaving the Royal Yacht that day, but will not learn result of St Leger until arriving in Aberdeen 2 days later. He bemoans the fact that there is "no telegraph here as I should have been on La Fleche".
Sends kind regards to 'Mrs Porter and all your belongings'. Yours very truly Henry Kepell.

3) Letter to Porter's son and letter to the Admiralty asking for another nomination indicates that in 1892, the son might receive Midshipman uniform. Also wishing Mrs Porter and family many happy returns of the new year. Complains that for the first time in 82 years, he is laid up with gout.

Letter March 1st (year unknown)
"Please let me know if you hear anything good for Lincoln Handicap – I can keep any information to myself"
He had been to Sandown that day but had not seen anyone from Kingsclere.

Letter from Royal Naval Club – Portsmouth – Nov 11th (year unknown)
"Please tell me a likely Derby winner that I may take the long odds about!"

Hoping you and yours are thriving.

Letter Jan 16th (year unknown)

1)   Barry – Porter's son – must work hard re naval commission.
2)   Still Suffering gout
3)   Overwhelmed with grief at what the good Prince and Princess are suffering.

Admiral Sir Harry Keppell, was according to Porter "one of the most delightful men I have met".
He paid a visit to Kingsclere nearly every year.

July 4

Dear Mr. Porter

I thought you might
be anxious to know
where you were to be
at the Naval Review
So write to Captain
Domvile onboard
the Collingwood, he

will have the chief
management and
you could not be
better placed
Do not reply to this
as I will write again
Yours very truly
Henry Keppel
By the bye I do not

know your Post Town
So please send me
the proper address

Copenhagen Wed 8 Sep
Ledger day

Dear Porter
Your kind invite of
5th just received —
Many thanks, Stephenson
& Self have been in
this neighbourhood
for the last fortnight

or we should greatly
have enjoyed the
Sunday with you.
& I leave this today
and shall not know
the result of the race
until I get to Aberdeen
in two days time —

No Telegraph here or
I should have been
on La Flèche, am on
Common —,
Kind regards to
Mrs Porter and all
your belongings —
Stephenson remains
here the Princess
Yours very truly
Henry Keppel

Bishopstoke

Jany 1 - 92

My dear Porter

I am so sorry about
your boy but hope it
will be all right in
June, I have written
to the Admiralty to ask
for another nomination.

Many thanks for kind
invitation to your
charming High Kingsclere
but I am, and have been
for the first time in
eighty two years, laid
up with the gout. —
I mean to try to get up
to London next when
I hope to write again.

Wishing Mrs Porter
yourself and family
many happy returns
of the new year with
about you in his
Midshipman Uniform,
Believe me
Sincerely yours
Henry Keppel

March 1st

Dear Porter

Weather has been too
bad for me to visit
you

Please let me know
if you have any thing
good for Lincoln
Handicap. I can keep

any information to
myself.

Was at Sandown
today but could find
no one belonging

Hoping you are all
flourishing & kind regards
to Mrs Porter
Very truly yours
Henry Keppel

Nov. 11

Dear Porter
Please tell me
a likely Derby winner
that I may take
the long odds about!
Hoping you & yours
are thriving
Believe me
Yours truly
Henry Keppel

Jan. 16

Dear Porter

Barry is to have another
chance but the good
boy will have to work
hard the next six
months

I am still confined
with gout but hopes
to visit you, as you

kindly propose, when
the days get longer

We are overwhelmed
with grief at what
the good Queen & Empress
are suffering

My kind regards to
Mrs Porter
Yours truly
Henry Keppel

155

Daisy Greville – Countess of Warwick
Frances Evelyn "Daisy" Greville – Countess of Warwick

Was a socialite and long term mistress of HRH Albert Edward, Prince of Wales, Later
King Edward VII. She was the inspiration behind the popular music hall song 'Daisy, Daisy'.

She and her husband were members of the Marlborough House Set – ie close friends of HRH
Prince of Wales. She had an affair with Lord Charles Beresford whose brother
Lord Marcus Beresford was racing manager to HRH Prince of Wales. This caused a rift between
Lord Charles and the Prince which lasted all their lives.

At a Crichel House party in 1894.
Those present include John Porter, the Earl of Warwick, Lord Alington (host) Countess of Warwick
sitting next to HRH Prince of Wales, Lady Alington.and others

The letter to Porter from Warwick Castle February 1892 concerns votes for candidates to the
board of Royal Agricultural Benevolent Institution, founded in 1860 for the benefit of workers in the
Agricultural Industry. An industry that the Countess always had an affinity with because of the
agricultural holdings of her family in East Anglia. Porter and the Countess clearly knew one
another well enough to correspond on such matters (see letter).

The Countess was friendly with Elinor Glyn, the novelist who was to become the mistress of Lord
Curzon sharing Montacute House, Somerset with him 1915 – 1925.

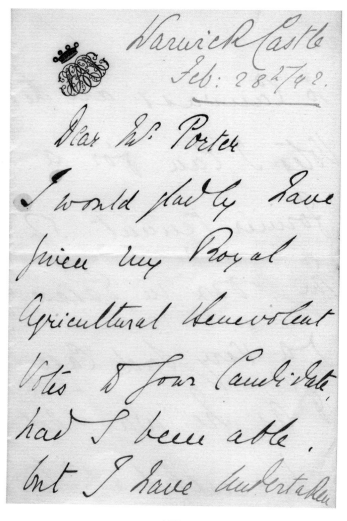

to Canvass all the
votes I can for a
former tenant of
my own in Essex,
a very sad case,
as he was not
successful at the
last two elections.
I am bound to go
on until he is elected.
Otherwise should have
been happy to help y'
Case. Believe me,
Very faithfully y'rs
Frances Evelyn Brooke

Evelyn - Duchess of Wellington
Wife of Henry - 3rd Duke

A letter of 24th September 1890 written on notepaper of Tresco Abby, Scilly Isles, Cornwall, thanks Porter for sending to her home in Berkshire - Strathfield Saye, a "setting of eggs". She hopes "she" may succeed in rearing some chickens. It is very kind of you remembering to send them to me".

The Wellingtons and Porter had a close friendship and each visited the other at Strathfield Saye and Kingsclere. This shows Porter's affinity with horticulture, agriculture which he had throughout his life. Here he sends eggs – to others he shares his plants, quite a different side to his training career.

Evelyn finishes the letter hoping Mrs Porter and your daughters are quite well. A hint that his two sons had by that time flown the nest.

(See letter)

A letter of 3rd March 1898 from Strathfield Saye.
Evelyn encloses with her letter details of a boy in whom she is interested and who is devoted to horses, asks Porter if he could take him into his establishment, as she knows how well he looks after his lads – if not perhaps finding him a placement with another trainer. Another letter indicating the quality of friendship.

The reference to his lads being well looked after was an aspect of this yard, acknowledged by many. In his design he had prioritized that the accommodation should be of the best standard.

A letter of 9th June 1910 from West Green House

Evelyn had moved to this address, having become a widow.

Again the letter shows the closeness of the relationship – this letter being some 20 years after the 'egg' letter.

See letter

This property is of historical interest. Evelyn lived there until her death in the 1930s. Shortly before her death it was purchased by Sir Victor Sassoon who in time gave it to the National Trust. Lord McAlpine became the National Trust tenant. In 1990, the Irish Republican Army looking for Lord McAlpine and his friend Lady Thatcher, blew it up.

Tresco Abbey
Isles of Scilly
Cornwall
Sep. 24. 98

Dear Mr. Porter —
I hear from Strathfield Saye
that you have very
kindly sent me a sitting
of eggs — Thank you
very much indeed
I hope I may succeed
in raising some chickens
It is very kind of you
remembering to send them
to me —
Thos. Mr. Porter

& your daughter
are quite well

Believe me

Marshal
Duke of Wellington

EVELYN

Strathfieldsaye
March 3. 98

Dear Mr Porter -
I am very much
interested in the boy
referred to in the
enclosed. -
He is devoted to horses
& his great ambition

is to be in a racing
stable. Would you
kindly help me to
get him into one?
Of course I would
rather he went to
you than to anyone,
as I know how well

your boys are looked
after; but if you
have no room for
him, perhaps you
would give me a
helping hand in
placing him somewhere
I hope Mrs Porter
is quite well -

Please give her my
kind regards & I
hope you will forgive
my troubling you

Yours very truly
Eustace Wellington

June 9. 1910

WEST GREEN HOUSE,
WINCHFIELD,
HANTS.

Dear Mr Porter -

We were so very sorry to
hear of your accident & hope
that by this time you have
quite recovered.   I would have
written before, but curiously
enough I heard of it for the
first time in a letter received
from Mr Money -   I hope
before long, that you & Mrs Porter
will pay us another visit -

What terrible storms we have
had lately!

Yours very truly

Eupl Wellington -

161

Henry - 3rd Duke of Wellington

Letter of 27th April 1886.

To Porter from Wellington enclosing donation for £20 for the Reading Room in Kingsclere that Porter was establishing.

Letter 11th February 1888 written from Strathfield Saye House inviting Porter to a rabbit shoot on Wednesday and Friday. Thursday can be spent "looking over the place". The invitation is also extended to Mrs Porter.

Letter 13 February 1888
Porter had obviously advised he could only do Thursday. Wellington advised they come by train to Mortimer and he will send a carriage to meet them.

Letter of 12 December 1888
Letter to Porter advising visit of Lord Fitzhardinge and Captain Thoroton to Strathfield Saye the following week. Wellington enquires if they could visit Park House and have a look at the stables – letter asks if Wednesday or Thursday would be convenient, also time etc.

Lord Fitzhardinge had been in the Royal Horse Guards – MP for Cheltenham and was a Fellow of the Society of Antiquarians.

Letter 13 February 1890

Concerns the wishes of a Mrs Walker – both Wellington and Porter wish to know what she wants.

Letter 6th April 1894
To Porter enquiring if Wellington Lord Hardinge and Captain Thoroton could visit Park House Stables on 23rd April. Lord Fitzhardinge has only 23rd available. Porter to advise another day when Wellington and Captain Thoroton might visit.

Letter April 20th 1896 from Strathfield Saye House. From Wellington asking if he and Captain Thoroton could visit Park House. Apologies for short notice but he had been rather unwell.

Letter 11th May 1896 from Strathfield Saye House.

This letter accompanies a gift of "an old Dutch silver box which ought to belong to Porter as it has the initials of your place on the lid. Inside is a Dutchman's idea of a Derby winner, although I am not quite sure whether Baron Max de Tuyll would agree or not"

Separate note: (accompanying box)

In memory of many very pleasant visits paid to Park House.
Truly, Wellington
NB Tuyll is the name of a noble Dutch family with familial and historical links to England. The full name is Van Tuyll van Serooskerken.

Letter 9th January 1898 from Strathfield Saye House

Thanks Porter for good wishes for the New Year which Wellington and the Duchess reciprocate along with Captain Thoroton who is staying with them.

Has wintered well and much enjoyed the shooting. Will have great pleasure in coming over to Kingsclere in the Spring to have his usual look around.

Letter 4th March 1900 – from Strathfield Saye House. Written just 3 months before Wellington's death.

Wellington thanks Porter for invitation to the sale of the Duke of Westminster's horses, but regrets he cannot on doctor's orders. He hopes to be quite fit in 10 days and that when the weather is nice invites Porter to come for a visit.
A p.s. says that it is unlikely that Captain Thoroton and Lord Buchan may attend the sale.

Before inheriting as Duke in 1884, he had been educated at Eton, joined and left the Grenadier Guards and was MP for Andover from 1874 to 1880.

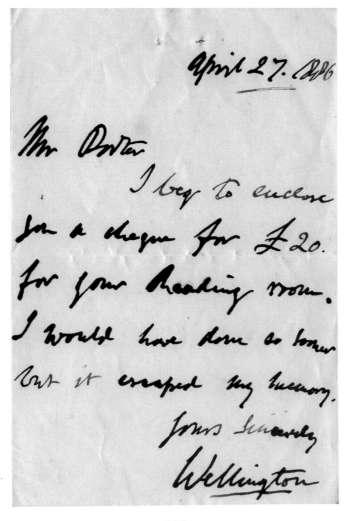

STRATHFIELD SAYE HOUSE,
MORTIMER, R.S.O.
BERKS.

11.2.88

Porter

If you are not too
busy will you come here
on Tuesday next till Saturday.
We shall have a little rabbit
shooting on Wednesday & Friday
& on Thursday you can look
over the place. If Mrs

Porter would like to come
also we shall be delighted
to see her.

Yours sincerely

Wellington

STRATHFIELD SAYE HOUSE,
MORTIMER, R.S.O.
BERKS.

13.2.88

Porter

By all means come
on Thursday I am sorry you
cannot stay longer. If you
come to Mortimer by train,
let me know what time you
there. & I will send to meet
you. Yours very truly

Wellington

164

Guiston
Dec 12. 1880

Porter

Lord Fitzhardinge &
Captain Thornton are coming
to stay with me next week, &
I know they would very much like
to go over & have a look at
your stables. Will you kindly
send me a line to Strathfield Saye

Mortimer; whether Wednesday
or Thursday would suit you.
also the time, etc.

Yours sincerely
Wellington

STRATHFIELD SAYE HOUSE,
MORTIMER, R.S.O.
BERKS.

Feb: 13. 90

Porter

I am much obliged
to you for your letter.
I have not heard yet what
Mrs Walker wishes to do.
When I am informed, I will
communicate with you.

Yours very truly Wellington

165

STRATHFIELD SAYE HOUSE,
MORTIMER, R.S.O.
BERKS. April 6. 94.

Porter

If by chance you
are not going to New-
market on the 23.rd would
it suit you if Lord
Fitzhardinge, Capt Thornton
& I came over to
Kingsclere on that day—

If it is inconvenient will
you let me know when
you would like Capt Thornton
& I to come. the 23rd
is the only day Lord F.
will be here.

Yours very truly

Wellington

STRATHFIELD SAYE HOUSE,
MORTIMER, R.S.O.
BERKS. April 20. 96.

Porter

If you are at home
at the end of the week
& not too busy, would it
suit you if Captain Thornton
& I came over to see you.
I should have written before
but a short time ago
I was rather unwell, & I

did not know if I could
manage it. Please let
me know what day to
come, if you can receive
us.

Yours very truly

Wellington

166

Strathfield Saye House,
Mortimer, R.S.O.
Berks.

May. 1896

In Memory of
Many very pleasant visits
paid to Park House
by
Wellington
—

Strathfield Saye House,
Mortimer, R.S.O.
Berks.

May 11. 96.

Potter
I send you an old
Dutch Silver box which
clearly ought to belong
to you, as it has the initials
of your place on the lid.
Inside is a Dutchman's
idea of a Derby winner,

although I am not quite
sure whether Baron Max
de Tuyll would agree
or not.

Yours very truly
Wellington

167

STRATHFIELD SAYE HOUSE,
MORTIMER. R.S.O.
BERKS.   Jan 9. 98

Porter

The Duchess & I beg
to thank you very much
for your good wishes, &
to return them most
heartily to Mrs Porter &
yourself, as does Capt
Thornton who is here

I have been very well
this winter & have enjoyed
the shooting very much.
It will give me great
pleasure to come over
to Kingsclere again in
the Spring & have my
usual look round—

Yours very truly
Wellington

STRATHFIELD SAYE HOUSE,
MORTIMER. R.S.O.
BERKS.   Mar 4. 00

Porter

Many thanks for asking
me to come to the sale
I should like to immensely
the the Drs says no. I
hope to be quite fit in a
week or 10 days, & some day
when it is fine you must
come over & see us—

Mrs Hatter is lying in
wait for you— I hope
you will have a good sale.
Yours very truly
Wellington

I think it not unlikely
that Capt Thornton &
Lord Buchan may
go over from here to
the sale.—

168

Charles - 6th Duke of Richmond, Lennox, Gordon & Aubigny.
1818-1903

Letter June 26th from 49 Belgrave Square (Duke now aged 78).
Thanking Porter for sending him a copy of 'Kingsclere'. Tells how it will help him recall memories of a time he was more intimately connected with racing. Pleased to hear of his good account of the horses coming to Goodwood.

Letter July 5th 1897 from 49 Belgrave Square
(Duke now aged 79)
Duke of Richmond informs he asked Duke of Westminster to let Porter know he could have the stables at Goodwood as usual. Poland (an employee) died in winter 96/97, but his widow continues to live in the cottage and would I have no doubt be happy to take you and do for you as she has done on former occasions.

Letter June 6th 1899 from 49 Belgrave Square
(Duke now aged 81)
Congratulations on having once more won the Derby, and with what from all accounts must be a very good horse and very well trained (Flying Fox) ridden by Mornington Cannon.
(N.B. this was the last Derby to be started by the flag. Horse owned by Duke of Westminster)

The stables at Goodwood will be, as usual, quite ready for you. As the time draws near and you know what you will bring, I have no doubt you will let me know.
Letter Jan 2nd 1900 from Goodwood, Chichester (Duke now 81)
Thanks Porter for good wishes for the New Year which he returns most sincerely.

"I was sure you would feel the death of the Duke of Westminster very much. I consider his loss as a national calamity. He always made such admirable use of his great wealth. I have known him well for a number of years and could appreciate his merits. I am sure* the Racing Stud is to be sold but I suppose the Duchess could not manage it. It will be a great thing if the Breeding Stud is to be continued. *he probably meant 'sad'

Letter Marsh 5th 1900 from 49 Belgrave Square

Thanking Porter for sending him the list of the late Duke of Westminster's horses to be sold on March 8th. Regrets he will be unable to attend and thanks Porter for offering to meet him.
NB the sale was held at Kingsclere.

Letter July 9th 1900 from 49 Belgrave Square. Confirmation that the stables at Goodwood will be available. Asks for numbers Porter will be buying so that he can have everything ready for them.

Letter Dec 26th 1900
Many thanks for season greetings which Duke of Richmond reciprocates wishes Porter "a good year and pull off some big things, especially if you do not put up American jockeys. If I was on the turf again, Morney Cannon and others like him would be quite good enough for me."

Letter July 8th 1903 from 49 Belgrave Square. Duke now 85 (written two and a half months before he died).

Apologises that he will not be at Goodwood for the races this year.
He writes a line to say the stables will be available as usual
"I wish you all luck".

June 26
1896.

49, BELGRAVE SQUARE.

Dear Sir

I am extremely obliged to you for sending me the Book you have written on Turf matters. I shall read it with much interest: I have no doubt it will recall to my recollection many circumstances which I have almost forgotten connected with the days when I was

more intimately connected with racing than I am now.

I am very glad to hear a good account of your string for Goodwood

I remain

Richmond & Gordon.

July 5.
1847.

49, BELGRAVE SQUARE.

Dear Sir

I asked the Duke of Westminster to say you could have the Stables at Goodwood as usual

Poland died last winter, but his widow continues to live in the Cottage, and would I have no doubt be happy to take you, and do for you as

She has done on former occasions.

I remain

Richmond & Gordon

49, BELGRAVE SQUARE.

June 6
1899.

Dear Sir

I congratulate you on
having once more won the
derby. with what from all
accounts must be a very
good horse. and very well
trained.

The Stables at Good-
wood will be, as usual,
quite ready for you. As the
time draws near, and you

---

know what you will bring
I have no doubt you will
let me know.

I remain
Yours faithfully
Richmond & Gordon

49, BELGRAVE SQUARE.

March 5
/1900.

My dear Sir

I am much obliged to you
for sending me the list of the
late Duke of Westminster's
horses that are to be sold on
March 8.

I am very sorry I shall
not be able to attend the Sale
and am much obliged to you
for offering to meet me.

Yours faithfully
Richmond & Gordon

49, BELGRAVE SQUARE.

July 9 1900.

Dear Sir

I write a line to say that
the Stables at Goodwood will
be ready for you as usual.

When you know how many
horses you will have there, if
you will let me know I will
see that everything is ready

I remain
Richmond & Gordon

To
Mr. Porter

Dec. 26
1900

Dear Sir

Many thanks for your
letter containing good wishes
which I return to you.

I hope you may have a
good year and pull off some
big things Especially if you
do not put up American
Jockeys. If I was on the Turf
again. Morny Cannon and
others like him would be
quite good enough for me
I remain
Richmond & Gordon

July 8 1903.

Dear Sir

I am sorry I shall not be
Goodwood this year for
The Races.

I write a line to say
you are welcome to the
use of The Stables at
Goodwood as usual.

I wish you all luck
I remain
Richmond & Gordon

January 2
1900.

Dear Sir

I am much obliged to
you for your good wishes
Contained in your letter which
I received this morning, I
return them most sincerely

I was sure you would feel
the death of the Duke of
Westminster very much. I
Consider his loss as a National
Calamity. He always made
Such admirable use of his

Great wealth. I have known
him well for a number of
years. and could appreciate
his merits. I am sure of
The Racing Stud is to be Sold
but I suppose The Duchess
Could not manage it.

It will be a great thing if
if the Breeding Stud is to be
Continued.

Yours faithfully
Richmond & Gordon

Charles Gordon Lennox - 7th Duke of Richmond

Letter 6th January 1904

"I much appreciate your letter continuing to me the good wishes you had been in the habit of sending to my father – wishing you all prosperity"

Letter June 26th 1904 from 54 Lowndes Square.

"If you are coming to Goodwood with any horses this year, I hope you will bring them to the stables at the house as usual.

Edward Stanley 15th Earl of Derby
1826 – 1893

Was a British statesman. He served as Secretary of State for Foreign Affairs twice – 1866 – 1868 and 1874 – 1878.

A letter 9th May 1866

Regretting a letter from Porter advising that a colt he had sent him proved unsatisfactory. Requests he contact his stud groom – Forshaw, to make arrangements for the colt to be returned to Knowsley.

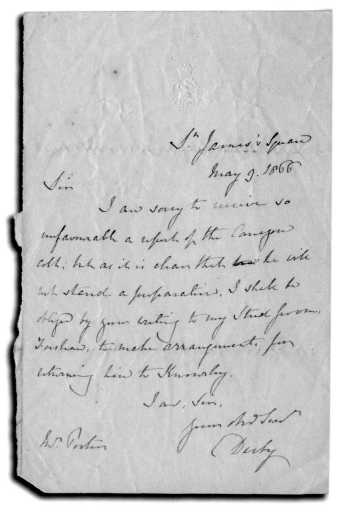

Edward Baldwin Courtenay, 12th Earl of Devon

A letter (undated as to year, likely to be 1866) Monday 6th February form 23 Lower Brook Street, London.

"I congratulate on the birth of a son and hope that Mrs Porter is doing well. I shall be very happy to act as Godfather etc. re name

Letter Tuesday 21st March

Regrets not being able to attend Christmas – all good wishes, small present for Edward John. Trust Porter has picked a representative for him at the christening. Also encloses £5 note for presents for Edward John's sisters.

Letter 20th August 1866

Thanks for photo of Mrs Porter and my godson. Regret he has not been at a race this year, though a deprivation may have been good for his pocket! May go to Doncaster where they might see one another – he would like to meet as they have not seen one another for a long time.

Being away from the racing does not much weaken his liking for it.

Letter 25 March 1867 – Black surround-notes in mourning.
Advice a toy sent by train to Overton Station – for collection. Hopes it will amuse Edward.
Asks Porter to visit him in London
"I am much obliged for what you say as to the death of my mother which was indeed a great affliction on our family".

William Courtenay 12th Earl of Devon had as his country seat – Powderham Castle.

There is no evidence that he owned racehorses and if he did they were not trained by Porter. He evidently had a very keen interest in racing and must have been known to Porter for some years – to be asked to be 'Godfather' to Porter's eldest son.

It is a matter of record that the Earl invited Fred Archer and his wife to visit him at Powderham Castle whilst on honeymoon in Torquay in 1883. However, they appear not to have accepted.

23 Lower Brook St.
London W

Monday 6 Feb

Porters,

I congratulate you on the birth of a son and hope that Mrs Porters is doing well. I shall be very happy to act as godfather although I am afraid that as I am a good deal engaged now in London, I shall not be able to get down to the ceremony. As regards names, if you and Mrs Porters have no objection, I should suggest his having one of my names (whichever you & she prefer) Edward or Baldwin. Will you let me know which you choose and when the Christening is to be; in order that even in my absence, I may send some gift to buy for son to whom I wish every luck and that he may turn out as good a fellow as his Father.

I don't mean to race much this year and shall certainly not begin early.

If ever you happen to be in London I hope that you will come and see me. I am nearly always in till one or two and shall be glad to see you.

You will receive in a few days the photograph for which you asked. With best wishes for Mrs Porters and yourself

believe me

Yours truly
Courtenay

23 Brook Street
London
Tuesday. 21 March

Dr Porter/

I am sorry that I cannot manage
to get down for the Christening of my
Godson to whom however I wish every
success and prosperity in life; which
if he follows in your footsteps he
will most certainly deserve...

I have ordered the sent down to for to day
a small present for him which I
hope that you and Mrs Porter will like.

I have also sent down a photograph
for which you asked last year —
I hope to see you soon and to hear a capital
account of the progress of the boy, Edward John,
and that you and his sisters are well.

With best wishes I am
Yours truly,
Courtenay

I trust that you have provided a representative for me tomorrow!
I also enclose a 5£ pound note with which

I shall be obliged if you or his mother would
buy some little present for the boy sisters
now or at some future time, according as
you think best; as I had a difficulty
myself in knowing what to choose for
him... although I hope that what I have
sent will please...

177

23 Wrok Pl.
20 Aug. 1866

Sir, Many thanks for the
photograph of Mrs. Porter and
my Godson which was forwarded
to me from Porterham and
which I shall value much.
I hope that he is going on
all right and is a healthy
and promising young one and
likely to "train on". — Remember
me to Mrs. Porter and tell her
that I think it is the likeness
of a very pretty child.

I have not been at a race
this year which though a
deprivation one way very possibly
has been an advantage to my
pocket. — I shall however
very likely go to Doncaster
where perhaps I may see you. —
I should be very glad to see
you as we have not met for
a long time; and if possible
have a look at the boy. —

I am afraid that I do not
find that staying away from
racing weakens much one's
liking for it! I am

Yours & truly
Courtenay

178

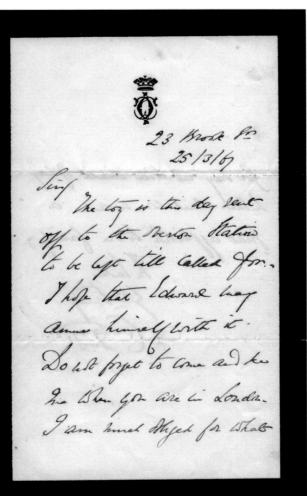

23 Brook St.
25/3/87

Sir,

The toy is this day sent off to the Newton Station to be left till called for.

I hope that Edward may amuse himself with it.

Do not forget to come and see me when you are in London.

I am much obliged for what

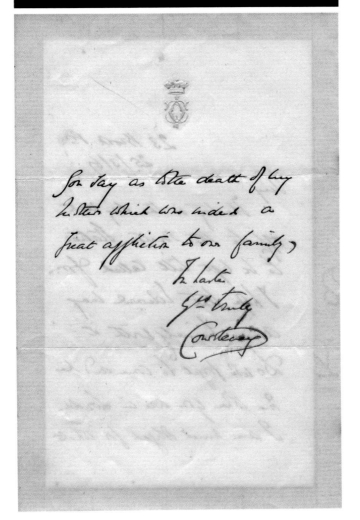

you say as to the death of my sister which was indeed a great affliction to our family,

In haste

Yrs truly

Courtenay

Charles Russell, Baron Russell of Killowen
1832-1900

An Irish statesman who became Lord Chief Justice of England. As Lord Chief Justice, his portrait was painted in 1900 by John Singer Sargent.

Correspondence with Porter covers the years 1891 – 1899. Written before he became Attorney-General in 1892, the first letter, 24th November 1891, refers to an old Racing Cup he is sending by rail, as an expression of his thanks for Porter's kindness and courtesy to him. He hopes Mrs Porter will not think it too lacking in artistic merit to adorn their sideboard!

Russell was born in Newry, County Down, to a family in moderate circumstances, their ancestors having suffered much for their Roman Catholic faith in C17 and C18. Following schooling he joined a Newry law firm in 1849 and then moved to another in Belfast in 1852. He became a qualified solicitor in 1854 and became a champion of the Catholics.

He was so successful that his friends urged him to become a barrister and in 1856, aged just 24, he entered Lincoln's Inn in London. He was called to the Bar in 1859. His success in the northern circuit led to his recall to London where he became a Queens Counsel in 1872, dividing the mercantile business of the circuit with Lord Herschell. So successful was he that his fees rose from an average of £3000 per annum between 1862-1872 to £32,826 in 1893-1894 when he became Attorney General. He became regarded as the first advocate of his age.

His letter of 24th November 1891 asks how a horse shapes and "Have you sent the name to Weatherbys".
A clear acknowledgement of a horse (Heather Queen) being run by Porter rather than under the patron's name. Russell did not want his ownership to be publicly known because of his profession.

Letter of 27 July 1892 from Tadworth Court.
Requesting Porter to send to Lady Russell some cuttings of his choice varieties of carnations – if you can spare them. Asks if Heather Queen has gone or is out of training. Implying the horse was no good.

Letter 9th August 1892 from 10 New Court, Ludlow Inn. Thanks for carnations. Reference to Orme in the betting.

3rd April 1894. House of Commons notepaper written 10 New Court.

Inviting himself hopefully for the weekend 14th April Saturday – Sunday – Monday morning, so he can see horses on the gallops.

13th April 1894. Attorney-General's Chambers, 10 New Of.

Giving Porter his travelling arrangements for 14th April. Assures him he will arrive in time for dinner!

28th April 1894 – Attorney-General's Chambers
Letter about visiting stables in Downs Road (?Epsom) Paragraph saying "I am sorry to say Lord Northbrook does not intend at present to make you a JP. He will see Lord Alington and Lord Hawkins to put pressure on Lord Northbrook.

21st November 1894 – Royal Courts
"Asking to send Porter a yearling filly to try and see if any potential – if not, sell her".
"Begging that I may be kindly remembered by Mrs Porter and your daughters".

Undated – Royal Courts of Justice 1899.

Ref to Flying Fox 1899 Derby, following prior race. Also to Mercenary which ran under Porter's name but owned by Russell who would like to see her run at Epsom before he has to go abroad.

27th November 1894

Letter about sending filly to Porter from his own stables – accommodation in village for his man.
Could his man see the stables. Leasing documents being sent to Weatherbys.
Cannot spend weekend at Kingsclere because of work commitments.

31st December 1884 - 86 Harley Street
New Year greetings and good wishes. Ref to filly mentioned in letter 27 November. Ref also "How melancholy about Lord Randolph but I have long foreseen it must come to this". This refers to the death of Lord Randolph Churchill following a long illness – he died aged 45 on 24th January 1895.

very Dear Mr. Porter,
Faithfully,
C. Russell

10, NEW COURT,
LINCOLN'S INN.

24th Nov: 1891.

Dear Mr. Porter,

I am sending by Rail an old Racing Cup, of which I beg your acceptance, as a slight expression of my sense of your uniform kindness and courtesy to me. I hope Mrs. Porter will not think it, in point of artistic merit, unworthy of a place on her Sideboard.

How does Heather Queen shape? Have you sent the race to Weatherby's? Begging to be kindly remembered by your family circle,

I am

Tadworth Court,
Epsom,
27th July 1892.

Dear Mr Porter,
Will you kindly send to Lady Russell, as above, some cuttings of your choice varieties of Carnations — if you can spare them? Lady Russell will be very much obliged if you can do this.
Begging to be kindly remembered by Mrs Porter
Believe me
Faithfully
C. Russell

I hope Heather Queen has gone or is out of training
C. R.

9th Aug. 1892.

Dear Mr Porter,
My wife wishes to thank you for the promised carnations. She hopes you will send them in good time.
I see our horse is back in the betting.
Faithfully
C. Russell

---

10 New Court,
Lincoln's Inn,
3rd April 1894.

Dear Mr Porter,
I should like very much to run down for a day to Kingsclere if Mrs Porter and you will have me.
I hope if in any way or for any reason this is inconvenient I hope you will say so.
If I might I should like to go down on Saturday

Saturday the 14th April seeing the Horses on the Downs on Monday morning and returning after breakfast on that day.
Begging that I may be kindly remembered by Mrs Porter —
Very faithfully
C. Russell

ATTORNEY-GENERAL'S CHAMBERS,

10, New Court,

Room 543.

Lincoln's Inn,

Royal Courts of Justice,

London, W.C.,

Strand, W.C.

13th April 1894.

Dear Mr Porter,

Availing myself of your hospitality – I hope to be at Kingsclere sometime tomorrow (Saturday) afternoon probably about stable time – but I cannot be certain of the time. You may be sure I shall find my way by dinner time. Always truly

C. Russell

ATTORNEY-GENERAL'S CHAMBERS,

10, New Court,

Room 543,

Lincoln's Inn,

Royal Courts of Justice,

London, W.C.

Strand, W.C.

28th April 1894.

Dear Mr Porter,

at Mr. Merricks, Down's Road (near Jardine's training stables) you can certainly get stable accommodation and I think, house accommodation also. I enquired there yesterday. You will do well to run over one day and look round for yourself.

I am sorry to say Lord R does not intend at present to make you a J.P. I will see Lord Alington and the Lord Chancellor and put pressure on him.

Faithfully

C. Russell

184

Royal Courts,
21st Nov: 1894

Dear Mr Porter,

I have a promising yearling filly that I hope you will be able to take. She is by Poulet out of Miss Shylock (a winner) by Loclock out of Blushing Bride by Rosicrucian out of Gamos. She is on the small side but she has good substance and moves well.

She has been backed and ridden but is not yet perfectly broken.

As I could not race her in my ~~own~~ own name I propose you should lease her in the ordinary way and if after you have got her into condition and galloped her you should think her worthless for racing I am willing that she should be entered in a selling Race and let go for anything she fetches. If on the other hand you would wish, after trying her, to buy I am willing to sell her for whatever you think she is worth. I think she will race. I hope you will be able to do as I ask. It

this time she is taken in hand with a view to seeing if she is worth anything and therefore I should like to send her as soon as possible if you will take her.

Begging that I may be kindly remembered by Mrs Porter and your Daughters,

I am faithfully

Russell of Killowen

What has Mr [?] done if anything?

1869

Dear M. Porter,

Bravo!

If temper does not interfere
T.T. will win you your
7th or 8th Derby.

Cold prevented going to
Stables on Tuesday.

Is there any little race
for Mercury at
Epsom? I shall be

going abroad very soon (in
June) and I should like
to see her run for
a race when she
has a chance. But
of course you will do
just as you think
right. Thankfully
[signature]

going abroad very soon (in
June) and I should like
to see her run for
a race when she
has a chance. But
of course you will do
just as you think
right. Thankfully
[signature]

27th Novr 1894.

Dear Mr Porter Thanks.
Kindly tell me by
what route I ought to
send the Filly. I propose
to send my own head man
with her and as I am
sure he would like to
see your string of
Horses in the Stable and
on the Hill perhaps you

will kindly allow him
to do so. Further ask
one of your people, please,
to direct him where in the
village he can put up.
I will write to Weatherbys
for the Lease forms &
after signing them send
them to you.

There is nothing I should
like better than to go
to your hospitable

House from the Saturday to
the Monday but I cannot
do so at present I am
sorry to say. By & by
by I shall be glad to
run down when the
Filly is under your
skilful hands,
Somewhat in shape.
Begging that I may be
kindly remembered by you
and Miss Porter
Yours faithfully
Russell of Killowen

187

31st Dec: 1894.

Dear Mr. Porter,

Let me, on the eve of
the New Year, wish you
and Mrs. Porter and all
your family health &
continued prosperity in the
time to come. I hope you
will allow me later, in the
new year, to run down for
a day when you will
know a little more
about the Filly than you

you can know yet.
How does she shape?
How melancholy about
Lord Randolph but I
have long foreseen it
must come to this!
Very Dear Mr. Porter,
Faithfully
Russell Reynolds

188

On Circuit,
Durham,
27th Feb: 1897.

Dear Mr Porter,

How have you wintered? I hope you and Mrs Porter are very well.

On my return to Town in the of March I hope I may go down to see you.

Is St Lucia dead? I have not seen her name either in the List of Horses you train or in the Training Reports.

I hope you think

better of her than you did. Probably she will want time.

If you are not too busy pray let me have a line at your leisure.

With kind regards to Mrs Porter

I am
faithfully

Russell of Killowen.

189

15th Dec: 1898

Dear Mr Porter,

I am about to go abroad for a Holiday till 14th January but before going I write to wish you, Mrs Porter and your daughters a merry Christmas and a happy new year and many of them.

If you have time pray drop me a line to
Hotel Metropole,
Monte-Carlo,
France -
to say how your Horses generally and particularly your 2.year olds are going on and particularly the filly "Necessary". all things considered I think

you have had a fair year - altho', no doubt, some disappointments.
With all good wishes

I am
Dear Mr Porter,
Faithfully

On his return to London in March hopes he may go down to Kingsclere.

Enquires about St Jessica who won one race in 1897. This was probably one that Russell owned but ran in Porter's name. If you are not too busy please drop me a line.

15th December 1898

Lets Porter know he is going abroad on holiday until 14th January 1899. Sends him, Mrs Porter and daughters a merry Christmas and happy New Year. If you have time please write to him at Hotel Metropole, Monte Carlo. Let him know about 2 years and the filly Mercenary. All things considered 1898 has been a fair year for the stable, though no doubt with some disappointments.

Lady Ellen Russell

Letter 30th May 1902

Writes her condolences to Porter on the death of his wife. 18 months after loss of her own husband. Heartfelt in expression.

Exemplifies the empathy that Porter built up with his patrons and friends. Follows on the theme of Lord Russell's letters.

30th May

6, HYDE PARK GATE,
S.W.

Dear Mr Porter,

I should like to express to you. My sincere sympathy in your great loss. Only those who have experienced it, can realize the pain of such a parting, or know what it means, to the one who is left behind, and only God Himself, can help us

to endure what He sends. I trust your own health is good, and with kind regards I am.

Yours very sincerely
Ellen Russell of Killowen

Margaret Cambridge, Marchioness of Cambridge
1873 – 1929

Born: The Lady Margaret Grosvenor, sixth child and third daughter of 1st Duke of Westminster. She also became known as Princess Adolphus of Teck and later the Duchess of Teck. Sister of Lord Henry Grosvenor.

1)   Letter from Eaton, Chester November 30th 1894.
         *To Mrs Porter

         Thanking the Porters for their lovely wedding present and confirming wedding day as 12th December.

2)   Letter from Frogmore Cottage, Windsor 24th January 1913.
         To Mr Porter
         Telling him that her husband has mislaid a letter about the races and could he write again. Hopes he and Mrs Porter are well. She is at   Windsor until May when they go to London. She likes being in the country and getting plenty of riding. Signed Margaret of Teck.

During the First World War in 1917 her husband renounced all his German titles and became

Adolphus Cambridge 1st Marquess of Cambridge. Teck was a Dukedom in the Kingdom of Wurttemberg.

*A pearl locket with a heart shaped diamond in the centre.

Friday

Eaton
Chester

Nov. 30th
1894

Dear Mrs Porter,

Very many thanks
to you & Mr Porter
for the lovely
present you
have so kindly
sent me, it

is so kind of
you giving me
such a charming
present, which
I shall for
ever value. —
Our Wedding is
now settled

for the 12th of December
Thanking you
again very much
indeed,

I remain
Yours faithfully

Margaret Grosvenor.

194

Jan. 24th
1913

Dear Mr Porter.

My Husband tells
me that some little
time ago you wrote
to him about
some races, but
unfortunately he
has mislaid
your letter & cannot

remember what
it was. — Would
you very kindly
write again? —
I hope you & Mrs
Porter are keeping
well. — We are
here till May,

& then move up to
London. I like being
in the country
& getting plenty
of riding. —

Yours sincerely

Margaret of Teck

Lord Arthur Hugh Grosvenor
1860 – 1929

2nd son of 1st Duke of Westminster
Brother of Margaret, Marchioness of Cambridge and Lord Henry.
Letter undated, from horses mentioned, probably 1887 or 1888.

Wishing Porter and family good wishes for the New Year and best of luck for you and the horses. Those named being Orbit, Ossory, Friar's Balsam, Ormonde and a boy colt out of Lily Agnes – a brother or Orbit and a sister of Ormonde. Some horse a trifle lame but nothing serious. Had a good hunt.

Letter undated but either 1886 or 1887. Ormonde won the Hardwicke in both those years, but probably 1887 per contact. Letter asks for one of Ormonde's racing plates won in the Hardwicke. Drank Ormonde's health at dinner and yours also. Hopes Ormonde will have a rest now.

Educated at Eton and Oxford

Gained the rank of Lt. Colonel in 3rd Battalion Cheshire Volunteer Regiment. Was a Justice of the Peace and Deputy Lieutenant for Cheshire.
He served in the Boer War 1900 – 1901.

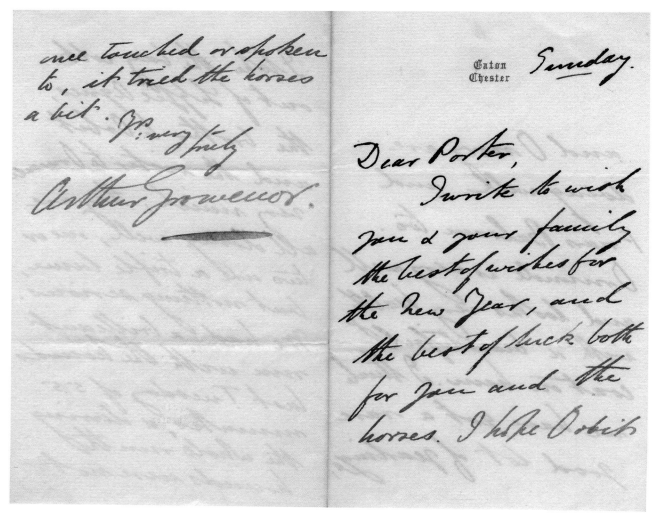

and Ossory are
doing well and
Friars Balsam too.
Ormonde is very well
and looks very healthy
with a beautiful
coat on him. I think
we have got a rare
good lot of yearlings,

I like the bay colt
out of Lizzie Agnes,
the brother to Orbit
and the sister to Ormonde
very much, they are
all doing well, one or
two are a trifle lame,
but nothing serious.
We had a brilliant
run with the hounds
last Tuesday of 55
minutes, during
the whole run the
hounds were not

Friday

Dear Porter
         I wish you would
keep me a plate that
Ormonde ran in for
the Hardwicke Stakes if
possible, I should so
like to have one, if it
is not giving you
any trouble. I never

saw such excitement
after a race before.
We all drank Ormonde's
health at dinner, and
yours was included
in it. I hope Ormonde
will have a rest now
                  yrs truly
                  Arthur Grosvenor.

197

Victor Alexander Grosvenor
1853-1884

Owner of Reprieve – trained by John Porter.

Eldest son of the 1st Duke of Westminster, brother of Margaret Marchioness of Cambridge, Arthur Hugh Grosvenor, Henry George Grosvenor. Educated at Eton and was styled Earl Grosvenor between 1869 and 1884.

Letter 2nd January 1883, just a year before he died. Seighton Grange, Chester.

Letter to Porter
"We have just heard about Lord Stamford's death – what a terrible blow it is, but one could hardly hope after the bad report yesterday. If his horses are to be sold (as I suppose they will be), do you think it would be worth my while to get a 2 year old cheap? If you could buy it and train it for me – I think it would be worth my while to get one. I think I am going away to the West Indies in about a month, but I shall try to get down to Kingsclere to see Loch Maree, who I hope is going on well."

Victor Alexander knows Porter has trained 31 winners for Lord Stamford between 1880 and 1882 and it seems he sees his death as an opportunity to buy something on the cheap. Lord Grosvenor did in fact own a two year old – the only horse he ever owned and it was trained by Porter – Reprieve. During 1883 it won 5 races and was placed second twice. Prize money was £4188.

Victor Alexander died aged 30 on 22nd January 1884.

Saighton Grange.
Chester.

Jan. 2 /83.

Porter.

We have just heard
about Lord Stamford's
death — What a ter-
~~rible~~ blow it is, but
one could hardly
hope after the bad
report yesterday. If his

horses are to be sold
(as I suppose they will
be,) do you think it
w.^d be worth my
while to get a 2 y.^r
old cheap? If you
c.^d buy it, & train
it for me — it

I think w.^d be worth my
while to get one. I
think I am going away
to the West Indies in
about a month, but
I shall try & get down
to Kingsclere to see Loch
Maree — who I hope
is going on well.

Grosvenor.

Lord Henry Grosvenor
1861 – 1914

Son of 1st Duke of Westminster, brother of Marchioness of Cambridge and Arthur Hugh Grosvenor
Married Dora Erskine-Wemyss

Letter to Porter from Bullwick Park, Wansford (Mourning black trim) dated 1st March 1895

Suggests a name for a filly - Chinkara. She did run, but not in Grosvenor's name. She ran in Porter's name. She was a bay filly by Galopin and won one race in 1895 worth £222.00
Grosvenor says he will not be on the racecourse in 1895 – he is in mourning for Dora who died on 24th December 1894. He is packing up at Bulwick Park and moving to Tittensor Chase, Stoke on Trent, close to the Duke of Sutherland's place. Hopes George Williams the vet is getting on well at Newmarket. Awful weather. He will go to Scotland with the children at the end of May for the Summer.

"Life now seems to wretchedly sad and empty. I hardly know what to do. It is too terrible"

Letter 29th December 1899 – from Tittensor Chase, (mourning black trim).

Relating to death of 1st Duke of Westminster and the funeral. The Duke died on 22nd December – just 7 days prior to this letter. Refers to Lord Arthur and how touched family were by Porter's letter. Sorry to hear that both he and Mrs Porter are unwell. Horses will be sold but part of the stud may be kept.

Hoping you are all well

Believe me

sincerely yours

Henry Grosvenor

Bulwick Park
Wansford

~~Feb~~ March 1. 95.

Dear Porter

I've got a real good name
for the filly. "Chinkara"
with first a — pronounced
long as in the word are.
It is an Indian antelope
that goes a most terrific
pace. I have shot some.
How is she going on? and
the others. I shall not
be on a racecourse this

year and so shall be unable
to see her run, but you will
let me know when she does.
And of course run her in
Your name always. I am
very busy packing up and
moving. for I am leaving
this for Tittensor Chase,
Stoke on Trent, and close
to Trentham — the Duke of
Sutherland's place. almost
in the park. a lovely place.

I hope you are all well at
home, & that George is getting
on well at Newmarket.
What awful weather it has
been, all the horses must
be backward I expect.
About the end of May I
go to Scotland with my
children for the summer.
Life now seems so wretchedly
sad and empty I hardly
know what to do. It is
too terrible.

TELEGRAMS.
TITTENSOR.
STATION.
BARLASTON, N.S.R.

Dec 29. 99.
TITTENSOR CHASE,
STOKE-UPON-TRENT.

My dear Porter

I only got your kind letter the morning of the funeral, as it had followed me about. but dear Arthur told me he had written to you. It was kind of you to write and we were all

much touched by your kind sympathy. It is a terrible blow and came so suddenly and it will be hard to get on without Him. He was everything to all of us.

I am so sorry to hear you are ill too. and Mrs Porter. I only hope you will soon both be well again. I fear the horses will be sold but there is some talk of keeping on part of the stud.

It is all so sad and such a break up.

Yours sincerely

Henry Grosvenor

Lady Dora Grosvenor
1856-1894

Born Dora Erskine-Wemyss, wife of Lord Henry Grosvenor and daughter-in-law of 1st Duke of Westminster, she died aged 38.

Letter 4th December 1881 from Berkeley Castle, Gloucestershire writer Dora Grosvenor.

A request on behalf of husband Henry, requesting if any racing plates from Ormonde, Friar's Balsam etc. are available. Four would do so they can be mounted and given to a charity.

Creator of the Wemyss School of Needlework in 1877 to provide work for miner's daughters, Dora took an active role as a designer and business manager.

She married Lord Henry Grosvenor in 1887 and they lived at Bulwick Park, Wansford, Northamptonshire.

Frederick Campbell - 3rd Earl Cawdor
Politician

From 1895 – 1905 was Chairman of the Great Western Railway

Letter, undated asking Porter if he could buy a filly and train it for him. Written to Porter at Kingsclere, so was written no earlier than 1903. The connection was a very helpful ingredient in Porter's plans for Newbury Racecourse – it gave him direct access at the highest level to the Great Western Railway, who agreed to build a racecourse station and run special trains from Paddington within the hour. The distance approximately 53 miles. The agreed first class fare – 10 shillings return. As Porter put it "they virtually ensured the success of our venture".

Refer to this under 'Newbury' along with letters from patrons.

Stackpole Court
Pembroke
South Wales

BURWOOD HOUSE,
COBHAM,
SURREY.

Dear Sir I am quite in
Earnest, in asking you
to buy me a yearling -
a filly . if you should
light upon a promising
one at from £500 to £700
but not beyond that -
I do not know what
your arrangements with
those who train with you are
& whether you could &
would take charge of

a yearling for me - I
should not care for
you to purchase for me
if I had to send the
animal elsewhere.
I move about a good deal
but letters addressed
as above will always
be forwarded to me -
I should prefer a late
(April or May) Foal, not
made up for Sale - If
it should turn out

as likely to be able to
gallop a bit - I should
leave it to you to enter
it by & bye if you thought
it worth while - There is
plenty of time. perhaps
a better chance than some
of these purchasers at
high figures have got
all they want -
J.
Candor

Mr John Porter
Kings Clere
Berks

Henry Cadogan - Viscount Chelsea
1868 – 1908

Letter – undated but must have been between 1892 when Cadogan married Lord Alington's daughter Cecilia and 1903 when Porter left Kingsclere.
Thanks Porter on behalf of himself and Lady Chelsea for their very pleasant trip to Kingsclere.
Reference to Cadogan's possible interest in Clwyd and possible run in the Derby – to be kept a secret.

31ª, Green Street,
Park Lane, W.

Sunday night.

Dear Mr Porter,

I am writing on behalf of Lady Chelsea as well as myself to thank you very much for our very pleasant trip to Kingsclere yesterday. We all enjoyed ourselves very much & think it was very nice of you letting us come

I hope you won't say a word about getting 'Clwyd' & make him running for you in the Derby till the matter is absolutely settled. Please remember me to Mrs Porter, & wishing you the best of luck in the Guineas & Derby

I remain

Yours truly

Chelsea

Anthony Ashleigh - Cooper, 9th Earl of Shaftesbury
1869 – 1961

Letter – April 18th from White's – London Club
Asking Porter to visit Woodyates where William Day trained. Shaftesbury asks Porter to advise on what needs to be done to the house and stables that would make it lettable to a trainer. Suggests he could get there and back in a day and could meet Shaftesbury's agent. Suggests Porter take the train to Salisbury and then a ten mile drive.
Shaftesbury was going to Ireland that night so could Porter write to him at Tipperary. Hopes he is not asking too much.
He was a philanthropist. In 1928 he provided a financial grant to establish Bryanston School and was its first Chairman of governors. The school consisted of Bryanston House and 450 acres of grounds. Bryanston House was designed and built by Norman Shaw for Viscount Portman. The Portmans had occupied it for 30 years at the time of its sale, but death duties necessitated the sale. The building and estate was the biggest in Dorset and the last of the grand stately homes to be built in England.
In 1934 the Earl gave Belfast Castle to the City of Belfast.

April 18

WHITE'S

Porter

I am writing to
ask you if you will do me
a great favour -
You remember Woodgates
I daresay where William
Day used to train -
Well at this moment it
is without a tenant and
I am anxious to let
it again as a training
establishment -
But of course the place
and stabling especially
would want a lot doing to
it -
I want to get some idea
of what a trainer would
expect done to it supposing
he thought of taking the
place -
So do you think some off
day soon, when you leave, some
times to spare you could
manage to go over there and
look at the place - I
should arrange for my
agent to meet you there and
you could point out to him
what would require altering
or doing up.
I think you could manage
to get there and back
in the day - Your way would
be to go to Salisbury by train
and it's a ten mile
drive from there -
I go to Ireland to-night
a letter addressed to me to
Cahir.
Co Tipperary Ireland
would find me -
I should be awfully obliged
if you could manage this
for me and hope I am
not asking you too much
Truly yrs
Shaftesbury

Carnegie St Vincent, 3rd Viscount

Owner of Lord Clifden, undefeated as a 2- year old winning both the Woodcote and Champagne Stakes. As a 3 year old was beaten a short head in the Derby, but went on to win the St Leger. He was retired at the end of his four year old season and became champion sire of Great Britain and Ireland in 1876. As a two and three year old he was trained by Edwin Parr.

An undated letter to Porter advises that St Vincent has sent by post a pin of Lord Clifden's head. The letter is addressed from "Godmersham Park, Canterbury".

Godmersham Park was owned by the family of Edward Austen Knight (Jane Austen's eldest brother). He had died in 1852 but the property had passed to his son. Confusingly also Edward (Austen) Knight (1794-1879). It seems highly probable that St Vincent was his guest in 1863 when Lord Clifden won the St Leger.

It is widely accepted that Godmersham Park became Jane Austen's" Mansfield Park" and it is known that she made many visits to her brother's house.

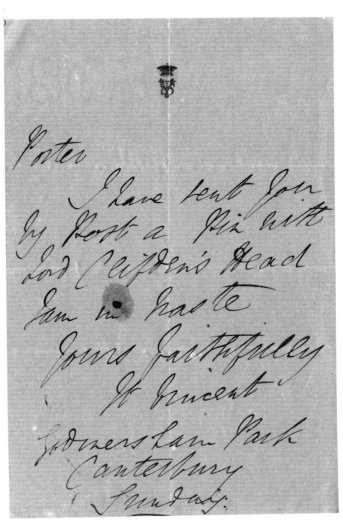

Henry Walter Gilbey 2nd Baronet
1859-1945

Director and Chairman of W & A Gilbey, wine merchants. He was also an influential figure in horse breeding and sports.

He had visited Kingsclere as referred to in the letter dated 24th May 1902.
Letter addressed from 28 Seymour Street, London W.

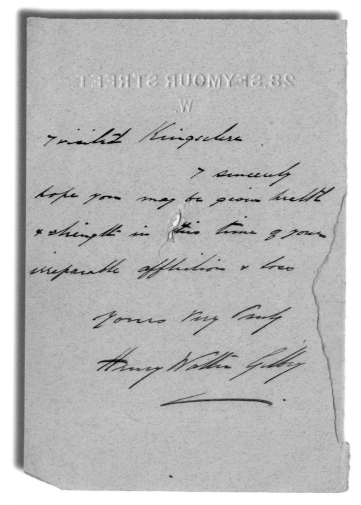

John Gubbins 1838 – 1906
High Sheriff of C. Limerick, 1886
British Crown Judicial Representative

Breeder and owner of racehorses. After being educated privately he inherited the Knochasy Estate and purchased the estate of Bruree, Co Limerick.

The letter to Porter of 24th December 1887 is written from Bruree House, Bruree, encloses a cheque for £3000 in payment for a horse.

From a young age he took a keen interest in horse racing – initially for steeplechasing. Horses he bred won 2000 Guineas, Derby and St Leger and the Eclipse Stakes. In England his horses were trained by Joussiflfe at Lambourne and Sam Darling at Beckhampton.

He was a warm hearted genial man, a kind and indulgent landlord and employer and a sportsman of the best type.

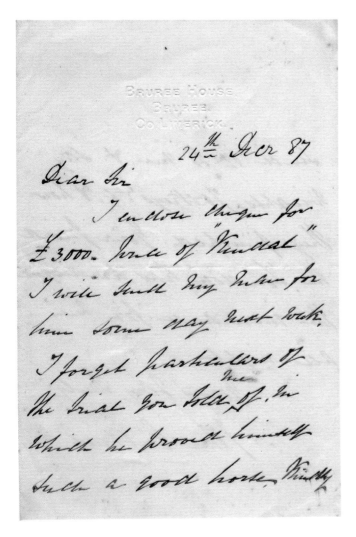

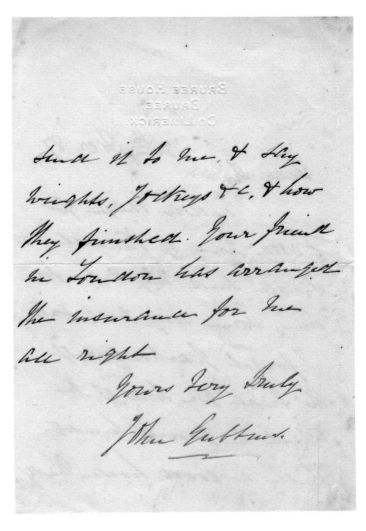

Henry Montague Hozier
1838 – 1907

Father of Clementine Spencer Churchill, wife of Winston Churchill.
This is a belated letter of condolence as Hozier was in Africa at the time of Porter's wife's death and only learnt of it on his return. The reference to 'daughters' indicates that the writer was reasonably well acquainted with the family.
This contact indicates the very wide spectrum of people that Porter had come to know over the years and who wanted to offer their support at that time.

Sunday.

Dear Mr. Potter.

As I was in Africa in the early part of this year I never heard of the sad loss that you had sustained, I deeply sympathize and condole with you: and am most sorry that in

my ignorance I recalled your sorrow to you.

I deeply sympathize with you: but I hope that the affection of your daughter may to a certain degree compensate for your heavy loss: and that time may

gradually alleviate the pain that you must have suffered

Yours most sincerely

Henry M. Hozier

Edward Moorhouse

Collaborated on the writing and publishing of 'John Porter of Kingsclere' with Porter.
This letter from Moorhouse updates Porter on the book sales, through both Grant Richards, publishers and the British Bloodstock Agency Ltd, for whom Moorhouse worked as Editor of the Bloodstock Breeders Review.

Letter dated 26th April 1920.

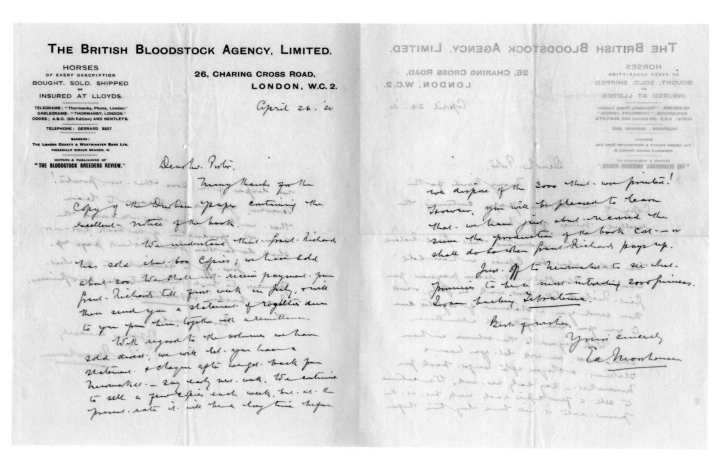

Colonel Sir George Maude

Held the post of Crown Equerry for 35 years from 1859-1894. He was a distinguished army officer and had lost an eye fighting at Balaclava in the Crimean War. He was a fine horseman and he later had great success as an owner, winning the Derby, the Oaks and the St Leger. Maude was robust in his defense of the position of Master of the Horse. He worked closely with Queen Victoria's private secretary (see letters) – Sir Henry Ponsonby. He was Crown Equerry for no less than 10 Masters of the Horse.

Letter from Royal Mews 12th December 1892
Asks Porter to write to the Queen's Private Secretary at Windsor Castle, to reply to a note HRH Prince of Wales has written and which Maude encloses with his letter, whilst acknowledging that Porter may be in Paris.

Letter from Royal Mews 3rd January 1893
Refers to removal of Prince of Wales's horses and those of Baron Von Hirsch from Kingsclere.

Letters from Royal Mews 23rd December 1893.
To Mrs Porter asking for information on Porter's serious illness.

Letter – 10th August 1989
Refers to Sainfoin winning his first race – the Astley Stakes at Lewes.

Letter from Royal Mews – 6th June 1890
This is a request from the Queen for a photo of Sainfoin, following his Derby win. As Maude does not know the owner's address (Sir Robert Jardine), he asks Porter to seek the necessary permission and to get it carried out as soon as you can. He thinks the horse will be drawn soon by some of the sporting painters – then we could get a print of it. He congratulates Porter on sending the horse out so fit.
Sainfoin had been bred at the Royal Stud
This last comment is appropriate as the race was run in appallingly wet conditions.

Letter 25th September 1892 from the Stud House, Kington.
Congratulating Porter on La Fleche's win in the St Leger and of Porter's training of her.

Kingsclere
Decr. 4th/92

To
Col. Sir George Maude. K. C. B
                    Sir

                    I beg to acknowledge
with thanks your letter
of the 1st inst. in which
you inform me Her Majesty
the Queen has graciously
accepted the two
photographs of "Sainfoin"
and "La Flèche" which

I ventured to submit.
I feel deeply grateful for
the honour conferred upon
me.

                    Trusting I may again
have the honour of training
a Derby winner bred by
Her Majesty.

            I remain.

                    Your Obt. Servant
                    Porter

216

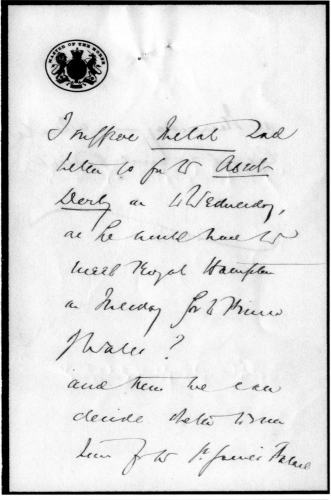

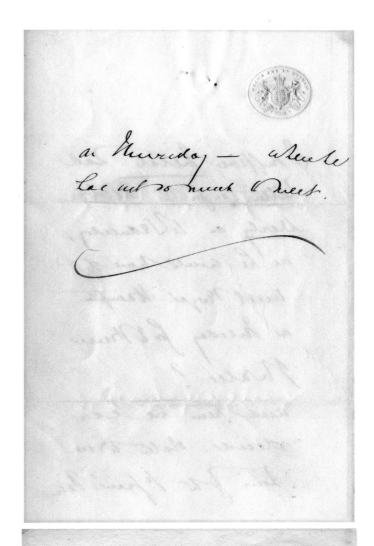

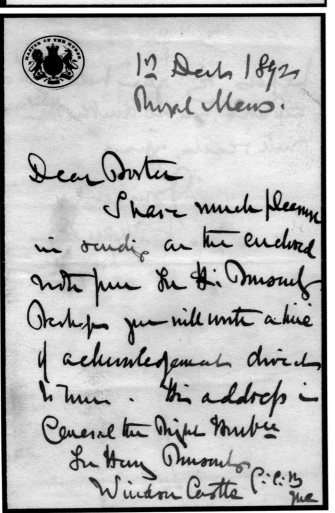

12 Decbr 1892
Royal Mews.

Dear Porter

I have much pleasure in sending on the enclosed with you for Sir Henry Ponsonby. Perhaps you will write a line of acknowledgement direct to him. His address is General the Right Honble Sir Henry Ponsonby Windsor Castle

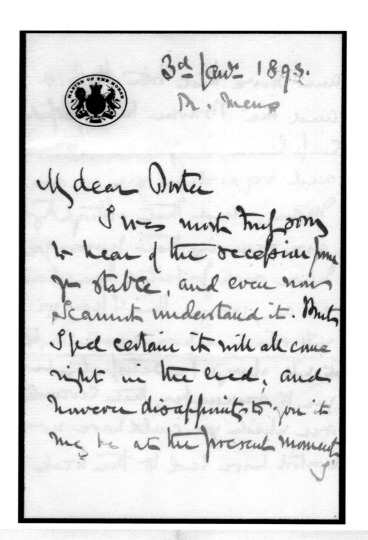

3d Jany 1898.
Dr. Mens

My dear Porter

I was most truly sorry
to hear of the secession from
yr stable, and even now
I cannot understand it. But
I feel certain it will all come
right in the end, and
however disappointing to you it
may be at the present moment, I

am sure that both H.R.H. &
and the Baron have perfect
confidence in you as a trainer,
and regard for you as a
man; and that although they
are removing their horses, you
have not forfeited their esteem
in any way. This I feel you
will see is a poor consolation, but
it will always be satisfactory to
you to remember, that circumstances
over which you could have no
control have led to this break

up — circumstances which are very
well understood by the racing
world in general, and that yr
character stands as high as ever.
I am particularly sorry that
Jn Hèche to whom you have
done so much justice in leaving
yr stable. With kind regards
to you and Mrs Porter and
all your family I remain

Yours sincerely

Gmande

218

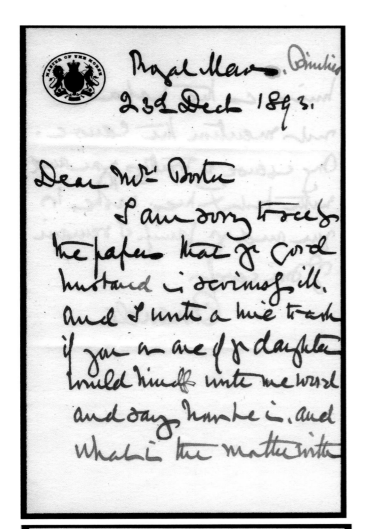

Royal Mews. Pimlico
23rd Decr 1893.

Dear Mrs Boston

I am sorry to see by the papers that yr good husband is seriously ill. And I write a line to ask if you or one of yr daughters would kindly write me word and say how he is, and what is the matter with

him, as the papers do not mention the cause. Ony cause y troubles you and with best wishes to you and yr family I remain yr sincerely

Amanda

—

10th August
189

Dear Boston

I must write a line to congratulate you on winning a nice race with "Samson" Velocet. and I hope he may win many more for you, in that

you will be able to part with him at a good price. I wish you had him in better for Bend'or which I thought a very fine yearling.

Yr sincerely
Amanda

6th June /90.
Royal Mews

Dear Porter

I have received a telegram from the Queen saying she should like to have a Photo of "Fairfire". As I do not know the owner's address, I must ask you to be good enough to obtain the necessary permission

and to get it carried out as soon as you can, for H.M. I daresay the horse will be drawn soon, by some of the Sporting painters, and then we could get a print from it. I did not half congratulate you on standing up the horse &c. Yes.

Yours very
[signature]

one of the few who can do justice to them.

Yours very
[signature]

220

Sir Henry Ponsonby

Ponsonby was Queen Victoria's Private Secretary
Again, Porter kept a handwritten copy of his letter – this on the same subject matter as the one to Maude.

Kingsclere
Dec. 4th/92

To
Sir Henry Ponsonby
          Sir

          I beg to
acknowledge with thanks
the receipt of your letter
of the 30th inst. in
which you inform me
Her Majesty the Queen
has graciously consented
to accept the two

photographs of "Sainfoin"
and "La Flèche" which
I ventured to submit

          I would that Her
Majesty might know
how deeply grateful
I feel for the honour
thus conferred upon
me.

          I have the honour to remain
          your Ob. Servant
                    J. Porter

Byron Webber
1838-1913

Webber was a sporting journalist and author. He wrote for, amongst others, the Sporting Gazette and the Sporting Life. He also founded and edited the Illustrated Sporting and Dramatic News.
He also wrote the famous and patriotic song "Hands Across the Sea".
As a London literary writer he had a wide circle of friends and acquaintences, amongst them being Porter.
Byron Webber's letter of condolence following Mrs Porter's death in 1902 is very expressive of his feelings to Porter and the family.

33, Oxford Gardens
North Kensington
W
Sunday night

My poor dear John

I couldn't write to you — words failed me, and so kept putting it off. Some sorrow is unspeakable. If I could have met you I will I will not dwell on it. A sweeter lady, a kindlier gentler creature, a better woman never lived than the wife you loved with such wonderful affection — the wife you were devoted to. I cannot fathom the depth of your loss.

I feel that it is unfathomable. Such women are the rarest of God's gifts and when they are wives and mothers the noblest. From my heart of hearts my dear John I sympathise with you on your irreparable loss, and with her children, and pray that you may be given strength and fortitude to sustain it. My wife joins me in this expression.

I remain, my dear John,
Yours faithfully
Byron Webber

John Porter Esq

Mathew Dawson
1820 – 1898

Racehorse trainer at Newmarket – contemporary with Porter.

*letter from Melton House, Exning 14 May 1894.

In 1885 Dawson retired from large scale racing and moved to Exning Manor – which he renamed Melton House. Although having charge of a smaller number of horses, he continued to have considerable success winning Classics and the Grand Prix de Paris. He had intended to retire completely in 1891, but was persuaded to train a few horses for Lord Roseberry. Being in his 70's and often unable to walk, due to gout, he still managed to train a further few classic winners for Lord Roseberry, including the Derby's of 1894 and 1895.

He died at Newmarket in 1898. Although the sport was tainted with corruption and dishonesty he left behind "a reputation which an Archbishop might envy".

He was significant as one of the first public trainers rather than being the employee of a wealthy patron. His career was mostly based at Newmarket.

He started training in Scotland in 1840 where his main patrons were Lord Kelburn and William Hope Johnstone. In 1846 he moved to England, training for Lord John Scott at Compton, Berkshire. When Scott sold his horses to James Merry in 1857, he continued to train them at Russley Park, Lambourn.

In 1886 he moved his stables to Newmarket, first at St Mary's Square and then to Heath House where he had his greatest successes. Initially he trained for Lords Newcastle and Hamilton but were quickly followed by Lord Falmouth. Between 1870 and 1883 he trained no less than 14 classic winners for Falmouth, including two Derbys. In 1868 Fred Archer had come to him as an apprentice and he became stable jockey in 1874. He had other important owners, the Duke of Portland and Lord Hastings.

*See correspondence between Portland and Porter re switch of horses from Dawson to Porter at Kingsclere.

Although being rivals as trainers, Matthew Dawson and John Porter clearly had a very high regard for one another.

May 14. 1894

My Dear Sir

There is only one John Porter &
he lives at Kingsclere — I thank you exceedingly
for your very kind & welcome letter, & assure you I
thoroughly reciprocate your sentiments & good feeling,
which are those of a gentleman & sportsman, & not
of a mere trainer of race horses —

With kind regards & best wishes to you
& yours

Believe me

My Dear Sir
very faithfully yours

M. Dawson

P.S. I am very sorry to hear of poor Lord Alington's
illness M. D

224

Col. Wilfred Lloyd

Wilfred Lloyd was private secretary to Bendor, 2nd Duke of Westminster so was in close contact with Porter regarding the Duke's horses at Kingsclere.

The letter of 4th August 1905 expresses his sorrow on hearing that Porter is retiring from training and thanks him for his hospitality on all his visits to Kingsclere. The letter also refers to a serious error made by Weatherby's regarding entries for the Duke's yearlings.
In 1910 Wilfred Lloyd was instrumental in saving the Duke's life following a boating accident when the Duke was trying out a new 40 foot speedboat, when it broke up, during trials. He had been following in the Duke's old boat and with help, pulled the Duke, unconscious, from the water.
Lloyd resigned from his post in 1915 to re-join the Army.

Dear Mr Porter, I
must write a line to
say how very sorry
I am to hear that
you are retiring - You
have one consolation
at all events, namely
that no trainer up to
date has ever had such

marked success with
his horses on Junhave -
written or Yspand
Classical races ~~won~~,
or in Stakes won -
I wish to thank
you also for your
kindness to me
personally during
the last nine years.

I can only say that
one and all of my
visits to Kingsclere
have been thoroughly
enjoyed, thanks to your
hospitality -

This is a very
serious error which
has been made regards

the entry of his Duke's
Earlings - and very
slack on the part of
Messrs Weatherby who
said have seen that
matters were put right.
The best of luck to you
in the future &
Believe me
yours
Wilfred D. Lloyd

226

William Day
1823-1908

Day was a member of the widely known Day racing family. He was a jockey, trainer and author. His father John Barham Day was Porter's first employer when he became apprenticed to him. William Day was one of 12 children. His brother John was a successful trainer, winning 12 classics, his brothers Samuel and Alfred were successful jockeys. William was in 1845 'warned off' having been involved in the 'Old England' Derby nobbling scandal. His ban was eventually revoked.

William, having had his ban revoked, set up as a trainer at Woodyates on the border of Dorset/Wiltshire in the late 1840s. His first major training success was in the Chester Cup of 1852. A month later he won the Gold Cup at Royal Ascot.

In 1855 the Days were involved in further controversy when it became known that William and John Barham Day had come to an arrangement over their horses in the 2000 Guineas and the Derby. It ended with Mr Padwick, John Barham Day's patron, sacking him and effectively ending his training career. William, to his dying day insisted that his horse had never been considered as a Derby horse and his lack of condition was the consequence of a respiratory condition.

Despite the scandal he continued to train successfully until the early 1880s when he retired, living in Salisbury until his death in 1908. During that time he wrote two volumes of memoires as well as books on breeding and training racehorses.

His letter of condolence to Porter dated 30th May 1902 shows a man far removed from the scandals of his earlier life. A man of religious belief - caring and compassionate.

See letter from 5th Earl of Roseberry re visiting Woodyates in 1895, also from Earl of Shaftesbury, seeking Porter's views on the possible redevelopment/refurbishment of William Day's old yard.

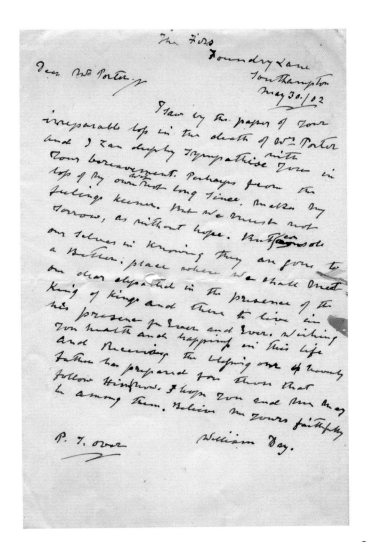
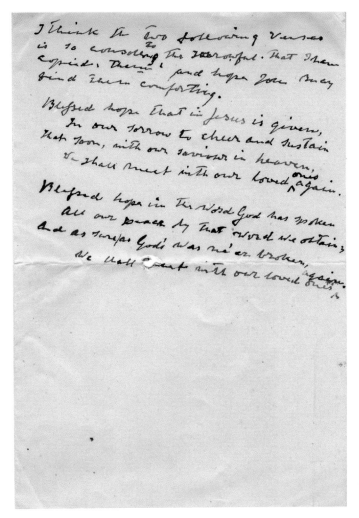

Herbert Sullivan
1868 – 1928

He was the nephew and from 1877, the ward of Arthur Sullivan – the Sullivan of Gilbert and Sullivan.

Sadly from the 1880s onwards, Arthur Sullivan's health was precarious and Herbert essentially looked after him and when necessary accompanied him to the South of France and other resorts where the composer rested.

The letter to Porter dated 23rd September 1892, refers to a meeting between Arthur and Herbert Sullivan with Porter. The interruption referred to as the Duke of Edinburgh was in fact Alfred, Duke of Saxe-Coburg and Gotha, second son of Queen Victoria and Prince Albert, who was known as the Duke of Edinburgh from 1866 to 1893.

The same letter introduces Herr Richard Van Vogel from the Swiss Government who would like to see Kingsclere. Both Vogel's and Sullivan's letters are written from Tottenhall Towers which suggests they were there as guests of Col. Thomas Thorneycroft an inventor and engineer – this being the connection with Sullivan who was also an engineer at one time.

Sep 23rd 1892

My dear Mr Porter

Would you allow
my friend Herr Richard
von Vogel, accredited
from to the Swiss
government, to go over
your stables. He loves
to see fine horses
although he takes very
little interest in
racing. He will present

himself with this letter
and I hope you will
not mind him seeing
your famous quarters

Believe me
Yours faithfully
Herbert Sullivan

P.S. The last time we
met was when my
uncle Sir Arthur, was
so ill; the Duke of

Edinburgh came &
interrupted our interview.

Sir Ian Mortimer Singer
1863 – 1920

Was the eldest of the children of Isaac Singer – founder of the Singer Sewing Machine Co. Isaac died in 1875 and the family inherited substantial wealth. His sister married into French nobility, while his brother Washington was a philanthropist and racehorse owner.

Ian studied at Cambridge, but left without a degree. Although born in America, he became a British subject in 1900.

Ian's first passion was thoroughbred horses which he began breeding and racing in 1881. This is no doubt how he came to be acquainted with Porter. He was also a pilot and became the 8th person to hold a licence from the Royal Aero Club in England in 1910. In subsequent years he offered a series of awards for the development of British Aviation and may well have met "Mrs Gretton" who was likewise interested in the development of British Aviation – see Fred Gretton owner.

He lived at Milton Hill, Steventon, Berkshire from where he wrote to Porter thanking him for his book – letter dated 5th October 1914. So was a copy of Kingsclere, written some years earlier. The tone of the letter suggests they knew one another pretty well, including their wives.

MILTON HILL,
STEVENTON,
BERKS.

5th October, 1914.

Dear Mr. Porter,

I am so sorry that I missed seeing you last time you called.

Thank you very much indeed for the beautifully got up book which you left for me, giving a history of all the races that you won in the many years you acted as a public trainer. It is indeed a record of which any man could justly be proud, and I cannot believe that it has ever been beaten by anybody else, and it must be a delightful feeling for you, in your old age, to think that you have conquered on so many glorious fields and been able afterwards to retire with such a splendid character for honourable dealing and the affection and respect of those for whom you have trained and of those who have had the pleasure of your friendship.

Mrs. Singer joins me in kind regards to Mrs. Porter and yourself.

Yours sincerely,

Mortimer Singer

John Porter, Esq.,
    Ormonde House,
        NEWBURY.

Marquess of Hartington
Later, Spencer Cavendish 8th Duke of Devonshire

British statesman – declined to be Prime Minister on three occasions, not because he was not a serious politician, but because the circumstances were not right.

Took great pains to parade his interest in horse racing, so as to cultivate an image of not being entirely obsessed in politics.

Nonetheless he did have the distinction of leading three political parties –

Liberals in the Commons 1875 – 1880, Liberal Unionist Party in the Commons 1886 – 1903 and The Unionists in the House of Lords 1902 – 1903.

He was not one of Porter's winning owners but sent him a cheque on account for his fees to 31st March 1885, dated 14th July 1885 and asking Porter to send an account for anything else due.

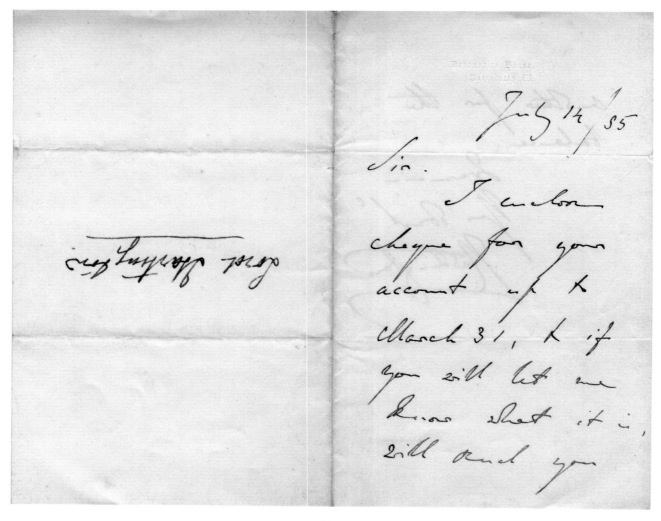

another for the balance.

I remain
Your obedt
Wellington

George Cadogan, 5th Earl Cadogan
1840 – 1915

Conservative Politician
Lord Lieutenant of Ireland 1895-1902

Letter – addressed from the Jockey Club Rooms Newmarket dated 29th October 1888 to Porter.
The letter seeks to obtain a good second veterinary opinion on the treatment of a horse he has purchased – his own vet, Barrow advised that it should be blistered but his trainer Gilbert has begged him to get a second opinion. Cadogan asks Porter if he can suggest a thoroughly reliable vet who could go to Newmarket and give advice – please reply to Babraham Hall, Cambridge with apologies for troubling Porter.
Babraham Hall was the home of the Adeane Family.
Cadogan was a member of the Jockey Club.

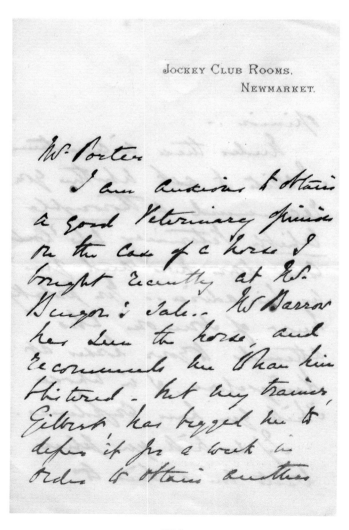

opinion ..

Under these circumstances
I write to ask whether you
recommend a thoroughly
reliable Veterinary who would
come down here and give
us his advice .. You probably
know of some one who
attends to your horses at
Kingsclere, & in whose
skill you have confidence.

If so will you please
write him a line to

Babraham Hall
Cambridge,
Apologizing for troubling you,
I am
Yrs truly
Cadogan

Oct 29/88

Archbishops of York

Letter dated 7th November 1884 from Bishopthorpe, York from William Thomson, Archbishop 1862-1890 re Distribution of prizes 25th November.

Letter dated 16th October 1891 from Bishopthorpe, York from William Dalrymple Maclagan, Archbishop 1891-1908 re Distribution of prizes at Archbishop Holgates School on 23rd November.
Both letters addressed to Rev A.W. Welch – Headmaster of the school.
Quite why these letters should be in John Porter's archives is a mystery.

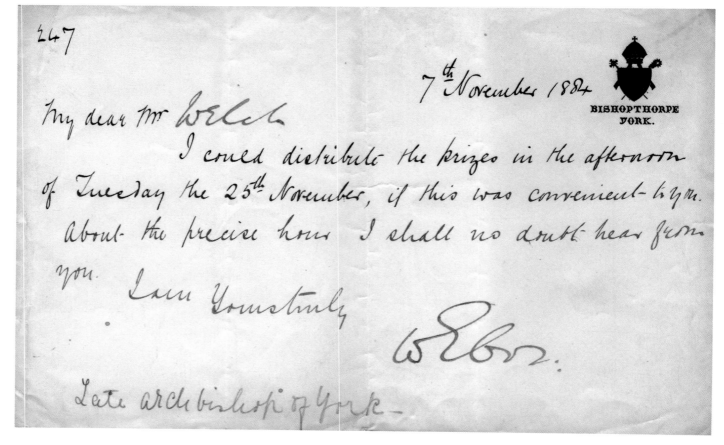

BISHOPTHORPE .
YORK.

16th Oct: 1891

My dear Sir,

I will gladly distribute
the prizes at Archbishop
Holgate's School, and if
Monday the 23rd November
would be convenient for
you I could provisionally
fix that day, subject
however to change if
any urgent duty should

BISHOPTHORPE
YORK

make it necessary.
I should however be able
to tell you definitely by
the middle of November,
if you will write to me
again at that time.
Three o'clock will do
very well.

Yours faithfully
William Ebor:

The Rev:
A. W. Welch

237

Constance Baxendale

14th July 1901, from Greenham Lodge, Newbury.

Constance was the 2nd daughter of Lloyd Baxendale (Snr). She was the elder sister of Lloyd Baxendale (Jnr) who sold the land for Newbury Racecourse to John Porter, he also became a director of the Newbury Racecourse Co at its inception.

The above letter thanks Porter for a Baxendale family visit to Kingsclere to see the horses and stables. It makes reference to Mrs Porter being so ill, and what an anxiety it must be for the Porter family. Reference to interrupted conversation about Mr Winston Churchill's lecture and offering any help they can give, let them know.

This letter implies that the two families were well acquainted and it seems likely that Porter already had in mind plans for making a new racecourse at Newbury and that he was aware that the land he would need was owned by the Baxendales.

Lloyd Baxendale (Senior) was a Partner of Pickford & Co, carriers, as declared in the Census of April 1861, when he was aged 39 living in Totteridge, Hertfordshire.

The Census of 1871 shows him still there. He is also shown as a Magistrate and Partner in Pickfords.

The Census of 1881 shows the family at Greenham Lodge. He is now a JP and partner in Picfords. Lloyd Baxendale (Jnr) is also shown as partner in Pickfords.

The 1891 Census shows the household included 14 servants which indicates they had become a family of much wealth.

It also showed that Lloyd Baxendale (Snr) had died in 1882 aged 60. His will finally proved in November 1883 shows he left an estate worth £411,535,14.3. At today's value in excess of £33,000,000.

it is such a dreadful
anxiety for you all.

With many thanks
& best regards to Mr & Mrs
Porter Yours v. Sincerely
Constance Baxendale.

We were interrupted
in our conversation
about Mr Winston Churchill's
lecture, if we can be of
any use to you please
let us know, but we go
away on the 8th August
for some weeks —

Captain J.O Machell
1837 – 1902

Newmarket Trainer – see biography 'Captain Mac-Hell'. Contemporary of Admiral Rous, Duchess of Montrose, Fred Archer.   He came to Newmarket as an outsider and with little money. However with his extraordinary understanding of horses, good judgement and bold risk taking, he became the doyen of the racing circle and wealth and influence followed.

His letter of January 2nd 1888 refers to one of his owners – Warren de la Rue, grandson of Thomas de la Rue, who had founded the stationery company of that name. The family came from the Island of Guernsey. His own Father, also Warren, was a well known astronomer, chemist and inventor.

The grandson's horses were trained by Machell at Newmarket, with some success. The best known being Traylers which won the Ascot Gold Cup and the Goodwood Cup in 1889 ridden by W.T. Robinson.

In 1867, Captain Machell trained Hermit to win the Derby. It was conservatively estimated that he was owed £400,000 by the bookmakers – in today's value in excess of £32,000,000.

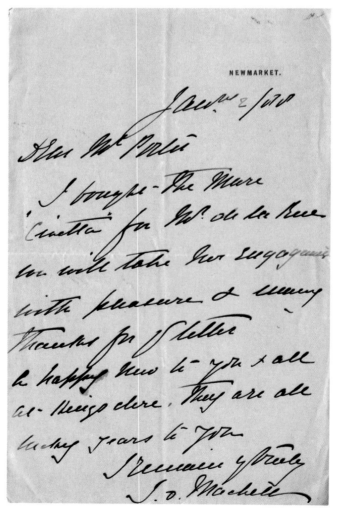

E. Somerville Tattersall

A member of the Tattersall family, he was a senior partner.
He has a race over the Rowley Mile at Newmarket named after him.

The letter dated 22nd May 1902 is addressed Tattersalls, Albert Gate, Hyde Park, London S.W. which in those days was their headquarters.
It is a letter of condolence to Porter on the death of his wife – not just from Somerville, but all at Tattersalls.
The headquarters and sales were consolidated at Newmarket, following Somerville's death in 1942.

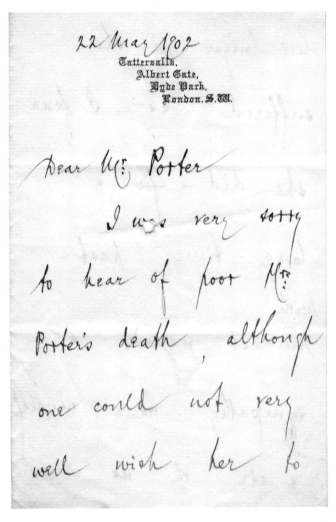

live longer if she
suffered as I fear
she did for a
long time past.
With
Kindest regards +
sympathy from myself
+ all of us

I remain

yours very truly

E. Somerville Tattersall

—

Thomas Baring - 1st Earl of Northbrook

Two letters from Northbrook to Sir Charles Russell dated 17th and 19th April 1894.
Lord Russell and Lord Alington had been promoting Porter for the position of magistrate (Justice of the Peace). Northbrook is not prepared to put forward a recommendation to the Lord Chancellor, he has other plans.

Lord Russell must have forwarded the letter of 19th April to John Porter – as in Porter's hand there is a note 'Return to Sir C.R.' in the top corner.

STRATTON,
MICHELDEVER STATION.

April 17/94

Dear Sir Charles

I am much obliged to you for your letter about Mr Porter – Alington had already mentioned to me his wish to become an M.P. and I am well aware of his

high reputation as a trainer –

There is no doubt a want of a magistrate at Kingsclere, but I think I have an arrangement in hand which will meet it for the present – I am

Yrs faithfully

Northbrook

STRATTON,
MICHELDEVER STATION.

April 19/94

Dear Sir Charles

I am sorry that
my letter was not
clear, I intended
that you should
infer from it that
I do not see any
way at present
to recommend no
Patie to the Lord

Chancellor for
the Commission of the
Peace. Yrs faithfully

Northbrook

244

George Edwardes
1855-1915

An English theatre manager and producer who brought a new era in musical theatre to the world. Edwardes began work in theatre management. By the age of 20 he was managing theatres for Richard d'Oyly Carte. In 1885 he became manager at the Gaiety Theatre.

For the next 30 years Edwardes ruled a theatrical empire including the Gaiety, Daly's Theatre and Adelphi to name but three. He also sent touring companions around Britain and abroad. In the 1890's Edwardes identified the audience movement away from Burlesque type shows to the Edwardian comedy.

Edwardes raced horses which is how he came to know Porter.

Letter from Bad Nauheim 12th June 1914.

Edwardes was making his annual visit to a German spa when World War 1 broke out. He was imprisoned in Germany for several months which made his health problems worse.

This letter suggests to Porter he should go to the spa for the good of his health. It was as well he did not, as he might have ended being imprisoned like Edwardes.

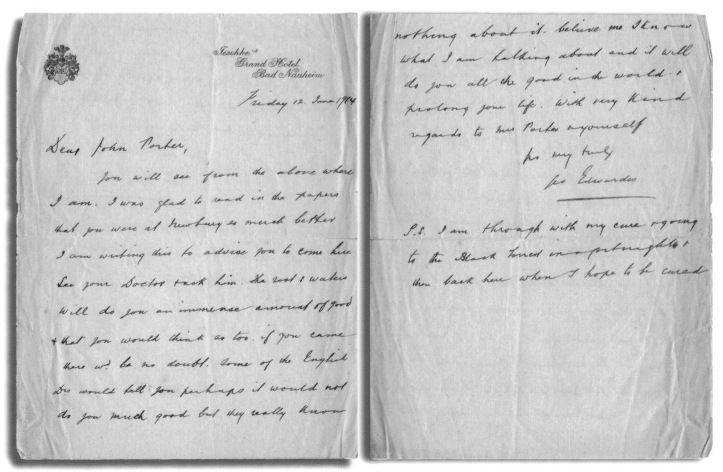

Douglas Graham, 5th Duke of Montrose

He was a military man and served in the South African War. He was Aide de Camp to King George V.

Letter 10th July 1895
He appears to have had a share in a horse Le Var with Sir Frederick Johnstone. After it won the Prince of Wales Stakes in 1895 the owners wanted to make a gift to Porter the trainer and Mornington Cannon, the jockey. This letter confirms that Weatherby's will be instructed to transfer £500 from Montrose's account to that of Johnstone's.
A handsome contribution to a generous gift.

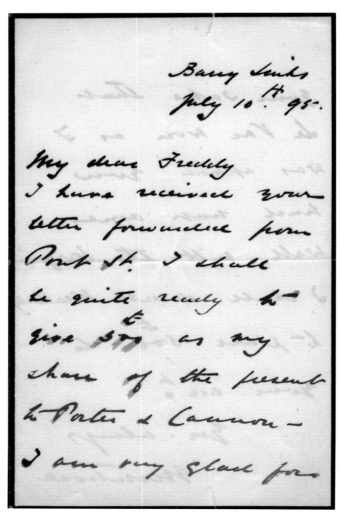

your sake that
he has won as I
was afraid you
had not done
well with the bargain.
I shall direct Weatherby
to place 500$ to
your acc^t.
Yrs. always
Montrose

Adolphus Cambridge - 1st Marquess of Cambridge
1868 – 1927

Was a member of the British Royal family, being a great grandson of King George III and a younger brother of Queen Mary – wife of George V. In 1900 he became Duke of Teck in the Kingdom of Wurttemberg, Germany. He relinquished his titles in 1917 to become Marquess of Cambridge. He married Margaret Grosvenor in 1894.

Letter from Eaton Hall, Chester, where he was staying with his future brother-in-law, the Duke of Westminster. Believed to be written in November 1894, a month before his marriage to the Duke's sister, Margaret Grosvenor. His letter thanks Porter for a gift – some of Ormonde's hair mounted. Porter had got the Duke of Westminster to take the gift back to Eaton with him.

Letter 2nd January 1904 from Gloucester House, Park Lane, written by the Duke's secretary thanking Porter for his kind thoughts and good wishes, which he reciprocates to Mr & Mrs Porter.

Letter 23rd May 1909

Declines bidding for a mare which he had seen a month previously – replying to Porter's letter of 22d May

Letter 13th March 1913 – from Frogmore Cottage. Telling Porter he and the Duchess will come to the races with Sir Richard Sutton, one of the richest men in England at that time. He was the 6th Baronet.

Nov. 30th

Dear Mr Porter

The Duke
of Westminster
has just given
me your most
charming and
useful present
& I hasten to

write and thank
you for it. Your
idea is I think
quite charming of
putting some of
Osmonde's hair in
it. Believe me
Yours faithfully
Adolphus Drexel.

Jan. 2. 1904

Gloucester House.
Park Lane. W.

Dear Mr Parker

The Duke of Cambridge
desires me to write & thank
you for your letter & for your
kind thoughts of him.
His Royal Highness wishes that
Mr Parker many happy New
Years – a wish in which I
Cordially join & remain

Yrs truly
Albert Williams

Letter
Relating to King Edward
& others.

250

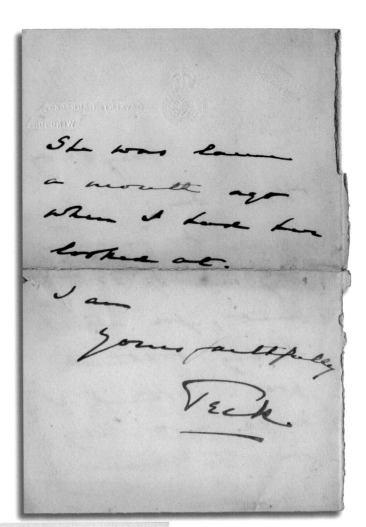

TELEPHONE,
38 WINDSOR.

CAVALRY BARRACKS,
WINDSOR.

May 23. 09

Dear Sir

In answer to yours of 22nd inst, for which I beg to thank you — I think I will not try for the mare —

She was lame a month ago when I have her looked at.

I am

Yours faithfully

Teck

FROGMORE COTTAGE,
WINDSOR.

March 13. 13

Dear Mr Porter

The Duchess & I are coming tomorrow after lunch to the races with Sir Richard Sutton from Denham Valence —

Yours sincerely

Teck

251

H.R.H. Prince Charles Alexander Edwards Theodore of Abyssinia.

Letter to Porter asking if he could forward 'the enclosed' to Baron von Hirsch. Letter dated 28th October 1892.
Letter written from Exeter House, 16 St Nicholas Road, Brighton.
No information on the writer has been found.

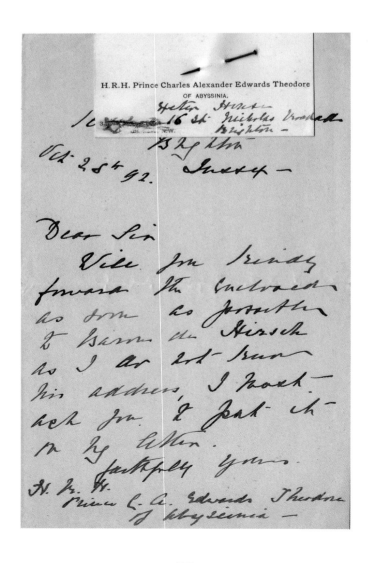

Henry Hawley Smart
1833 – 1893

Nephew of Sir Joseph Hawley.

Novelist and friend of John Porter although he does not appear to have had any horses trained by him. Something of a gambler and incurring losses, he turned to writing. They were 'novels of society', military life, racing and hunting. He served in the Army from 1849 to 1864, serving throughout the Crimean War and during the Indian Mutiny.

Budleigh Salterton– letter November,1883 – quoted in Porter's autobiography pages 306/307. Refers to Porter liking a book – either 'At Fault' or 'Hard Lines' both published in 1883. Refers to being at Egglesford last week where Lady Portsmouth was pleased with it – Hawley Smart refers to her being a 'clever woman'. Compliments Porter on having done well but sorry to hear he has nothing promising for next year. Refers to Friar's Balsam and the Lancashire Plate. Enquires as to races at Stockbridge in1884 as he has no calendar in Budleigh Salterton.

Regrets he and Mrs Hawley Smart cannot manage a visit to Kingsclere, but hopes in Summer 1884 he will have a spare room for them. Mrs Hawley Smart reportedly got quite tired of heavy praise of 'The Master' at Egglesford.

Stockbridge Racecourse was developed at Danebury Hill in 1839 and closed in 1898 when the land at the eastern end of the course was purchased by Marianne Vandry who strongly disapproved of gambling and would not extend the lease.

Letter 29th July 1888 – written from the Garrick Club, quoted in Porter's autobiography pages 305-306.

Congratulations on Eclipse Stakes where Porter trained horses were first and second – owned by Duke of Westminster. Refers to a message from 'Matthews' – refers to Sir C. Matthews, one of Porter's legal friends. As a result of receiving a message, Hawly-Smart had a 'tenner' on Orbit that came first. More about racing – shows Hawley-Smart's interest in the sport.

Letter 24th February from an address in Cheltenham.

Commenting on Porter's son losing a leg and how sad it is – drawing attention to another friend of Hawley-Smart. 'Toole, the actor, lost a daughter, wife, brother and business manager within a year.'

Letter 29th November 1887 from Budleigh Salterton. Sends Porter two books 'A False Start' and 'Saddle and Sabre'. Refers to Mrs Porter and daughters.

Letter 5th February 1887 (incomplete) from Cheltenham. Refers to scandal of Durham, Chetwynd and George Wood - Gimcrack speech – Resignation from Jockey Club and being 'warned off' – Woods.

Clearly a close friend of Porter's and one not afraid to let him know his perspective on his horses.

Rousemont
Budleigh Salterton
S Devon Nov 4th

Dear Porter

I am glad you liked the book — it promises to be a great go before the month's out. It has come out just in the nick of time — it was like having a colt thoroughly ripe in the Epsom on Ascot week — Every one speaks highly of it and all notices so far are most laudatory — At Eggesford last week they were all full of it — Lady Portsmouth is ~~[crossed out]~~ specially was pleased with it and she's a clever woman —

No I've spent 4 years in Iceland but it was long ago and I don't think I shall trouble it again —

might find myself unpopular you know —

Yes you have indeed done well It all over now and we see what undifferent material you had to work on and I am sorry to hear that you have nothing very promising for next year — I don't know whether Trois Balsam can stay, and even you may not be quite certain on that point, but if he had only kept well what a sheep of the board it would have been — Last year he was always master of Ayrshire and Stalleap He no doubt had very bad luck in the ~~[crossed]~~ Lancashire Plate or else I suppose he would have finished in the first three at all events —

I am miles from a Calendar down here — Will you let me know what Races you won at Stockbridge in 84 — I remember Luminous & Gehazi — hey but forget the others — tho' I think De White Nun was another I want to know particularly —

I am sorry to say he cannot manage a visit to Kings Clere at present but do hope that next summer we may find you with a spare room —

With kindest regards from us both — (Mrs Hawley Smart says she got quite tired of hearing the praises of "The Master" ~~sung~~ at Eggesford)

Believe me
Sincerely Yours
Hawley Smart

254

Garrick Club
Covent Garden WC
London July 29th

Dear Porter

No End of congratulations
on the Eclipse Stakes
If your team was a little
backward they came with
a rattle ~~rattle~~ when they did
come and about 13600 £
in two "pops" must make
the Duke think keeping race
horses about the most Econom
-ical sport out —
I couldn't get down to see it
but what a good race it
was between your pair and
~~for~~ ~~XXX~~ Ossory, to make
all the running, give away

3 lb and stick as from
all accounts he did so gamely
to his work, was a good performance
I got a message from you
by Matthews for which many
thanks and had a tenner on
Ot but in consequence. They
may not be first class horses
but they are an uncommonly
useful pair they stay so well
and whichever you think the
best in September is sure to
bother the horses at Doncaster
if he don't beat — Ossory was
about ~~last~~ last all the way to the
Stansley turn at Ascot but the
further he went the better he
liked it —
By the way I came up with
a gentleman on the Hunt
Cup day who I perfectly

remember your introducing one
to on the training ground
when I came down to Kingsclere
He said you told him on
the Saturday previous you
fancied your chances for
the Prince of Wales and the
Hunt Cup that he did so
down on Tuesday and so declined
back Ossory but that he did
back Candlemas — As I had
done likewise we mutually
lamented —
Kindest regards to Mrs Porter
and wishing you all sorts
of success at Goodwood
Believe me
Yours Sincerely
Hawley Smart
I'm afraid you won't be at the
~~breeze~~ in the Sussex —

Top right

8 Imperial Square
Cheltenham
Feb 24th

Dear Porter

I did not hear of the trouble that had befallen you until some little time after the accident occurred and am glad to see by the papers that your son is going on well — Still it is a very bad business the losing a leg at the commencement of life and it must come hard upon a young fellow who judging by the cups you showed me was a peculiarly active man — It has been a sad winter among my friends — Poor Toole the actor for instance. Only last autumn I wrote to him about the loss of his daughter and

Top left

falling quite into the back ground —

Kind regards to Mrs Porter and trusting your son's accident will not preclude his following up his profession

Believe me

Yours Sincerely

Hawley Smart

I don't know whether you like Napoleon but he's a rare bred one —

Bottom left

Now I am writing to him about the loss of his wife — In the last few years he has lost son daughter wife brother and his right-hand friend and business manager — In short all belonging to him and though with countless friends is left practically alone in the world —

I am sending you a new story which may kill an hour or two reading for some of you — My stupid publishers in their hurry to get it out struck off heaps of copies without sending me a revise the consequence is it is full of blunders — bad stuff I think but "Short of Work" if the errata had only been put into the book instead of

Bottom right

on the slip of paper it would sell slower now like a half trained one it may but is not worth backing —

I hope the horses are going on well — With Jews Balloon Gay Hampton, Napoleon II you ought to make a bid for some of these big stakes which threaten to discount and swamp the Derby — As you said some time back the Epsom authorities ought to pile at least 5000£ a dozed — it would be a thousand pities if the famous race should lose its pride of place but what with the big race at Leicester the Royal Prize at Kempton &c it looks this year like

of the Sir Tatton Sykes year
& Bell & Scott's Derby fiasco —
Don Fonellon Yes he was
one of the cracks of the old
school when I think they rode
as a rule a deal better and
a deal straighter than they do
now — Cannon's the only
one of that sort we have now

Kind regards to Mrs
Porter and your daughters
and with all the compliments
of the season and wishing
you luck for next year
 Sincerely yours
 Hawley Smart

Spar Cottage
Budleigh Salterton
South Devon Nov 29

Dear Porter
 The curtain's down at
last and the racing season of
87 a thing of the past
and Kingsclere at all
events can't complain of
being left out in the cold —
What is Ascot & Goodwood
you had while Newmarket
has seen you to the fore all
the year —
St Mirin didn't run quite
up to your estimate nor
the Cambridgeshire tho' I
dare say Cannon could

---

have been beaten if he'd liked
but probably raced his horse
when he found he couldn't-won.
I stood him to win for a
fiver & clothes-back him for
the Liverpool Cup though I
had a conviction he would win
that — oddly enough I did
exactly the same thing last
year with Melton —
What a Derby horse you've got
I've no doubt Ormonde Balsam
is the best of the lot now but
both Orbit and Ossory must
be pretty smart and next
spring it might, tho' not likely,
be a case of Bendsman
and ~~Fitzland~~ Fitzroland
over again — I only hope they
will all winter well and

---

that next May you will land
your fifth (is it?) Derby —
21 lbs better than Mrs Porter
has a very Ormonde flavour
about it — we were over
at Egg'sford the other day
and Lord Portsmouth didn't
think Ormonde Balsam very
much behind "the great horse."
Still a horse that after he'd
turned roarer could polish
off two such horses as Minting
and Bendigo must have been
a wonder at his best —
You will get a couple of
books or little "A False
Start" and "Saddle and
Sabre" which I hope may
kill a few winters evenings
The latter story is the history

4 Queens Parade
Cheltenham
Feby 5th

Dear Porter

I have just got Bailey:
a very good likeness of you
but not quite a pleasing
one - like it is un mistake-
-ably but it makes you
look so serious and care
worn - That is the worst of
photography and I fancy
your picture is taken from
me - A man's natural
expression under those circum-
-stances is that of one about
to have a tooth out -
'an easy expression please'
says the artist -
'Result being an imbecile'

fashion -
Now I have got to tell you
a coincidence - A bit handicap
is always as amusing to me
as acrostics are to people who
that way - I after make no
bet whatever on it but I like
to calculate what should go
near winning on public form
I was studying the acceptances
for the City and Suburban
on Thursday Feby 2nd and
came to the conclusion that
Cordite was through the King
Philo running at Redcar
and Sandown Price at Glou-
-cester at about 7.5 and
that he was the best there
in the Handicap on book
form though Reed from looks
dangerous;

fun or an apparent bad
pain in the Stomach - I
have two photographs of myself
which exactly fulfil these con-
-ditions -
John Cole of course did keep
-clear - I have known him
for years and always liked
him - A good sort and of
the old kind - He apparently
is not in love with it but,
but while Friars Balsam
keeps up I don't suppose
the Duke's pain need trouble
our heads for the classic
races -
By the way it may interest
you to know that the
article 'Elephant Shooting in

Ceylon" in this month's Bailey is
by my brother in law - a judge
in those parts & a mighty
Nimrod - always killing some
-thing I can be sufficiently
thankful for not meeting -
I am very glad the Jockey
Club have put their foot down
at last and stopped those
two notorious scamps Wood
& G Barrett from riding - I
have no doubt they might have
enlarged their proscription list
but this will be a much needed
warning as also Lord Durhams
speech - I know nothing about
Sir George Chetwynd but
his horses do run in a
most marvellous un
uncertain

Henry Hawley (Sir Henry James Hawley) 4th Baronet
1815 – 1898

Sir Joseph Hawley's brother.

Letter 1875, from 34 Eaton Place
Re: Porter's attendance at Sir Joseph's funeral. Re. Lady Hawley and train journey for getting to the funeral. Refers to his personal feelings. Letter in black edging to note – ' in mourning.'

Feby 22^d 1892.

Porter

I am sorry I
shall not be able to
vote at the next Election
for Mr Arthur Dobson
as my votes are already
promised, but as soon
as they are free. I will

do so, unless she gets
in, at the May Election
It seems a very sad
case indeed.

I was pleased to see
your success last
year with Cowman,
I hope you will
have many such cases

years. I trust you
are well

Yours very truly

Henry Hawley

260

34 Gate Place
Saturday –

Porter,

If it would be any gratification to you to attend the funeral of Sir Joseph I shall be very glad for you so to do.

The sad ceremony is to take place next Tuesday at Leybourne

We leave the Snodland Station about 12 o'clock on that day. And there is a train for London at (Charing Cross) 9-55 by which myself and others who are going to attend. I shall go down –

I thank you much for the sympathy expressed for us in your letter Lady Hooker. I am sorry to say, is still far from well but the better to be present

at the Church on Tuesday –

I have been with my dear Brother so constantly the last eight months, a more patient invalid I never knew. And so thankful for all that was done for him; I shall miss him sadly, he was such a kind Brother, and we were so attached to each other. I am

Yours very faithfully
Henry Hooker

Lady Helena Gleichen O.B.E.
1873-1947

Daughter of Count Victor Gleichen also known as Prince Victor of Hohenlohe-Langenburg, a half nephew of Queen Victoria.

She was a painter and had a particular passion for horses.

She worked from her father's former studio in St James's Palace.

Her family home was a rambling estate Hellens Manor at Much Marcle in Herefordshire. During World War II it was used as a safe storage by the Tate, for works of art.

Letter re painting some of Porter's horses – undated.

Letter 14th July 1901 from St James's Palace re sorry at hearing of Mrs Porter's illness and hopes to hear of her recovery.

Letter undated from Crichlade, Wiltshire

Mentions a Mare 'Rainbow' she part owns and wants trained for winter chases. Porter gave her some guidance – trainers mentioned are Mr Hartigan – Porter's suggestion. He liked the mare but has no room and suggested Dollery - does Porter know of him. Thanks to Porter for all his help.

Wed. Berry down

Dear Mr Potter —

I must write you one
word to thank you for
allowing me to paint
in your Stables. I have
enjoyed it so much
besides having loved

Seeing all the horses —
I had hoped to have had
another morning's work at
the St Angelo filly but
found it impossible —
So I hope you will accept
the Sketch as it is, although
most unfinished — Please
do not trouble to answer

this — I will let you have
a p. c. when I send
off the Sketch. With very
many thanks again
I remain

Yrs sincerely
Helena Gleichen

263

1st November

Dear M! Porter —
I am sending off
tomorrow the portrait
of the yearling filly
I painted for you &
hope it will arrive

Quite safely —
Please remember
me to M!! Porter

Y!! sincerely

Helena Gleichen

When you have settled
a name for the

Yearling I should
very much like to
hear it — as it will
be interesting to
follow her career.

14th July 1901

St JAMES'S PALACE.

Dear Mr Porter —

I cannot tell you how
sorry I am to hear of
Mrs Porter's illness & I
do trust that by now she
is progressing favourably.
It is too sad for you having
so much trouble & I do
hope to hear soon that

She has turned the corner
& is well on the road to
convalescence.

Yrs sincerely

Helena & Crichea

265

your again so very much for your
help. Yrs very sincerely

Helena Gibbins

Dear Mr Porter –
We took the mare, Rainbow,
over to Mr Hartagan's on
Saturday & he seemed to think
she did quite well & that she
is well worth training. He said
she ought with luck to win us any

hunt race when she is in training!
Thank you so much for having
helped us. We think of entering
her for Oaksey, only the bother is
having to hunt her 8 times before,
as it may make her go light &
Mr Hartagan says she is just right
to go into training now – also she
pulls too hard for me to hunt.

So that will mean having to get a
man to hunt her.
I wish he could have trained her
but he says he is so full up now
he hasn't room – We are thinking
of Dollery, I wonder if you know him
& whether he would run us in for
a fearful lot – I wish I knew more
about it all, as for Mrs Hollings
& myself it is indeed the blind
leading the blind! Anyway thank

Sir Charles Willie Matthews
1850-1920

British Lawyer

A long term friend of Porter's. The archive letters cover the period 1884 to 1919, some 35 years. He does not appear to have ever been an owner, but enjoyed his racing and obviously valued Porter's friendship and hospitality.

Letter 28th September 1884

This accompanied a gift following a visit to Kingsclere.
Addressed to 'My dear Mr Porter'

Letter 8th May 1888

Invites himself and Sir Charles Renfell to stay at Kingsclere on 22nd May. Racing at Bath on 22nd, Manchester 23rd. Sorry Porter's horse did not win 2000 Guineas but he hopes his horse will win the Derby. A 'p.s.' asks if he owes Porter any money. It seems Porter may place the occasional bet for him.
Addressed to 'My dear John Porter'

Letter 11th June 1889

Congratulates Porter on a winner – had tried to find him on the course, but it was in vain. Hopes Friar's Balsam will prove only half as good, he will be good enough.
Addressed to 'My dear John Porter'.

Letter 26th December 1893

Very sorry to hear that Porter has been ill, had he heard earlier he would have written. "I know you will recover".
Addressed to 'My dear John Porter'

Letter 10th April 1899

Regrets that due to recent death of his Mother he will not be able to receive any friends – as has been the custom for some years. He will not be able to have his usual pre-Derby meetings, but will nonetheless drink to Porter's and Kingsclere success.
His wife joins him in sending very kind regards to Mrs Porter.
Addressed to 'My dear John'.

Letter 31st May 1899

Congratulations on Flying Fox's Derby victory. Addressed 'My dear John'

Letter 8th March 1907

Thanks for letter, the more so as it contained the welcome news Porter was once more himself. He had been unwell. Reference to the great work he had done at Newbury following on the great record he had left at Kingsclere.
Addressed 'My dear John'.

Letter 5th April 1914

Written to Mrs Porter saying –
"I have read with so much pleasure of John's progress towards recovery and I hope you will tell him so for his friendship and mine dates from very long ago".
The wording shows how deep a friendship it was and predating Porter's marriage to Isabel in 1902.

Letter 1st October 1914

This letter to be included in book.

Letter 23rd December 1918

Reminiscing and thanks
This letter to be included in book

Letter 20th December 1919

Porter had sent him a copy of his autobiography. Include letter in book – it sums up the meaning of their friendship to Sir Charles.
Sir Charles Willie Matthews was born in New York and was the child of his mother's first marriage. Following his Mother's third marriage, he changed his surname from West to Matthews.

He was educated at Eton and after three years in Europe he joined the chambers of Montague Williams as a pupil aged about 21. In 1886 he was appointed as a Junior Counsel to H.M. Treasury. Two years later – 1888, he was appointed Senior Treasury Counsel. Amongst the infamous cases he appeared in was Oscar Wilde's suit for libel against John Douglas, 9th Marquess of Queensbury and Lord Colin Campbell's divorce. Matthews was famous for his courtroom flair and aggressive advocacy.

Matthews was very sociable, he was a member of the Turf, Garrick and Beefsteak Clubs and was a good friend of Edward VII and King George V. He received his knighthood in 1907. In 1908 he was appointed the first independent Director of Public Prosecutions, a position he held until his death in 1920. He was made a baronet in 1917.

1. Essex Court. Temple. E.C.

May 8th 1888.

My dear John Porter,

I am going to
take you & Mrs Porter at your
word. I propose Sir Charles
Russell & myself for the night
at Kingsclere on Tuesday, the
22nd of this month. We know
you are very busy, and rely upon
your telling us if we shall be in
the smallest extent in your way.

I am there is some racing at
Bath on the 22nd, & at Manchester
on the 23rd, and you may be
taken to one or both of these
meetings. If it is likely to be so
again, you must let us know.

I am awfully sorry you didn't
win the £2000 prize, and
the more sorry when I read that
your best string has hit himself.
I hope he may be fit for the
"Oaks" & I shall if you can't win
contrive him, you will have no

good enough to take the big race
to Kingsclere.

Please remember us very
kindly to Mrs Porter, and
your family, &

Believe me.

Most faithfully yours.

Charles Mathews.

John Porter Esq.

P.S. Do I owe you any money. Did
you pay me on either Deviled or
Xmas Balsam? Please let me know.
I thank you very wrongs if you didn't.

1, Essex Court, Temple, E.C.

June 11th 1887.

My dear John Potter.

I was so
delighted to see you found
home on Saturday, and looked
long there for you to tell you
so, but, unhappily, in vain. May
"Friar Balsam" prove only half as
good, and he will be quite good
enough !!! Faithfully yours.

Charles N. Mathews.

5, LENNOX GARDENS,
S.W.

Dec: 26 1893.

My dear John.

I am very sorry
to hear there you have been ill.
I only heard of it this morning
or I should have written before.
A though his many friends this
will no give to hear good news
of you. I know you will reckon
Mr. always faithfully

Charles N. Mathews.

270

April 10th 1899.

My Dear Shee,

I greatly regret -
on every score - that dear
dear Mother's death is so
recent - that I shall be
unable to receive any
friends, as has been my
custom for some years, on

the day when the Derby is
run. I, believe me, there
is no one of them, whom
I shall miss more than
yourself. It is the one
occasion in the year when
I can rely on a quiet dinner
followed by a quiet rubber. On
the 3rd of May, well, it
would have delighted me to have

proposed your health if, as
I sincerely hope may be
the case, the "Blue Riband"
as again. I for the sixth
time, unless I am mistaken -
carried off by Kingsclere.
With very kindest regards to
Mrs Shee, in which my wife
joins. I am,
Most faithfully yours,

271

1, ESSEX COURT,
TEMPLE, E.C.

May 31st 1899.

My dear Shaw,

Accept my warm Congratulations upon Flying Fox's brilliant effort at Epsom this day afternoon, &

Believe me,

Very faithfully yours,

Charles E. Mathew.

5, LENNOX GARDENS,
S.W.

March 8th 1907.

My dear Shaw,

How very good of you to send me such a nice letter, which I appreciate more than I can tell you, & the more especially as it contained the welcome intelligence that you were

once more yourself. Long may you continue your leadership of Newbury. There you decided seem to create something like the great record which you left behind you at & still took till you from, Kingsclere. With our kindest regards to Mrs Shaw. I am,

Very faithfully yours,

Charles E. Mathew.

April 5th 1914

Dear Mrs Porter,

I have read with so much pleasure of Arthur's progress towards recovery, & I hope you will tell him so. His friendship & mine dates from very long ago.

With our kindest regards to you.

I am,
Very Sincerely Yours,
Charles W. Mathews.

Oct: 1st 1914.

Thank you, my dear John, for sending me "all the titles," & tell that pride must you contemplate the part you have played in the history of the Theif from 1863 until this very day. I learned, with so much pleasure that you were quite well again.

Yours sincerely Yours,
Charles W. Mathews.

---

move from our own homestead. We appreciate your kindness none the less. I send you every good wish for the Xmas which is so close. & for the bright New Year which be May life it in store for us.

Always, my dear John,

Very truly Yours,
Charles W. Mathews.

Dec: 23rd, 1918.

My dear John,

It was a great pleasure to see your handwriting & a greater to be assured that I still remained in your pleasant memory. It does indeed seem long since we last met.

[Top panel — embossed heading: 5, LENNOX GARDENS, S.W.]

& it must now be well over 4
years, for I have been to
no race meeting since the
war began, & it was upon the
race course that our meetings
have latterly taken place.

I hope all this may be
remedied in the coming years,
when, as I have heard with
so much pleasure, racing will
be revived upon the old pleasant

lines, & then if I go nowhere
else I am sure to pay a
visit to Newmarket, there
we are certain to meet.

Thank you so much for
your kind offer of hospitality
at Ormonde House, but my
dear John, it is only you
who grow younger, we are
getting, indeed have got old,
& it is very seldom now we

88, SLOANE STREET, S.W.1.

[printed: TELEPHONE VICTORIA 4334.]

Dec: 25th 1919.

Thank you, my dear John, &
most sincerely, for your kind
& thoughtful Xmas gift, which
I accept with very great
pleasure, & which I shall
read with very great interest.
Our association has been a long
one, & I am glad to think
I have retained throughout it a

friendship which I have ever
valued, & which has never
failed. Every good wish to you
at this & at all seasons.

Most truly yours,

Charles W. Mathews

John Porter Esq

Colonel Sir Robert Nigel Fitzhardinge Kingscote
1830 – 1908

Equerry in Waiting to H.R.H. Prince of Wales.

Letter 2nd March 1900 – Marlborough House.   Written for the Prince of Wales thanking Porter for sending catalogue of the Duke of Westminster's horses being sold on 8th March.   The Prince will be pleased to come to Kingsclere for the sale.   He will be accompanied by Lords William and Marcus Beresford and Kingscote.   Details of travel arrangements Paddington to Newbury arriving at 10.30 am, leaving 5.30 pm.   A landau to be at Newbury to transport the Prince to Kingsclere. Need for him to wash his hands before and after lunch.   Best wishes for good weather and successful sale.

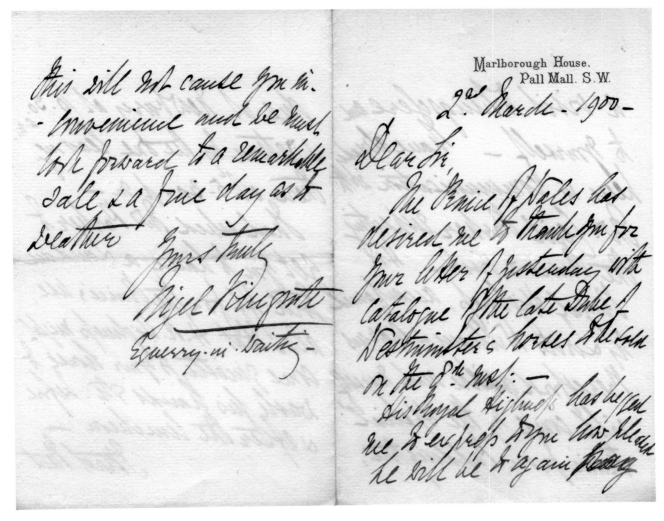

a visit to Kingsclere and
to yourself – I have already
been in communication with
Mr. Cecil Parker respecting
the Prince's visit – His
Royal Highness, accompanied
by Lords William & Marcus
Beresford and myself
will come by the special
train from Paddington,

due at Newbury at 10.30.
a.m.
& return by the one leaving
there at 5.30. p.m. –
I had asked Mr. Parker to
get you to have a Landau
told off for the Prince's use,
also that H.R. Highness might
come quietly to your house to
wash his hands &c: before
& after the luncheon –

Yours &c

276

Lord Henry Arthur George Somerset
1851 – 1926

Master of the Horse and was head of stables of H.R.H. Prince of Wales later King Edward VII.
He was linked to the Cleveland Street Scandal, involving several male prostitutes. He was
interviewed by the police in August 1889, twice. Following the second interview he fled to the
Continent, came back for a short time but believed he was going to be charged. He left for France
but travelled to Turkey, Hungary and Austria before a final return to France where he settled until
his death in 1926.

Letter 6th April 1887 from Marlborough House written before the scandal emerged, writing on
behalf of the Prince of Wales, requested Porter go to Sandringham on the Friday of the
Newmarket Craven meeting to see the West Norfolk Steeplechase on the Saturday and then visit
the mares on the Sunday.

Card 20th November from Sandringham

This is actually written to Somerset 'my dear Podge'. 'Podge' was a nickname for Somerset.
We have been unable to identify the writer and some of the text.

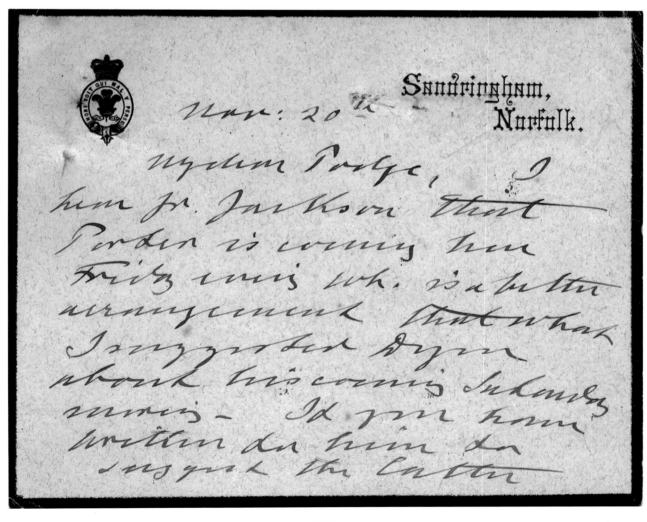

please telegraph that
I expect train here
Friday evening & work
Saturday morning —
Sunday morning —
Just going out shooting
here,
Yours very sincerely
[signature]

MARLBOROUGH CLUB
PALL MALL. S.W.
April 6. 87.

Dear Mr. Porter,
I am desired
by The Prince of
Wales to say that His
Royal Highness hopes
You will go to Sandring-
ham on the Friday
in the Craven Meeting
to see the West Norfolk

Steeplechases on the
Saturday & the races
on the Sunday —
Yours faithfully
Arthur Somerset
Marlborough House

Stables.
Marlborough House.
Pall Mall. S.W.

Nov. 21. 88.

Dear Mr. Porter.

I received the
enclosed just now,
& immediately write
to you — We shall
meet on Saturday
at Sandringham

yrs truly.

Arthur Somerset

279

Prince Christian of Schleswig-Holstein
1831 – 1917

Married Princess Helena, fifth child of Queen Victoria and Prince Albert.
Letter from Cumberland Lodge
Prince Christian asked if Porter could provide lunch at Newbury races on Saturday 8th April as previously, also for Sir William Portal with whom he will be staying.

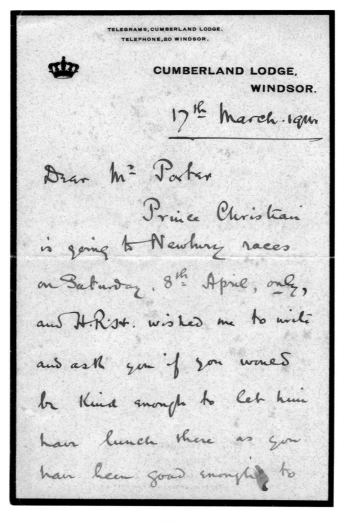

do on other occasions.

H.R.H. goes to stay with Sir William Portal that night, and would like to ask him & some of his party to lunch with him that day.

Would you be so kind as to let me know if you can arrange this. I think you know H.R.H. likes a pink

of champagne with his lunch!

Yours truly

Cyril Hankey.

Henry Hawkins, 1st Baron of Brampton
1817 – 1907

He was a Judge from 1876 to 1899

A letter dated 23rd March 1902

A letter of consolation and sympathy to Porter and family on the death of his wife.

A letter dated 1st November 1891, 5 Tilney St, Park Lane, thanking Porter and Mrs Porter for their sympathy with his ailment. Not yet fully fit but has been able to resume work. Congratulations on Orme's and his prospects.

Sir Henry Hawkins was one of the legal profession who visited Kingsclere on a regular basis. His legal career spanned the years 1843-1876, his judicial career 1876-1898.

He held for many years the office of Counsel to the Jockey Club and as an active member of that body, found relaxation regularly at leading race meetings. He was considered a capable judge of horses.

He died at 5 Tilney Street, Park Lane aged 90.

In Porter's view 'he was a very just and discriminating judge'.

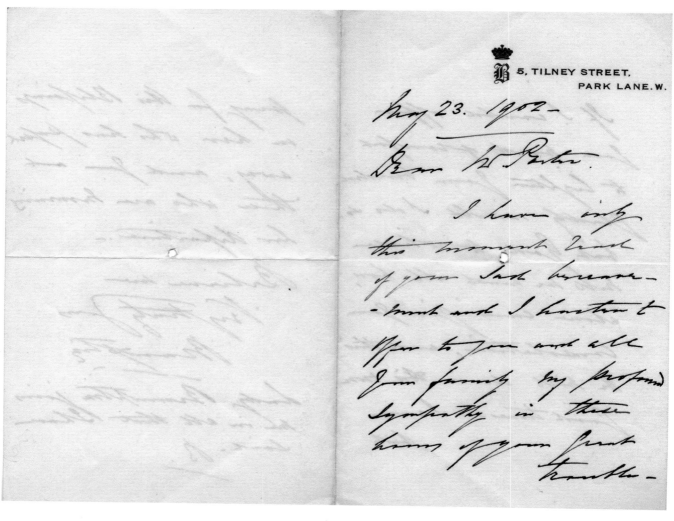

If I could offer
you words of comfort
to lighten your burden.
Gladly would I do so.
but God, to whose
will we must all bow,
alone can give you
consolation, and this
He will do in His own
good time. — I can
but

pray for His Blessings
on her who has passed
away, and you and
those who are mourning
her departure. —

Believe me
Very truly yours
Brampton

Lady Brampton joins
me in all that I have
said. — B.

Richard Vesey Hamilton

Admiral of the Fleet
A letter 3.7. –
From Hamilton to Admiral Henry Frederick Stephenson. Referring to "Sir Harry (Keppel) about receiving and returning nomination paper. It seems likely this was to do with Porter's son hoping to join the Navy.
A letter 3.7. –
Another letter of same date to Admiral Stephenson on the same subject.

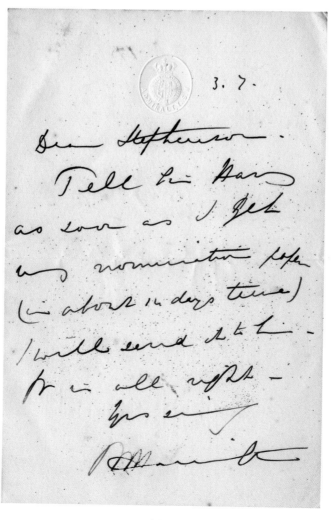

July 3rd

Dear Admiral Stephenson.

I have mentioned your visit to Sir Vesey Hamilton, and he quite remembers having promised Sir Henry Keppel that he would nominate young Porter for the Amateur Examination.

In the ordinary course the nomination would go not some time during the present month, but matters would be much expedited if I might have the enclosed form back again with the particular indicated filled in. — so as to be ready whenever Sir Vesey is called upon to send in his nominations.

I remain,
Yours very truly,
Geo H Hoste

General Sir Dighton Probyn, VC
1833 – 1924

Was a British Army Officer. He served during the Indian Mutiny, 2nd Anglo-Chinese War and Umbeyla Campaign. His Victoria Cross was awarded for his exploits during the Indian Mutiny. In 1872 he was appointed an Equerry to H.R.H. the Prince of Wales. He was appointed one of the first Knights Grand Cross of the Royal Victorian Order in 1896. He was appointed a member of the Privy Council in 1901.

He was in later life a grand figure of the Victorian age, being Keeper of the Privy Purse, as well as Secretary of the Prince of Wales and Comptroller of the Prince's Household. This was an important position as the Prince and Princess were both very free in spending and Sir Dighton had a hard job to keep them solvent. Probyn kept this role, throughout the Kings reign, right up to his death. He was appointed an Extra Equerry to the King in 1902. Probyn was totally devoted to the Princess, then Queen Empress. He had gardens built for her at Windsor Castle and Sandringham House.

His devotion to the Princess was reciprocated. He was occasionally suffering seizures and she always carried a small knife with her to be able to cut open his collar. He cut an impressive look in old age with a very long white beard.

Letter 23rd November 1903 Sandringham House

Best wishes to Porter in his 'newly married life'. Following his second marriage to Isabel Pilsbury.

Letter 10th May 1910

He encloses a ticket for the funeral of King Edward VII at St Georges Chapel, Windsor. Seat is in the choir, which Probyn believes is a good position.

Both above letters in book.

Letter from Sandringham dated 20th January 1900.

Re Persimmon injury – report's 'going on well, could not be doing better' – although useless for this season, believes he will return to stud next year with renewed energy. Was looking magnificent up to the accident. Has some good looking yearlings and 2 year olds that may be able to gallop a bit. Thanks Porter for good wishes for the New Year which he reciprocates.

Undated schedule of Porter's visit to Sandringham. Meeting with the Prince of Wales followed by visit to grounds of Park House etc. ending with visit to stables.

Letter from Sandringham House 23rd November 1903.

Congratulations on marriage.

Letter May 10th 1910.

Enclosing ticket for funeral of Edward 7th at St Georges Chapel, Windsor.

Letter from Marlborough House 11th June 1916

Ref King's collection of Vanity Fair Cartoons at Birkhall shooting lodge near Balmoral. Requests Porter's help in acquiring autographs of all who have been cartooned to place under their pictures – he is short of 19 signatures – refers to having Porter's autograph all ready to place beneath his cartoon.

Letter from Marlborough House – 15th June 1916 to Ormonde House. Thanks for Porter's reply of 14th. Porter referred to being unwell. Ref to having obtained Mornington Cannon's autograph.

Letter from Marlborough House – 17th June 1916

Letter advises omission of Fred Archer from list and adds he needs '3 of him' please!.

Letter from Marlborough House – 4th July 1916. Enquiring if Porter has had any success in Probyn's request for autographs.

Letter from Marlborough House – 7th July 1916 to Ormonde House thanking Porter for signatures and asks he keeps working on getting the rest as King is keen to complete the 1600 pictures by the autumn of 1916. Hopes Porter's health is improving.

List of outstanding signatures 9.8.16. Another list of outstanding signatures 23.8.16

Letter 13th October 1916 from Sandringham

Very anxious to get the signature of Sir Joseph Hawley for the King's collection – also that of Matthew Dawson, the trainer. Please reply to Marlborough House where he returns on Monday morning.

Letter 2nd October 1918 from Sandringham.

Include in book – a must. Dated by ref to when he joined the army – nearly 70 years – he joined up in 1849.

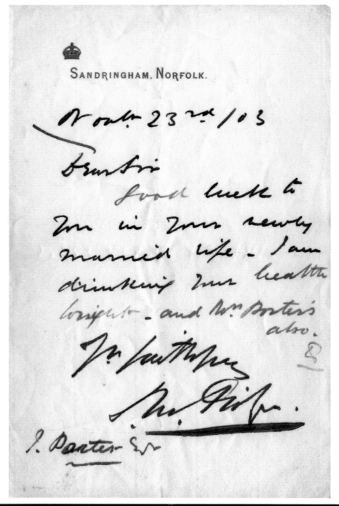

SANDRINGHAM, NORFOLK.

Nov. 23rd /03

Dear Sir

Good luck to
you in your newly
married life — I am
drinking your health
tonight — and Mr. Porter's
also.

Yrs faithfully

[signature]

S. Porter Esq.

BUCKINGHAM PALACE.

FROM

GENERAL
SIR DIGHTON PROBYN.

TO

Mr John Porter

May 15th 1910

Dear Mr Porter

I hope you may
be able to attend the Funeral
Service at St George's on
Friday — I enclose a ticket
for the Choir. which is
I believe a good position.

Yrs faithfully

[signature]

288

SANDRINGHAM, NORFOLK.

Nov 20th '05

Dear Mr Porter

Yes - it is a case of real bad luck about the great Horse "Persimmon" - but he is going on well - could not be doing better,

better, - and although useless for this season, I hope and believe he will return to the Stud with renewed energy next year -

He was looking magnificent upto the accident -

Yes - we have some good - looking Yearlings, and I hope also a few 2 year olds that may be able to gallop a bit -

Thanks for your good wishes for the New Year which I reciprocate.

Yrs faithfully

Sandringham,
Norfolk.

To be at the front door
to see His Royal Highness
at 10 o'ck. To view the grounds,
Park House, Tennis Court,
Church. Home Farm Dairy,
Gas works, Kennels, Water Works
Tower, & Sandringham Club.
Lunch at Mr. Prince's. & —
then go to Babingly Farm.
& Wolferton. do. to see —
the Prize Cattle. Where Mr.
Beck H.R.H. Agent met me.
Viewed the Stables afterwards.

MARLBOROUGH HOUSE.

FROM	TO
GENERAL SIR DIGHTON PROBYN.	John Porter Esq.,

June 11th 191 6.

Dear Mr Porter,

How are you ?   I hope well ? I have not seen you for ages.

The King has a very large collection of "Vanity Fair Cartoons" – all framed, classified, and catalogued – carefully arranged on the walls of Birkhall, a Shooting Lodge near Balmoral.

I am now trying to get for His Majesty, the signatures of all who have been "cartooned", to place under their pictures.

I find there are still 19 Jockeys – professional and amateur – whose signatures I have not yet been able to procure.   A thought has struck me that you perhaps might

be

be able to get some of the signatures for me. I shall
feel obliged therefore if you will kindly look through the
list, and just mark off on it, on the left hand side of the
paper, opposite the man's name, the words, "Yes" "NO" or
"perhaps".

"Yes" will mean you know, or think you can get
the signature. "No" that you are sure you cannot get it,
and "perhaps" that it is doubtful, but you will try.

You of course are in this big Gallery, and your
signature I already have, to place under your picture when
the work of affixing the signatures is taken in hand, as it
will be very shortly I hope now.

Yours faithfully,

D. M. Probyn.

FROM

GENERAL
SIR DIGHTON PROBYN.

TO

J. Porter. Esq.
Ormonde House.

June 15th *191*6   Newbury.

Dear Mr Porter,

Just a line to thank you for yours of yesterday received this morning.

I am indeed sorry to hear you have been so unwell, but
hope as you appear now to be on the mend, that you may soon
be all right, and that we may meet again ere long.

By the bye, I should add that since I wrote you, I have
obtained Mornington Cannon's signature, so you need not
think of that. Any of the others that you think you may
probably get, I shall be very grateful for.

M. faithfully

D. M. Probyn

MARLBOROUGH HOUSE.

FROM

GENERAL
SIR DIGHTON PROBYN.

TO

John Porter. Esq.
Ormonde House.

June 17th 1916   Newbury.

Dear Mr Porter,

On looking through the list again, I find
I omitted the name of FRED ARCHER from the one I gave you.
Will you please therefore kindly add it to my roll of
requirements and tell me whether I may record him on your
part as "Perhaps" "Yes" or "No".

I want three of him, please.

Yours faithfully,

MARLBOROUGH HOUSE.

FROM

GENERAL
SIR DIGHTON PROBYN.

TO

John Porter Esq.
Ormonde House

July 4th 1916   Newbury.

Dear Mr Porter,

I am now making a supreme effort to get
every signature I can for the King's Vanity Fair Collection,
I shall therefore be glad to hear from you if you have had
any success in procuring some of the signatures which you
so kindly said you would endeavour to get hold of. If so,
will you please send me what you have already got.

Yours faithfully,

292

FROM	TO
GENERAL SIR DIGHTON PROBYN.	John Porter. Esq. Ormonde House. Newbury.

July 7th   1916

Dear Mr Porter,

    I am very much obliged to you for the 3 signatures, of Fred Archer, George Fordham and James Woodburn, you have kindly sent me with your letter of the 4th inst., which reached me yesterday.

    They are most encouraging, as you were doubtful about getting the signature of the "Grand old Jockey" George Fordham, and Woodburn you were afraid there was no chance of getting. This therefore gives me great hopes for the future.

    I shall indeed feel very much obliged if you will kindly continue in your persevering search to get hold of some more of them, and I shall be glad if as you get one or two even at a time, you would let me have them, as the operation of sticking them on the pictures at Birkhall is shortly to commence, and as every one of the 1600 pictures

                has

FROM	TO
GENERAL SIR DIGHTON PROBYN.	

191

has to be unframed to have the signature stuck on the Cartoon, it will take time. The King being most interested in this work gives me an urgent desire to complete it as far as possible during this summer and autumn.

    I do hope your health is improving, and that if you are not already, you may soon be as well as you were years ago when we first met.

        Yours faithfully,

Names of Jockeys, Professional & Amateur, whose signatures are
still required for the King's Gallery of Vanity Fair Cartoons
at Birkhall.

Names.	Soubriquet.	Date.
2 Archer Fred.	"The Favourite Jockey."	1881.
Barrett Fred.	"Fred Barrett".	1889.
Catena Count Della.	"Count Strickland".	1893.
Dillon Bernard.	"Bernard"	1906.
Johnstone Capt: W. Hope.	"Wenty".	1897.
Loates Sam.	"Sam Loates".	1896.
Maher Danny.	"Danny"	1903.
Owen Capt: Edward Rodney.	"Roddy".	1891.
Reiff John.	"Johnnie"	1900.
Reiff Lester.	"Lester"	1900.
Sloan Tod.	"An American Jockey".	1899.
Templeman Arthur.	"A rising Star".	1908.
Thursby Mr George. J.	"Mr George".	1907.

augt 9. 116.

List of Jockeys whose signatures are still required for the

Vanity Fair Gallery at Birkhall.

Archer Fred

Barrett Fred.

Catena Count Della.

Dillon Bernard.

Johnstone Captain Wentworth.

~~Loates Sam.~~

Maher Danny.

Owen Captain E. Rodney.

Sloan Tod.

~~Templeman Arthur.~~   *Mallid*

~~Thursby George.~~

23.8.16

294

BIRKHALL,
BALLATER, N.B.

FROM   TO

GENERAL   John Porter. Esq.
SIR DIGHTON PROBYN.

September 6th   191 6

Dear Mr Porter,

In the list of Jockeys still required which
I sent you on September 3rd, I am glad to say I have since
received from other quarters,

Sam Loates, Arthur Templeman, and George Thursby.
Please therefore scratch them out of the list I gave you,
and also John Corlett's name if he was amongst the Racing
Men.

Yours faithfully,

SANDRINGHAM.

Friday night
Octr 13th/16

Dear Mr Porter
I am very
anxious to get
for the King's Collection
of Vanity Fair Cartoons
which you have
already helped so
much, the signature
of Sir Joseph Hawley -

It has been suggested
to me that you pos=
=sibly might have
one, or be able to get
one for me — perhaps.
I know if you can
help to secure this
signature you will —
Then the signature
of Mr Matthew Dawson.
"Matt", I also want,
and

and I shall be grateful
if you can get this
also for the collection —
Please reply to me
at Marlborough House
where I go on Monday
morning —

Yrs faithfully

S. W. Rolfe

Poor dear Lady! This
is a trying time for
Her Majesty — She is
of course very anxious
about her sister, the
Dowager Empress of
Russia — God only knows
what may not happen
to her in that wild
Country in which Satan
has lately been running loose.
Hoping you keep well
I remain

Yrs faithfully

S. W. Rolfe

SANDRINGHAM.

October 2nd 1910
(After post)

Dear Mr Porter
I ought long
ago to have acknow-
ledged and thanked
you for your letter
which I received some
10 days or more ago —
It was forwarded to
me in Scotland, where
I have lately been spending
some weeks in the
Highlands

Highlands, at Birkhall,
as usual — For the last
quarter of a Century, I have,
through the kindness of
our Sovereigns, the late
Queen Victoria, and
King Edward, and
since their Majesties'
deaths, by the kindness
of King George, ~~have~~
been allowed to occupy
Birkhall for a good
part of the Summer during
the last 25 years — It

is a delightful little
Shooting Box, and
the change to that de-
-lightful air always
does me good —

Yes — poor Jackson
has gone! He was a real
"institution" in this
place — all miss him
much — He was getting
on in years, though a good
bit my junior — In a
very few days I shall be
entering my 70th year since
I "took the Shilling" — I am
now well advanced in
my 47th year since I en-
-tered Queen Alexandra's Service.
Poor

297

Montague Corry – 1st Baron Rowton

Generally known as "Monty". He was private secretary to Benjamin Disraeli from 1866 until Disraeli's death in 1881. He was private secretary, even when Disraeli was not Prime Minister. The two men worked closely together. He was Disraeli's executor.

Letter 17th August 1894 from Rowton's London home

Asking Porter if he could possibly take his coachman's son into his stable or possibly find him a position with another trainer. Rowton's coachman had been with him for 10 years. Encloses some particulars about the boy, who is ready to go to Kingsclere at any time, for the purpose of "being inspected".

Letter 2nd September 1894

Thanks Porter for quick reply. Has spoken to his coachman and has ascertained the boy has no strong desire to be a jockey. He would however very much like to learn the job of being a stable lad at Kingsclere. Asks if boy could visit Kingsclere for approval by Porter or his deputy. Gives Porter his coachman's address to make direct contact.

An illustration of Porter's well-mannered way of dealing with matters and his wish to give youngsters a start in a new career.

Monty Corry was a friend of Queen Victoria and advised her to speak sensitively to H.R.H. Prince of Wales about his gambling.

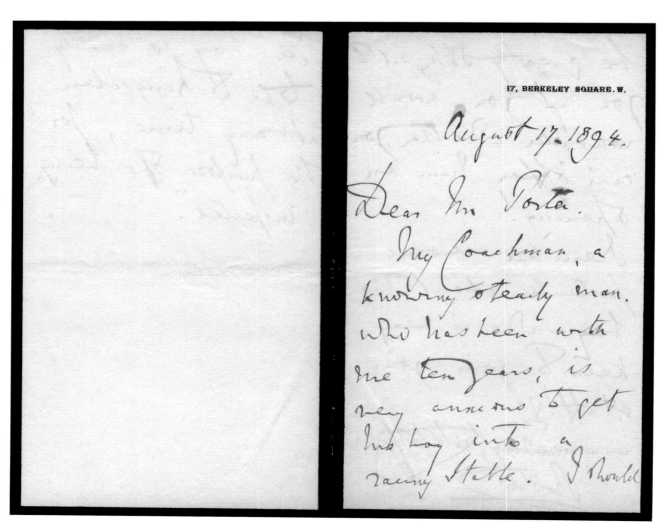

be greatly obliged to you if you would consider whether you can offer him an opening.

I enclose some particulars about the boy — who is very keen to join your staff. I am

very faithfully yrs

Rowton

The boy is ready to go to Kingsclere at any time, for the purpose of being "inspected".

may send.

The address is
Mr Harper.
3 Archibald Mews
Farm St
Mayfair.

I am very faithfully yrs

Rowton

17 Berkeley Square

Bolton Abbey.
Skipton.

Sept 2. 94

Dear Mr Porter.

Very many thanks for your kind and prompt attention to my recent letter.

I have, since I wrote you answer, seen my Coachman. I find the

299

boy has no special
wish to become a
jockey: — and, if
you would let him learn
stable work, in your
stables, I should be
very much obliged to
you.

Of course you are
very busy just
now! but, perhaps,

later on. you would
let the boy visit
Kingsclere, & be
approved of by you.
or any one you may
depute: or perhaps he
could be "looked over"
in London.

At all events. he
is ready to obey
any summons you

Francis Jeune - 1st Baron St Helier
1843 – 1905

Was a judge from 1891 – 1905. President of the Probate, Divorce and Admiralty Division of the High Court, 1892-1905 and Judge Advocate-General for the same period.

7th December letter from 79 Harley Street to Mrs Porter from Lady Jeune, inviting the Porter family to Arlington Manor on 27th December at 10 o'clock for a play. Please advise number so that Lady Jeune can arrange enough seats. Arlington Manor, Berkshire being the Jeune's country house.

Letter 1st June written by Lord Jeune

Congratulates Porter on Flying Fox. Consolation for "Orme". Sorry about French horse breaking its leg. They all won their money so were very pleased. Sending a small souvenir for Porter's daughter.

Letter 30th April written by Lord Jeune.

Ref. the Derby is coming to Kingsclere

Possible visit to Porter of his sister the Dowager Lady Tweedsdale to Kingsclere.

Sunday – undated

Letter to Mr Williams – Porter's son-in-law asking him to vet a horse at 10.45.

There is no indication that Francis Jeune ever owned a racehorse. The Porter and Jeune families were obviously good friends as well as being neighbours.

79. HARLEY STREET.
W.

[handwritten letter, largely illegible]

Dear Miss Porter upstairs

Dear Porter

Dear Mr

Brierly

M. Mure

Don't answer this

Dear Miss Porter I

must send you

one line to tell

you how glad I was

to see "Byng" the

[...] yesterday. I

was recently at the

[...] She said

you told her that

I was unkindly

... his leg. We all

how our money to

be were very pleased

... we got on at St Dun-

... the academy to

we did well. Her

you will have a

very cheery wedding

... sending you daughter

a small souvenir

today. Don't trouble

to answer this

... not feeling

... her he has

... the

... while ... you

... I was very

sorry about the

... have it

was hard ... feeling

April 30th

79, HARLEY STREET,
W.

My dear Mr Porter

I waited for a day or two to write & congratulate you on your victory in the two Thousand & now the Derby is coming to complete. I do like that

is a receipt, indeed I think it must be when you will be overwhelmed with congratulations from your many friends - I hope the Duke was pleased at having such a good horse. What a good horse must have been shown such a

pure sort. My sister the Dowager Lady Tweeddale is spending the summer at Arlington she is very anxious to see over the horses. May she do so some day it would be such a pleasure to her & you would like her for she is very clever & nice. Miss Porter is one of your daughters. When does his marriage

come off? Mr Francis joins with me in warm congratulations & believe me

Sincerely

M. [illegible]

Sunday

79. HARLEY STREET.
W.

Dear Mr Williams - I
have a horse want
you to it be can at
Talkmates Terminus
Stile be there about
10.45. can you come

truly

M. Allen

304

Leopold de Rothschild
1845-1917

Was a British banker, thoroughbred racehorse breeder and a member of the prominent Rothschild family.

On the death of his uncle Baron Mayer de Rothschild in 1874, he became head of the family's banking business in London.   He also inherited Ascott House in Ascott, Buckinghamshire.

An avid sportsman, he established Southcourt Stud in Southcourt, Bedfordshire. He put together a stable of some of the best thoroughbreds in Europe. His horses won a number of the prestigious races including the Epsom Derby, St Leger and the 2000 Guineas. He won the Derby twice – in 1879 with Sir Bevys and in 1904 with St Amant, a 25 year gap. The 1904 win was eight years after another of his horses – St Frusqui had been beaten by a neck by Persimmon owned by H.R.H. the Prince of Wales.

Letter 4th April from Ascot

Thanking for condolence on death of brother.

Letter 5th March 1912

Thanks for letter congratulating him on 'providential escape'.   Was this an attempt on his life or an accident?

Letter 3rd October 1914 from Gunnersbury Park

Thanks Porter for sending him the list of all his winners – marvels at his career as a trainer and that he has now founded the best race course in England – Newbury. Terribly sad to think this horrid war should cause so much misery to us all. "Ps thanks for enquiring about health. I am glad to say I am thoroughly well) again".

He and his wife attended Ascot in company with the Sassoons. Their trainer was Alfred Hayhoe. Leopold arranged the reconciliation of Sir George Chetwynd with Lord Durham following his libel case brought by Chetwynd. Leopold in 1893 had staying with him the Hon. George Lambton and Lord Stanley (later Lord Derby), who had just returned from Canada. He told of his father's plans to restore the Derby stables and asked Hon George Lambton to be his trainer. After some persuasion, Lambton agreed and was the Lord Derby's trainer for the next thirty years.

King Edward as a sportsman was by far the most popular man in England and in this respect Leopold de Rothschild was second only to him.

Leopold de Rothschild had a home in Newmarket Palace House – now home of the National Horse Racing Museum. They had a wonderful collection of racing pictures on display.

Leopold only had two trainers in his long career on the Turf – Alfred Hayhoe and John Watson.

Leopold was a busy man but had a great love for racing He managed his horses himself and arranged the trials. He always made his jockeys wear colours, boots and breaches in all trials.

He was very fond of betting and always liked to have his friends 'on' if he had a good win.   He was always proud of his horses and was at times guilty of over rating them.

He was emotional and excitable and at times quick tempered, but this was balanced with the ability to be generous and openhearted in making amends.

Leopold was always a staunch supporter of any jockey who rode for him – win or lose. Of those who rode for him, he probably liked George Fordham the best.

Ascott,
Wing,
Leighton Buzzard.

Dear Porter,

Pray accept my most grateful thanks for your kind letters of sympathy in our great sorrow. My brother always spoke so highly of you. & I feel sure that you realise the loss we have all sustained

Yours very truly
[signature]

New Court,
St. Swithin's Lane, E.C.

5 March 1912

My dear Porter

I thank you with all my heart for writing to congratulate me on my providential escape I am very grateful

I am very fortunate to have so many good friends especially you. Believe me

Yours truly
[Rothschild]

I hope you have quite recovered from the influenza

Gunnersbury Park.
Acton. W.

October 3rd, 1914.

Dear Mr. Porter,

I cannot thank you suffi-
ciently for sending me the list of
all your winners.   It is marvellous
the number of winners you have trained during your career - a great
record - besides which you have founded the best race course in England.
It is terribly sad to think that
this horrid war should cause so much
misery to us all, but we must hope
that it will soon be over and that
our favourite amusements will then

be resumed in the usual way.

With my kindest regards,

Yours truly,

Leopold de Rothschild

P.S.   Many thanks for your kind
enquiries about my health;   I am glad
to say I am thoroughly well again.

William Mansfield – 1st Viscount Sandhurst
1855 – 1921

British Liberal Politician & Colonial Governor
Succeeded to the title in 1876, aged 20, with entitlement to sit in House of Lords when aged 21.
1880, was appointed Lord-in-Waiting by William Gladstone, held office until 1885. From 1892 –
1895 he was Under Secretary of State for War.
In 1895 he was appointed Governor of India - a post he held until 1900.
He served as Lord Chamberlain of the household under George V from 1912 – 1921 when
Asquith and Lloyd George were Prime Minister.
He was appointed Viscount in 1917.
Letter written 9th February 1920, the year prior to his death in November 1921.
The letter is written on the paper of the office of the Lord Chamberlain.
From this letter he had clearly been a keen follower of racing all his life, reference to Matt Dawson
and the two Lord Falmouths. Porter's book obviously brought back many memories of horses. He
refers to some of Porter's and other horses, also referring to Porter's founding of Newbury
Racecourse.

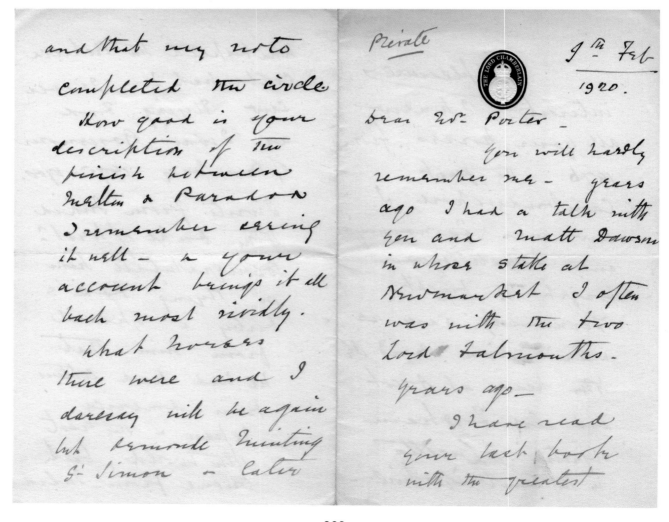

and pleasure

interest I knew
all your horses from
1876 the first
Cambridgeshire I
saw was Isonomy's
and I shall never
forget the fight
Fernandez gave us
when he ran Bend Or
to the head at Ascot
and also Fordham
objection to Lucetta
in the Cambridgeshire —

what speed the Rebecca
Colt had! I never
saw Flying Fox
as I was Governor
of Bombay 1895 - 1900.
I wrote from India
to the Duke of West:
to congratulate him
on Flying Fox's
Derby & I heard
from him that
he had had letters
from America
Japan & the rest
of the world, but
none from India

a most interesting
record —
Prices and
emoluments are
very different now
from what they
were in your
early days. !!
I hope Newbury
is turning out a
great success
Faithfully yours
Sandhurst

2

Barcaldine were giants.
Saraband had fine
speed I think saw
him win the Chesterfield
Cup I think with 8.8
& 8.7. but it is
long ago.
I remember a
famous quartette
in Matt's stable
Wheel of Fortune
Silvio Jannette
& Hampton — how

long Lord Falmouth used to look at them I was then with him often, Matt, & Archer — what a wonder Archer was to get "home".

Of course while it was impossible for me to compare I always thought

Osmonde the greatest wonder of all —

They were cheerful days and I used to love the early mornings & the early work.

Again — your book is truly delightful &

310

Archibald Primrose - 5th Earl of Rosebery
1847 – 1929

Liberal Statesman and Prime Minister 1894 – 1895
Letter 13th September 1872 from Danum House, Doncaster. Written as a young man of 25. He had approached Porter with the idea that he might seek Sir Joseph Hawley's acceptance of him as a patron at Kingsclere. Rosebery had evidently purchased 3 yearlings, but then had second thoughts about keeping them. He ends his letter thus "I hope you did not write to Sir Joseph before you got my telegram".
He was obviously very keen not to look foolish to Sir Joseph. He urged Porter to send him a line to 2 Berkeley Square London W. to clarify the situation.
Letter 16th June 1895 from 10 Downing Street, written 6 days before his resignation as Prime Minister.
"My dear Mr Porter, What have you done or decided about Woodyates?"
This letter seems to refer to a request by letter (18th April 1895) to Porter from the Earl of Shaftesbury concerning Porter visiting Woodyates – where William Day had trained – to give his views on the establishment and the viability of its refurbishment as a training yard.
Letter 4th October 1914
Porter had supplied Rosebery with a roll of honour containing all Porter's winners "It will form a valuable item in my racing library at Epsom". Expresses thanks for roll of honour.

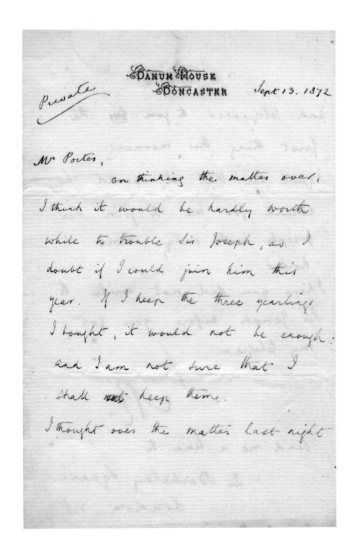

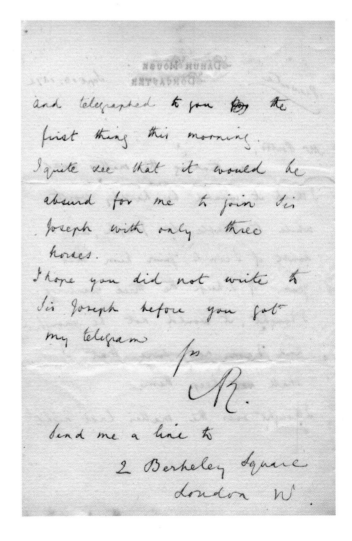

ROSEBERY
GOREBRIDGE
Dictated.   MIDLOTHIAN
                Oct 4th 1914.

My dear Porter,

            I am very much obliged
to you for the Roll of Honour, which
you have sent me, containing all your
many winners. It will form a valuable
item in my racing library at Epsom.

            I hope that all is well
with you.

            Believe me,
            Yours sincerely,

                Rosebery.
                        pp

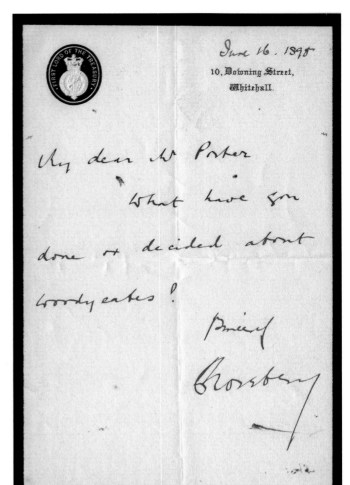

June 16. 1895

10, Downing Street,
Whitehall.

My dear Mr Porter

        What have you

done or decided about

Goodyeates?

            Briefly

            Rosebery

Caroline Agnes, Duchess of Montrose.
1818 – 1894.

Although there is only one letter written by her in the archive, she is too great a racing personality to overlook.

On the 'Turf' she was known as Mr Manton, due to the prevailing idea that owners, trainers and breeders were a male preserve. A view supported by the Jockey Club.

Whilst she could be warmhearted, cheery and genial she also had a virulent and often uncontrolled temper which explains her frequent change of jockeys, trainers and her domestic staff. She was overtly enthusiastic as a racehorse owner and breeder but was too impulsive and erratic to achieve the success her enthusiasm deserved. In course of time she found it impossible to obtain the services of the best jockeys to ride for her and trainers to train for her.

Her first husband, the Duke of Montrose, died in 1874. She married for the second time, William Stuart Stirling-Crawfurd, in 1878. He was a very successful owner and breeder of racehorses. Their marriage had all the appearances of being a very happy one. They moved into Newmarket having taken a lease on Sefton Lodge and stables in Bury Road. Additions to the original buildings were made to suit his new wife.

'Craw', as he was known, was very indulgent of his wife's behaviour, which over time damaged his good name amongst the racing community. An example of her erratic behaviour was her scratching of her horse Thebais shortly before it was due to run in the Cambridgeshire. Her reason being that its odds had shortened sharply before she had time to place her bet. This action by an owner was not acceptable and for some time she and her horses were booed when appearing on the racecourse.

Another example of her eccentricity was the berating of the vicar who offered prayers for fine weather for the harvest when her horse running in a Classic required soft going.

'Craw' died in 1883. She was distraught, selling the stable with its horses and retired from racing. To his memory she had built, St Agnes Church, in Bury Road a short walk from Sefton Lodge. She spared no expense in its building. For her it was a physical epitaph of a very happy marriage. It remains today a unique example of the high Victorian use of tile and mosaic.

Again her erratic behaviour was soon to manifest itself. Just eight months after her husband's death she was back on the racing scene.

She adopted the title 'Mr Manton' to get round the Jockey Club rule that only male's could be trainers rule. Nonetheless the rules meant she could neither own nor train horses, as it was with other women. Nor could she place a bet. Such activities had to be carried out by a male third party – a trainer or Head Lad.

In August 1888she eloped with Marcus Henry Milner, she was 70, he 24. It appeared she needed a man to advise her on her finances. He was after a generous marriage and life settlement. They soon parted but never divorced and he had little expertise in racing. She unsuccessfully attempted to have the settlements overturned. He followed a full time Army career.

She continued with her racing until her death in 1894. She was buried beside 'Craw' at the little Church she had built as a mausoleum to his memory.

Letters from her to Porter illustrate her handwriting to be as flamboyant as her character. Sometimes barely readable.

45, Belgrave Square,
S.W.

Dear Mr Porter

Your once said at Newmarket that you could tell me [illegible] [illegible] for my [illegible] [illegible] [illegible] would you would do me the great kindness if you would take an arrangement for [illegible] [illegible] the day [illegible] [illegible] [illegible] [illegible] [illegible] [illegible] [illegible] Travels to Newmarket I would send you a cheque for the whole expense. It is impossible to get [illegible] near Newmarket —

[illegible] [illegible] you [illegible] [illegible] [illegible] [illegible] [illegible] [illegible] [illegible] [illegible] [illegible] Hope [illegible] [illegible] [illegible] [illegible] pleasing [illegible] [illegible] [illegible] [illegible] [illegible] [illegible] "Charles Edward" is doing well

Yrs Faithfully
C. Montrose

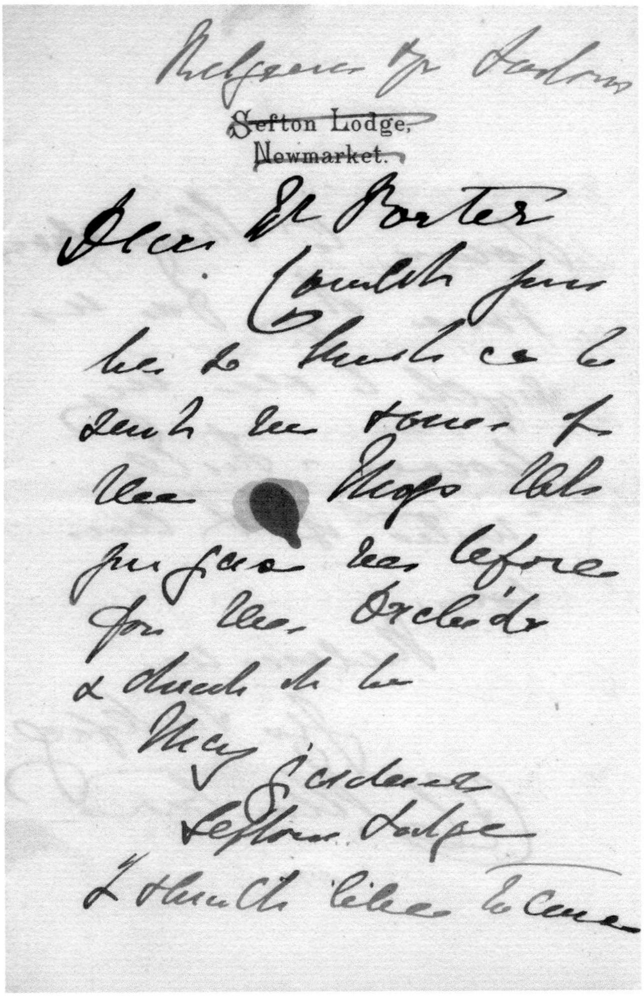

Sefton Lodge,
Newmarket.

Dear Mr Porter
[illegible]
[illegible]
[illegible]
[illegible]
[illegible]
My Address
Sefton Lodge
I should like to come

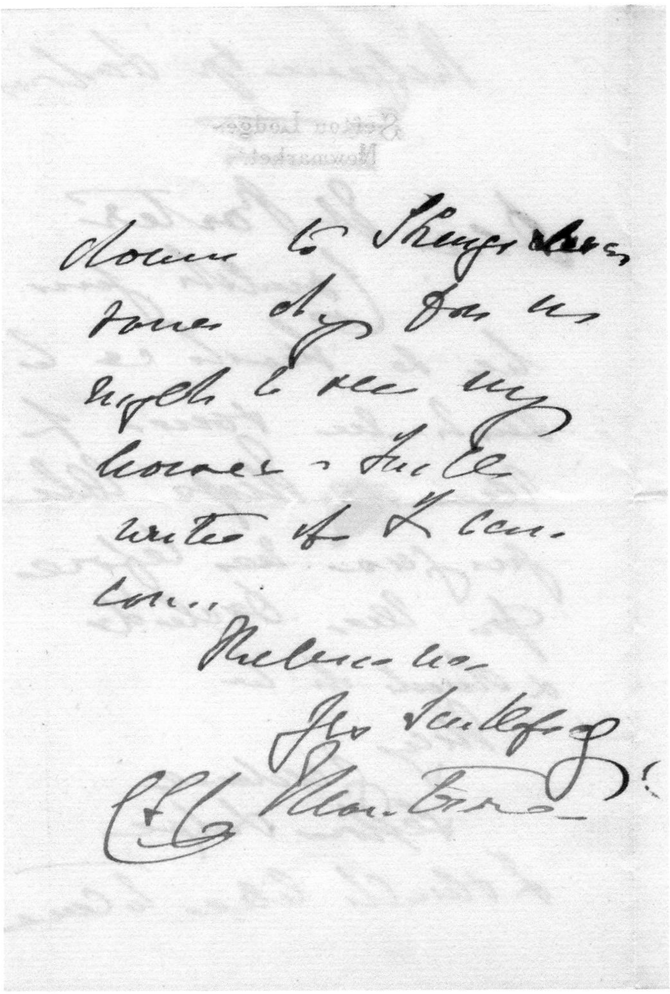

Sefton Lodge
Newmarket.

down to Kingsclere
some day for us
ought to see my
horses & will
write if I can
come...
Believe me
Yrs faithfully
C.L. Montrose

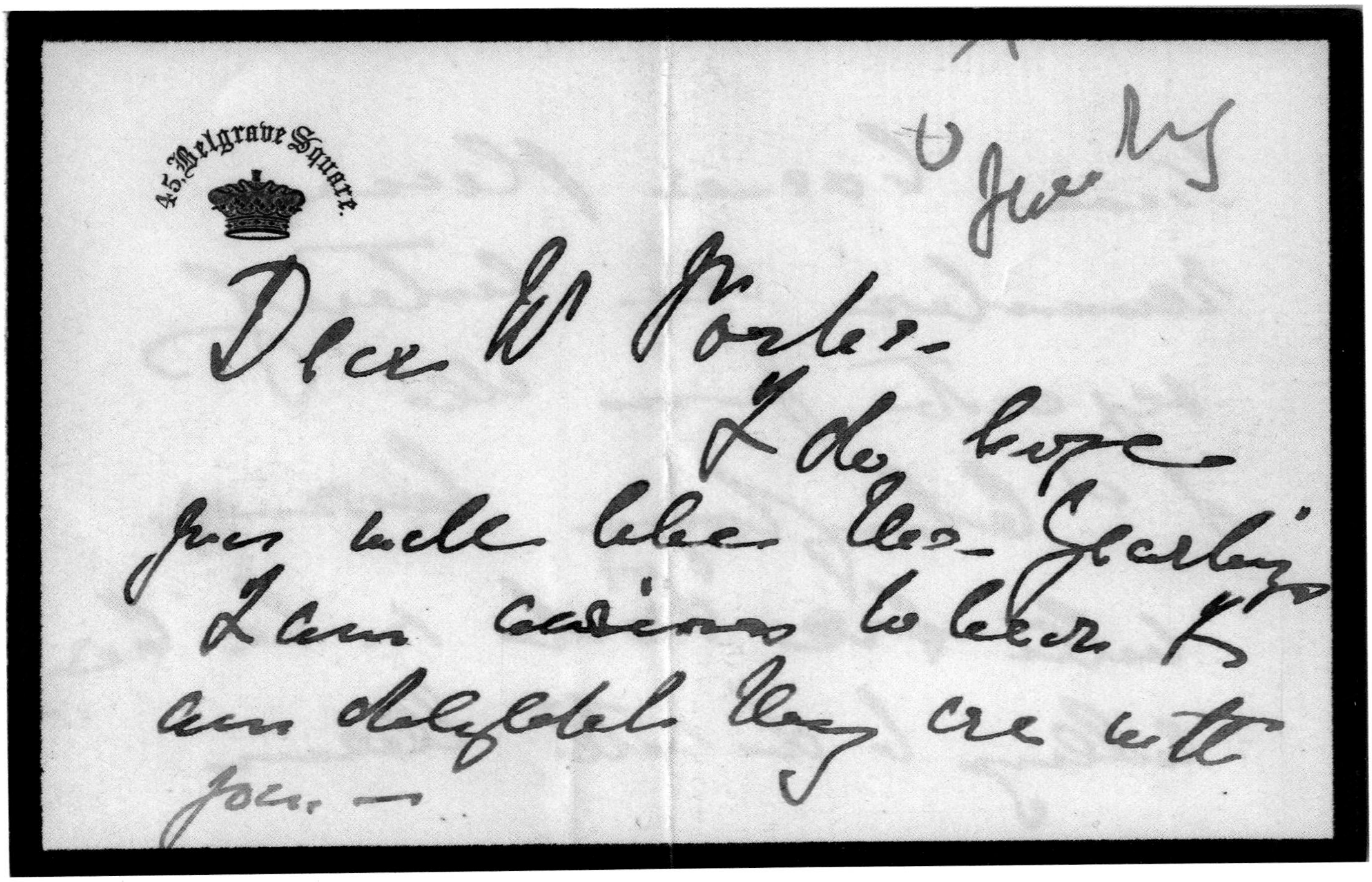

45, Belgrave Square.

[illegible]

Dear Mr Porter
I do hope
you will like the Yearlings
I am anxious to hear &
am delighted they are with
you.—

Newbury

For many years prior to his retirement from training, Porter had been mulling the idea of building a new racecourse at Newbury. At an early stage he had identified a parcel of flat land near to the town as being ideal. The land was owned by the Baxendale family who were long term friends of the Porters. Having got the permission of the Jockey Club, following the intervention of HRH Edward Prince of Wales, Porter had plans drawn up based on his considered requirements for a top class racecourse. He formed the Newbury Racecourse Company and made Lloyd H Baxendale one of the four directors.

Founding Directors of Newbury
John Porter
Lloyd H Baxendale
O. Rayner
J.J. Buchanan

Secretary of the Company – Mr G Gardner Leader
Clerk to the Company – Mr Bushby
Superintendent of Works – Mr Cotterell

Lloyd H. Baxendale was a director of Pickford's the transport company – as his father had been. He sold the land to Porter and the Company, which had formed part of the Greenham Lodge Estate. The Baxendales used to visit Kingsclere and it seems they were good friends. In the report of Thomas Barron Porter's death – he was Porter's youngest son – it refers to him playing cricket for his father's sides against the late Lloyd H. Baxendale's sides – an annual event.

Mr G Gardner Leader was a Solicitor, Mason and Vocalist, whose son Frank married John Porter's second daughter – Annie.

The Registered Office of the Company was Ormonde House, Porter's home.

Newbury
by John Porter
Something about the most up to date race course in the world.

Few things have been more gratifying to me in the whole course of a life spent on the turf than the enthusiasm of the fifteen thousand sportsmen who visited Newbury Race Course for the first time in September 1905, to witness the opening day's sport and who were obviously agreeably surprised and delighted with the perfection of the arrangements made for their comfort and convenience. The large field of twenty seven competed in the inaugural event (won by Trigg on Copper King), and no less than 177 horses ran on the two days of the first meeting. Newbury Race-course was an assured success from the very first and I think, deservedly so. It is not to be wondered at that sportsmen interested in the formation of new race-courses, and the improvement of existing ones, have visited Newbury from all parts of the world to pick up a few wrinkles.

No, I think I may claim without fear of contradiction, that the idea of a race-course at Newbury was originally conceived some twenty years ago by me and naturally it is with a certain amount of pardonable pride that I hear the completed course referred to as 'probably the most perfect racing venue in the world'. Nothing has been left to chance at Newbury. The thousand and one details necessary in the formation of a complete and thoroughly equipped race-course were carefully considered by my co-directors, Mr Lloyd H. Baxendale, Mr O. Rayner and Mr J.J. Buchanan, and myself, and were carried out with the able assistance of Mr G. Gardner Leader, secretary to the company, Mr Bushby, clerk of the company and last but by no means least, Mr Cotterell, who has superintended the whole of the work done in the formation of the course.

The precise situation of the course is in the parish of Greenham, in the heart of the Berkshire Downs. The Great Western main line runs past the back of the stands; and a new station, specially erected by the railway company, is only a few steps from the various entrances to the race-course. A splendid service of trains from Paddington, fifty-three miles away, lands the public on the race course within the hour and the return fares are extremely moderate. The three hundred acres of land comprising the estate of the Newbury Race-course Company are their freehold property, and were acquired cheaply enough for £30,000. Roughly speaking £100,000 has been spent on the undertaking, which has in so remarkable a manner immediately taken a high place in public favour. Newbury may be said to be in the very heart of the training country, something like 1,700 race-horses being located in the sixty establishments within a few miles. Kingsclere is seven miles away, Ilsley and Compton nine miles, Lambourn thirteen, Winchester and Beckhampton twenty-six, Burbage eighteen, Marlborough nineteen, Wantage eighteen, Chilton and Whatcombe twelve, Pewsey twenty three, Ogbourne twenty two, Swindon twenty three, Letcombe Regis eighteen, and Stockbridge twenty-six miles. It will be seen that the unique situation of the course in its close proximity to such a large number of stables has been a potent factor in its undoubted and speedy success.

As to the race-course itself, which is flat, everything has been considered to make it as perfect a racing track as possible. There is a straight mile as enacted by the Jockey Club, which is in reality as straight as if drawn by a ruler, therein greatly differing from some so-called 'straight' miles. The round course, which is pear shaped, is 166 yards short of two miles and every inch of the racing can be seen, all large trees that obstructed the view having been removed. Inside this is the steeplechase course. A great advantage here is a straight run-in of five furlongs to the winning post for all races. The finish of the straight mile, which is 105ft wide throughout is 8ft higher than it is at the commencement. At the distance there is a gentle fall of a hundred yards, and a gradual rise of fifty yards to the winning-post. It has some resemblance to the Rowley Mile at Newmarket in its "give and take". When the flat race-course was laid out it was completely re-turfed, and about three quarters of a mile of the steeple-chase track was similarly treated. There is a prepared exercise track parallel with the straight mile seven furlongs long.

Excellent arrangements have been made for artificial irrigation. A gas engine works two sets of pumps, which draw water from a borehole 150ft deep. This is conveyed through a 5in main to the centre of the two courses and there is a 4in main laid round the circular courses and a 3in branch main for the first three furlongs of the straight mile. Hydrants have been fixed all around the courses from 75yds to 100 yds apart. This very complete system of irrigation can be supplemented whenever necessary by the local water supply.

The stands are massively and prettily constructed They are of a pleasing design in red brick, with the woodwork and girders picked out in white paint and proudly towering into the sky from the emerald green of the race course, form a landmark which can be seen for miles around. The architect, Mr C. W. Stephens who had previous experience in this direction in the construction of the new stand at Ascot, was particularly ingenious in his plans for those at Newbury. These are built up against the sides of a large artificial hill. There are two floors for all departments, the upper floor being entered from the level of the rings, and the lower one from the paddock at the rear.

The various luncheon rooms are particularly commodious, and the bar accommodation is ample. The sanitary and lavatory arrangements throughout are complete and the fittings in every department as luxurious as those to be met with in a first class club. The cloak-room provided for the accommodation of fair sportswomen is unique.

Nowadays numerous members of the fair sex motor to the meeting (there is by the way a garage and repair shop attached to Newbury) – making extensive changes in their wardrobe on arrival. One side of the room under notice is fitted with large square pigeon-holes. These are specially adapted for the reception of the hat-boxes containing the latest thing in head-wear, which takes the place of motor-hats when Newbury is reached. In the event of any of the ladies' garments getting wet *en route,* a special steam drying range is fitted up, and here the clothing can dry during the progress of the racing. Large pier glasses and a thorough qualified ladies' maid in attendance, further gladden the hearts of the fair sex.

Each spectator, from the King down to the occupants of the spacious silver ring, can see every inch of the racing from start to finish, the angle at which the stands are constructed being excellent. There is no cramping in the rings here, there being ample accommodation for very large crowds. The member's lawn in front of the specially constructed and artistic royal box, is very spacious and Tattersall's ring is the same. Separated from the latter by an iron-railed police passage is the extensive silver ring, the inclusive charge to which is 5s. Like Tattersall's ring this is asphalted, and a splendid range of stands affords shelter in wet weather. The rings are nicely graded and wherever one may happen to be standing a complete view of the racing can be seen. Admissions to the park through which the general public can roam at will to see the various starts or finishes they list, is 2s 6d.

When the King paid his promised visit to Newbury last July, the directors reduced this low charge to the public to 1s. It may be remarked that his Majesty expressed the utmost delight with the perfect arrangements and there is no doubt that the new fixtures will in the future be frequently honoured by the ever-welcome presence of the first sportsman in the land. The special arrangements devised for the royal visitors are very complete and attractive. A covered stand from the station leads to a separated entrance to the King's suite of rooms. A short flight of stairs ascends directly into a retiring room, upon the walls of which hangs amongst other sporting pictures, a striking oil-painting by the famous horse-painter Herring, of the great match between Voltigeur and Flying Dutchman. The box from which the royal party witness the racing is very roomy and artistic. The front of it is bow-shaped, the windows being formed of movable glass panels. From this box, which is in direct line with the winning-post, a splendid view of the racing and the surrounding country is obtained. On the ground floor is the luncheon room, where the prevailing colour scheme of the decorations and furniture is green. Hanging on the walls are some very fine oil paintings of famous race-horses. These formerly adorned Park House, Kingsclere, when I resided there.

Leading off the apartment is the excellently equipped service room, where the royal lunch is prepared, with its numerous gas and cooking ranges etc. In a few years' time the exterior of that part of the stands containing the royal suite will be most picturesque, as the walls will then be hidden by the delightful clinging foliage of the climbing creeper Ampelopsis Veichii, several plants of which are already making rapid upward progress. Excellent and commodious stand accommodation has been erected for the general public in the principal ring, and special portions allocated for members of the Jockey Club, stewards of the meeting, owners, trainers, jockeys and members of the press.   The large number of private boxes for club members were speedily taken by prominent sportsmen. The jockey's commodious dressing-room has a bathroom attached and leading out of this is a lofty weighing room, with an enormous pair of jockey scales railed off in the centre under a domed skylight. There is an electric signalling board close by, and as each jockey is weighed out for a race the number of the horse he rides is worked on the switch-board and the corresponding figure instantly appears on the electric number frame in Tattersall's ring. Simultaneously, the number of the horse and the name of the jockey are telephoned to the official in charge of the large number board on the far side of the course and the public learn these important items of information as expeditiously as possible. At the back of the stands there is a very extensive and charmingly laid-out paddock with green-turfed, undulating lawns.

Lovers of flowers are well catered for; and numerous flower beds from the centre of which sapling poplars rise, are dotted here and there, brightening the scene with multi-coloured blooms. This year giant mignonette thrived splendidly here, and the paddock was filled with its delicate perfume at the September meeting. In course of time Newbury paddock bids fair to be a miniature Kew Gardens. Later on an extra dining room will be erected amidst these delightful floral surroundings, where a large tent now does duty, and a tea-house constructed on the lines of a Swiss chalet with over hanging eaves will be built a short distance away.

The safety of visitors in the paddock has been considered, and when the horses are brought in from the stables nearby, they parade in a spacious circular railed-off enclosure for inspection. All danger from the stray kicks of the spirited thoroughbreds is thus obviated. In fact there are two of these parading enclosures and they are very ingeniously utilised. The horses ready to run in the first race walk round in No 1 and those due to compete in the following event in No 2, the latter moving into No 1 when it has been vacated, and so on. This is one of the exceedingly numerous innovations to be found at this wonderfully up-to-date meeting.

Indeed, many ingenious contrivances are to be met with on every hand. Take, for instance, the winners' unsaddling enclosure. It is divided into three separate compartments, conspicuously numbered 1,2,3. There is a separate gate for each jockey to leave this enclosure after he has unsaddled. In an ordinary race the compartments or stalls are left as they are, but should it be a selling race, the winner of which had to be sold, a couple of the employees lift up the two dividing rails forming the separate stalls, swing them back on their hinges to the side of the enclosure and take out the posts upon which they rest. The post-holes are plugged, and in a few seconds the unsaddling enclosure is converted into a sale ring, inside which the horse to be sold is paraded for the inspection of potential buyers. The auctioneer's rostrum is just outside this. Another innovation is the steward's special observation stand, which has been erected on the members' lawn. This is copied from those in use on the Australian race-courses. From it the stewards obtain an excellent bird's-eye view of the racing and are able to detect any bumping or boring, or any other foul riding which may take place. This is the only one to be found on any English race-course, but I believe two of a similar kind have recently been erected on Kingsclere Downs to enable the trainer to watch the horses do their work. A hundred yards or so away from the stands, the stables have been erected and a very handsome pile of buildings they make. In this up-to date building modernism, completeness and comfort for everyone concerned are the distinguishing features. On the right of the entrance is the canteen, where the stable boys obtain their breakfasts, which by the way are like so many other things at Newbury – free. Stabling and provender for the horses are free and luncheons for trainers, jockeys, press and police are similarly provided. The stable-boys' dormitories are large and hygienic, comfortable beds being provided for those in charge of the horses running at the meeting. A glimpse into the hay and corn store proves that nothing but the very best of every kind of provender is provided for the thoroughbreds on the free food list. There are 146 large and lofty horse boxes each measuring 14ft by 10ft. The floors of these are constructed of impervious concrete, and there is a white enamelled bin and a horse's wardrobe in each one. The light is obtained from gas jets sunk in square holes in the wall. When required for use the brackets swing out from this hole and when finished with are replaced and for safety shut off out of the way by a sliding zinc lid. There is a drying room for horses' clothing, steam-pipe racks being run round the walls and upon these the wet rugs etc. are placed to dry.

In case of accidents there is a hospital in the front part of the stable with two beds. The patients' room, which is very lofty and well-lighted is tastefully furnished in fumed oak and attached to it are a bathroom and other offices. The nurse's room overhead is charmingly arranged in fumed oak.

The Newbury Race-course is perfect in every respect and he would be a fastidious man indeed who could discover anything to find fault with.

The racing so far has been productive of excellent sport and the Newbury Spring, Summer and Autumn Cups are already important events in the racing calendar.

Mr John Porter

A man who has made over a million pounds for other men.

With a modesty as pleasing as it is uncommon on the turf, Mr John Porter, in the interesting article on Newbury, which he has been good enough to write for this magazine, mentions himself once – possibly twice. But the racing man who is really a racing man and not in the journalese hallowed by custom "a popular turfite" knows that Newbury Race-course is almost wholly the idea, the work, and production of Mr Porter. That he was justified in putting his long-standing idea into execution is now proved overwhelmingly by its success. That he was justified in doing so before the success came is, I think, as easily proved by the turf record which he has behind him. How many men can equal this:-

In the month of July 1843 and at the age of twenty five, he took up his residence at Kingsclere (a place since grown famous all the world over) and became private trainer to that celebrated sportsman. Sir Joseph Hawley (the lucky Baronet as he was then called). Since this beginning Mr Porter has trained for:-

His Majesty the King	Lord Alington
Duke of Westminster	Sir F. Johnstone
Duke of Portland	Colonel Alexander
Earl of Crewe	Mr F. Alexander
Earl of Portsmouth	Mr J. Gretton
Earl Spencer	Mr F. Gretton
Baron Hirsch	Mr W. Lowe
And others	

He has won for them in stakes alone the enormous sum of £794,017 and the profits on the sale of horses he has under his charge would bring the total up to over a million pounds sterling, an amount which has never been exceeded by any other trainer living or dead.

He has written his name boldly in classic races, having won:

	No of times		No of times
The Derby	7	Doncaster Cup	4
The Oaks	3	Brighton Cup	3
The Two Thousand	5	Prince of Wales	
The St Leger	6	Stakes, Ascot	6
The One Thousand	2	Coronation Stakes	4
*The Eclipse Stakes	5	Hardwicke Stakes	5
*Jockey Club Stakes	2	Rous Memorial, Ascot	3
*Princess of Wales		Great Yorkshire Stakes,	
Stakes, Newmarket	2	York	4
Newmarket Stakes	1	Great Foal Stakes,	
Grand Prix de Paris	1	Newmarket	6
Ascot Cup	4	Champion Stakes, Newmarket	7
Alexandra Plate	5	Craven Stakes, Newmarket	3
Gold Vase	3		
Goodwood Cup	4		
*£10,000 Stakes			

TWO YEAR OLD RACES

	No of times		No of times
New Stakes Ascot	4	City of London Breeders,	
July Stakes, Newmarket	4	Kempton	2
Chesterfield Stakes	1	Champagne, Doncaster	4
Richmond Stakes, Goodwood	4	Middle Park Plate	1
Prince of Wales Stakes,		Dewhurst Plate	7
Goodwood	5	Criterion	10

HANDICAPS

	No of times		No of times
City and Suburban	1	Stewards' Cup, Goodwood	1
Chester Cup	3	Brighton Stakes	1
Jubilee Kempton	1	Ebor Handicap	1
Manchester Cup	2	Great Yorkshire Handicap,	
Ascot Stakes	1	Doncaster	3
Royal Hunt Cup	1	Great Eastern Handicap	1
Liverpool Summer cup	2	Cesarwitch	1
Liverpool Autumn Cup	7	Cambridgshire	2
Chesterfield Cup, Goodwood	6		

A truly wonderful record!

Many other lesser races were won. Too many to list.

Today's race followers - particularly those who attend meetings at the racecourse, are probably unaware that their enjoyment is very largely the result of one man's endeavours. Undoubtedly they owe a great debt of gratitude to John Porter and it seems ironic that the proposed course turned down by the Jockey Club at several meetings, before giving Porter permission, to develop it, remains one of the foremost dual grass racetracks for both Flat and National Hunt Racing.

Letters relating to the United Services Meetings are from the following:

General Sir Horace Smith-Dorien.
Field Marshal Frederick Roberts.
Field Marshal Lord Francis Grenfell.
Admiral Michael Culme-Seymour.
Mr J.A.T.Garratt.

1st Viscount Sandhurst, William Mansfield, Lord Chamberlain.
Lt-General Sir Reginald Pole-Carew.
Major-General J.S. Cowans.
Alfred Bingham p.p. Sir Richard Sutton.
Rear Admiral Sir Christopher Craddock.
Admiral Hedworth Lambton Meux.

F. Kerausch p.p.King Manuel 2nd of Portugal.
Field Marshal Sir John French.
Major Dermot McCalmont. (Jockey /Owner.)
Prince Adolphus of Teck.
David Lord p.p. Prince Christian of Schleswig-Holstein.
Lt.Colonel Sir Edward Barry.
Mr H.G. Miles.
H.M.Pryce-Jones A.D.C. to General Sir Charles Douglas.

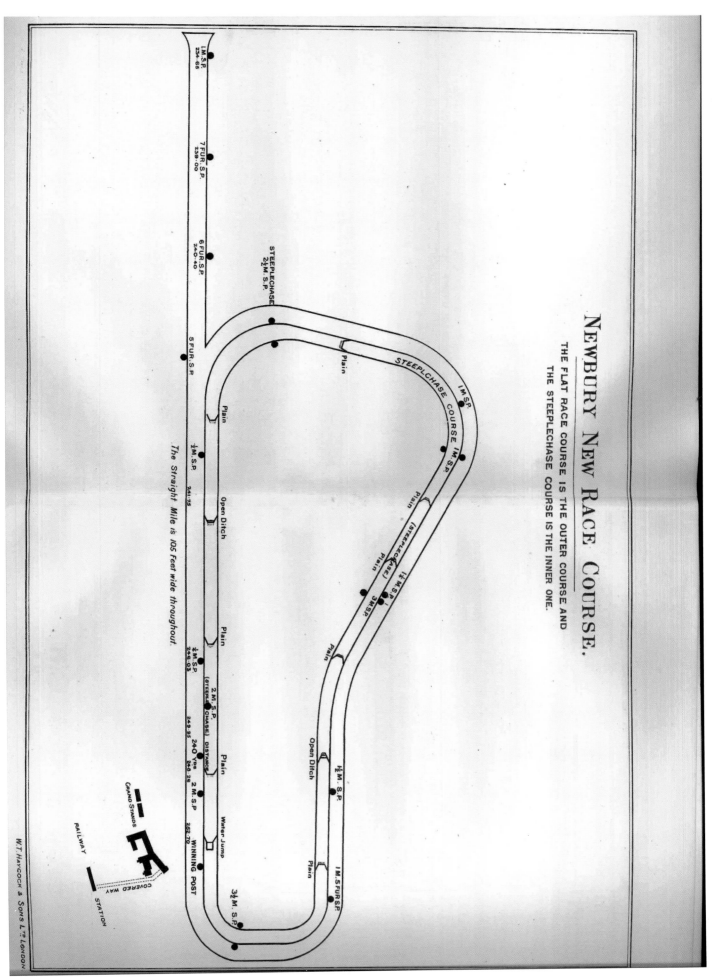

Layout of Newbury Racecourse, 1905

View of the Grandstand Newbury Racecourse, 1905.

The Directors, Newbury Racecourse Ltd, 1905
Back Row: Mr. W. E. Bushby (Clerk of Course), Mr. G. G. Leader (Secretary), Mr. C. W. Stephens (Architect)
Front Row: Mr. O.W. Rayner, Mr. John Porter, Mr. Lloyd Baxendale (Directors)

Looking up the straight mile. Newbury 1905.

ENGLEMERE.
ASCOT.
BERKS.

16 December 1910.

Dear Sir,

      I write in reply to your letter of the 14th instant to say that I am leaving home tomorrow for a visit, but I shall be glad to hear from you what it is you wish to see me about, and I will, if possible on my return arrange to meet you.

          Yours very truly

          Roberts

John Porter Esq.

ENGLEMERE.
ASCOT.
BERKS.

10 February 1911.

Dear Sir,

      I am much obliged to you for sending me the Programme of the United Services Meeting at Newbury on the 24th and 25th instant, but am sorry to say it will not be possible for me to be present at it, as I leave for the Continent on the 20th.

          Yours very truly

          Roberts Fm.

John Porter Esq.

Letters
Relating to Newbury
United Military Service
Steeplechases.
From Officers

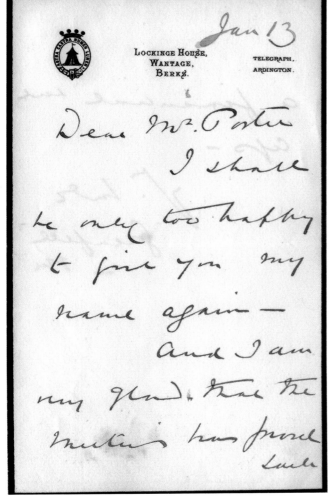

Jan 13

LOCKINGE HOUSE,
WANTAGE,
BERKS.

TELEGRAPH.
ARDINGTON.

Dear Mr Porter
I shall
be only too happy
to give you my
name again —
And I am
very glad that the
meeting has proved
such

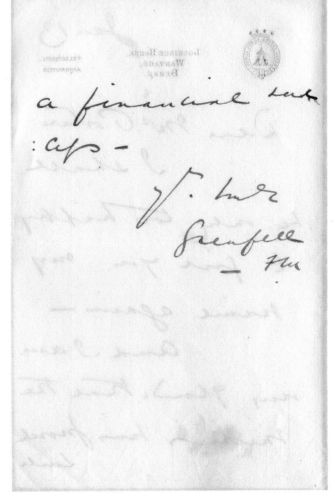

a financial
success —

J. mcr
Grenfell
— The

327

**WADENHOE HOUSE,
OUNDLE.**

Northants

28 Jan 1912

Dear Mr Porter

Your letter of the
6th only reached me this
morning, as it went out
by mistake to my son who
commands the "Argyll" &
who is one of the escort
with the King & he sent
it to me from Port Said —
If it is not too late, I
shall be glad to be one

of the patrons of the United
Service Meeting. on the
23rd & 24th Feb. & am much
obliged to you for thinking
of me. — I doubt if I
shall be able to attend
but will if I can — but
I am not always able
to get away. — We have
15° frost at present &
hunting stopped. — I
am glad to say, I get
3 days a week as a

rule. — I hope you are
keeping well.

Yours sincerely

[signature]

I wish I had a horse fit
to enter — but I have only
3 & none fast enough.

Jan 1st 1911

Dear Sir,

I shall be very
happy to act as a
Steward at your
"United Services Meeting"
I sincerely hope it
will be a success. I
think its a step in
the "right" direction &
if anyone can make

it a success you are
the man to do it.
Yours faithfully
J.A.T. Garratt

John Porter Esqr

9th Feb
1920.

Dear Mr Porter —

You will hardly remember me — years ago I had a talk with you and Matt Dawson in whose stable at Newmarket I often was with the two Lord Falmouths.

years ago —

I have read your last book with the greatest

and pleasure

interest. I knew all your horses from 1876 the first Cambridgeshire I saw was Isonomy's and I shall never forget the fight Fernandez gave us when he ran Bend Or to a head at Ascot and also Fordham objection to Lucetta in the Cambridgeshire —

what speed the Rebecca Colt had! I never saw Flying Fox as I was Governor of Bombay 1895 - 1900. I wrote from India to the Duke of West? to congratulate him on Flying Fox's Derby & I heard from him that he had had letters from America Japan & the rest of the world, but none from India

and that my note completed the circle

How good is your description of the finish between Melton & Paradox I remember seeing it well — & your account brings it all back most vividly.

What horses there were and I daresay will be again but Bermonde Mounting St Simon — Cater

330

a most interesting
record —

Prices and
emoluments are
very different now
from what they
were in your
early days. !!
I hope Newbury
is turning out a
great success
Faithfully Yours

Sandhurst

Bayardo were giants.
Saraband had fine
speed I think saw
him win the Chesterfield
Cup I think with 8.8
r 8.7. but it is
long ago.

I remember a
famous Quartette
in Matt's stable
Wheel of Fortune
Silvio Jannette
& Hampton — how

long Lord Falmouth
used to look at them
I was then with
him often, Matt.
& Archer — what
a wonder Archer
was to get "home".
Of course while
it was impossible
for me to compare
I always thought

Ormonde the
greatest wonder
of all —

They were cheerful
days and I
used to love
the early mornings
& the early work.

Again — Your
book is truly
delightful &

331

12 Jan. 1903

Dear Mr Euler

Very many thanks
for your kind letter
and good wishes – Please
accept from Lady Beatrix
and myself the very
best of every wish for
this New Year –

Of course, you are
more than welcome
to my name for your
list of Patrons for
the Newbury Spring
and United Services
Meeting – I wish you
every success, and
truly wish I had a

horse to Enter –
but, unfortunately
the devil of Poverty
prevents that –

[signature]

Your programme looks
Excellent –

War Office,
Whitehall,
S.W.

13th December 1911.

Dear Sir,

Many thanks for sending me your prospectus or card,
for the United Service Meeting in February, which I shall
most probably attend.

I shall be very pleased to be included in your list
of patrons, but I am only at the present moment Director
General of the Territorial Force, and do not take over
Quarter Master General until May.

Lieutenent General Sir Herbert Miles, K.C.B., C.V.O.,
remains as Quarter Master General until May, in case you
want to include him, but I have never seen him at a Race
Meeting!

Wishing your executive every success.

Yours
J Cowans.
Major General

The Secretary,
    Newbury Racecourse Co.,
    Ormond House,
    NEWBURY.

Jan 13. 1913

Dear Mr Porter

Certainly keep my name on
yr Patrons list for the United
Services Meeting — which I wish
could be its success I am sure it
is going to be with you at the helm.

Yrs
J Cowans.

14th Jany 1913.

TELEPHONE,
2008 MAYFAIR.

6 Bolton Street.
Piccadilly.
London.
W.

Dear Mr Porter,

Replying to yours of the
12th with programme of the
United Services Steeplechase
Meeting at Newbury
I have seen Sir Richard
Sutton and he is willing
that you should add his
name to the list of Patrons.

Faithfully Yours

Alfred J Brigham

I am anxious to bring
in the Navy.

Yours very
Christopher Cradock

P.S.
I will find lunch to
the Meeting &
I shall come if the
Secretary from our
Squadron

Telephone
2 Gilling-West.

Rear Admiral Sir Christopher
Cradock K.C.V.O—C.B

HARTFORTH GRANGE,
RICHMOND, YORKS.

Dear Mr. Porter
I shall be very
glad to accede to
your desire — it is an
honour.
I wish I had a house
myself to better — but
I must wait till

Yours faithfully
Christopher Cradock
The Admiral

Aug. 10

I am afraid there
will be no lodging from
me — as I am employed
& have no leisure at
present

TELEPHONE.
4827 GERRARD.

90, PICCADILLY,
LONDON. W.

Dear Sir.
I shall be happy
to have the honour of
my name appearing
in the list at the
best & Service Meeting
house Lib: if the
Naval Crew Company
desire it — & if the
Service permits —
hope to be there
myself.

TELEPHONE.
248 PADDINGTON.

48, BRYANSTON SQUARE,
W.

Dec 24th

Dear Porter.

I shall be very pleased
to have my name
added as a patron of
your February meeting

though I fear I have no
animal good enough to
enter.

My only jumper is
engaged in a selling
hurdle handicap Dec 29th

So kindly send me a pass
in case I can come &
see her run.

Wishing you a Merry
Christmas.

Sincere yours

Hedworth Lambton.

335

Glen Grove
Kingsclere
Newbury.
Feb. 16. 11

My dear Portie

Messrs Weatherby
have sent me
passes for Sandown
24th & 25th.
I am much
obliged to you &
the Directors –
I saw Hedworth
Lambton on 3rd –
and he said
he hoped to run
down for the meeting

With kind regards
to Mrs Portie,
Yours sincerely
W. Hemifurtle
———

Elm Grove
Kingsclere
Dec. 14. 11

My dear Porter,

I shall be highly honoured by my name appearing as one of the Patrons for the "United Services" meeting to be held at Newbury on 23rd & 24th of February next, and hope it may as successful as

it was this year. I notice that the first day is to be on my 79th birthday. Thank you for the two days shooting, also for the brace of pheasants & rabbits you kindly sent last night.

With kind regards to Mrs Porter & all good wishes to you & yours for Xmas and the New Year

I am yours sincerely
W. Hewitt Grubbe

ABERCORN,
RICHMOND,
SURREY.

Feb. 23rd 1912.

Dear Sir,

I am instructed by H. M. King
Manuel to acknowledge the receipt
of a programme of the Newbury Spring
and United Services Races, 1912, and
to express you His Majesty's sincere
thanks for your kindness.

I am, Dear Sir,

Yours very truly

F. Kerausch.

ABERCORN,
RICHMOND,
SURREY.

Feb. 15th 1911.

Sir,

I am directed by H. M. King
Manuel to express you His Majesty's thanks for the Programme
of the Spring & United Services Meeting on the 24th & 25th inst.

I am, Sir,

Yours very truly

F. Kerausch

July. 1. 1904.

My dear Mr Porter

I send on line
to thank you very
much for all your
kindness in connection
with the Cavalry
operations this week.

It is a very hopeful
sign for the future of
the Army that people
of influence
like you should set
so fine an example of
Patriotism.

You have rendered us

the greatest help in
the training of the
1st Army Corps and again
I thank you with all
my heart.

I hope an may help to
do you & Mrs Porter
over here from time to time.

Yours Sincerely
J H French

339

Horse Guards,

Whitehall, S.W.

Dec. 14th 11

Dear Mr Porter

I am directed by General Sir John French to acknowledge the receipt of your letter to him of the 11th Inst. & to assure you that he will be very glad to allow his name to be again included in the list of Patrons of "The United Services Meeting" to be held at Newbury.

Sir John wishes me to thank you for for the preliminary particulars of the events you kindly sent him.

Yrs very truly

A.F.Watt.   Major

P.S. to I.G.Forces

13th January 1913

Dear Mr. Porter,

I am directed by General Sir John French to thank you for your letter to him of the 10th instant enclosing a programme of the Newport Spring Meeting. Sir John wishes me to say that he is very glad to allow his name to appear in the list of patrons.

Yours very truly,

A.F. Watt. Major

Private Secretary to Chief of Imperial
General Staff.

General Sir Horace Lockwood Smith-Dorrien
1858 – 1930

A career soldier who served in the Zulu War – Egypt, India and Sudan. Had home postings at Aldershot and southern Command. In the 1914-18 War served at Mons, Le Cateau and Ypres.

At Aldershot he was under the command of Field Marshal Sir John French but they suffered from a personality clash going back some years.

Porter and Sir John French knew one another through common interest in the cavalry – see Sir John's letter.

An interesting letter to Porter from Smith-Dorrien dated 24th February 1911 asking Porter to show Sir John French "that bicycle ambulance tomorrow". It seems Porter had devised such a machine.

The letter from Government House Farnborough, thanking Porter for looking after Smith-Dorrien and his wife and were sorry they could not find him to thank in person. This was following one of the days of the United Services meeting at Newbury racecourse. The bicycle ambulance may have been for the use of jockeys injured on the course.

Letters confirming that both Smith-Dorrien and French were happy to be patrons on the Newbury Race Meeting.

31. 12. 11

KING EMPEROR'S CAMP,
INDIA.

Dear Mr Porter

Yours of 11th finds
me in India with the
King — I shall be proud
to have my name
included again amongst
the patrons of the
United Service Meeting
to be held in Feb'y.
next & am truly sorry
that I shall be too far
away on the 23rd & 24th
Feb'y. to be able to take
advantage of your kind
invitation to be present

Yrs truly
H S Smith-Dorrien

Harnham Cliff
Salisbury
12 Jan'y 13

Dear Mr Porter

Certainly keep
my name as a Patron —
I am only too proud
to have it there —
Wishing you a
Happy New Year
from my wife &
myself

Yrs v truly

H S Smith Dorrien

342

14.3.13

ROYAL HOTEL,
COLLEGE GREEN,
BRISTOL.

TELEGRAMS, "BANQUET, BRISTOL."
TELEPHONE Nº 3591.

Dear Mr Porter
Alas I am
away inspecting &
cannot get finished
until to-morrow
night so all
hope of my wife &
self being able to
make use of these
passes for your
Races is out
of the question.

The passes have
just reached me
here & I am
very much obliged
for your kind
thought in sending
them —
Yrs Truly
H L Smith Dorrien

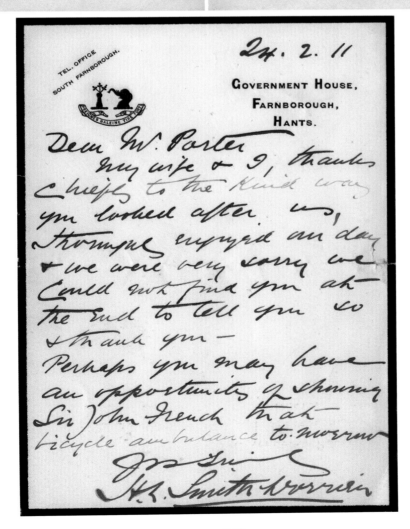

TEL. OFFICE
SOUTH FARNBOROUGH.

24. 2. 11

GOVERNMENT HOUSE,
FARNBOROUGH,
HANTS.

Dear Mr Porter
My wife & I, thanks
chiefly to the kind way
you looked after us,
thoroughly enjoyed our day
& we were very sorry we
could not find you at
the end to tell you so
& thank you —
Perhaps you may have
an opportunity of showing
Sir John French that
bicycle ambulance to-morrow
Yrs Truly
H L Smith Dorrien

343

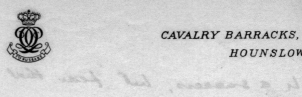

CAVALRY BARRACKS,
HOUNSLOW.

Jan. 28. 1911.
—

John Porter Esq.

Dear Sir

Very many
thanks for your letter. I
can see the meeting will

be a success, but fear that
Sandown will interfere with it
a little, what a pity it
could not have been held earlier
or later —

Yours faithfully.

Dennis N. Kelalenant.

344

4, DEVONSHIRE PLACE,
W.

Feb. 16. 12

Dear Mr Porter

I thank you
for your letter.
I shall be
most happy
to give my name
as patron to the
Westbury United

Service Meeting.
I fear that neither
the Duchess or I
will be able
to attend, as the
meeting takes place
just about the
time the Princess
Royal will be
returning to

England, with
the body of the
late Duke of Fife

Yours sincerely

Teck.

345

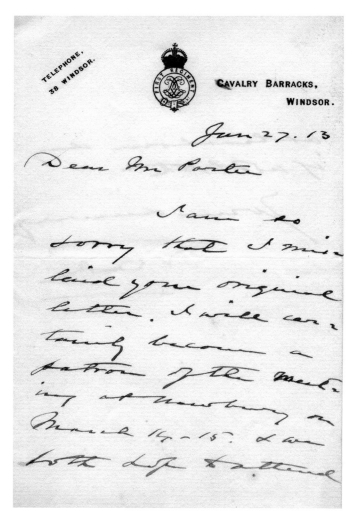

TELEPHONE,
38 WINDSOR.

CAVALRY BARRACKS,
WINDSOR.

Jan 27.13

Dear Mr Porter

I am so
sorry that I mis-
laid your original
letter. I will cer-
tainly become a
patron of the meet-
ing at Newbury on
March 14 - 15. & we
both hope to attend

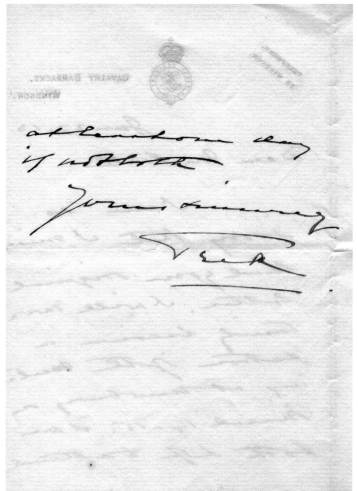

at luncheon day
if not both.

Yours sincerely

Seely

—

inform you that His Royal
Highness will be pleased
to give his patronage
to the United Services Meeting
to be held at Newbury
on February next.

Yrs faithfully
David N. Lord
—

TELEGRAMS, CUMBERLAND LODGE.
TELEPHONE, 20 WINDSOR.

CUMBERLAND LODGE,
WINDSOR.

Dec 27/10.

Dear Sir,

In the absence of the
Equerry-in-Waiting I am
desired by His Royal
Highness Prince Christian
of Schleswig-Holstein to

Ockwells Manor,
Bray,
Berks.

29 December 1910

"The United Services Meeting"

Sir

I have just returned home and before giving a definite reply to yours of the 14th inst would like to hear the names of those who have actually consented to become Patrons of your Meeting which takes place at Newbury on the 24th and 25th of February next.

Yours faithfully
Edward Barry

John Porter Esq
Ormonde House
Newbury

Ockwells Manor,
Bray,
Berks.

21 December 1911

Dr Sir

In reply to your letter of the 11th Inst I beg to state that I shall be pleased to allow my name to be included in the list of Patrons of the "United Services Meeting" as it was last time.

Yours faithfully
Edward Barry

J. Porter Esq
The Newbury Racecourse Company Ld
Ormonde House
Newbury
Berks

Ockwells Manor.
Bray.
Berks.

11 January 1913

Sir

I shall be pleased to allow my name to appear on the list of patrons of the United services steeple Chase Meeting to be held at Newbury on Friday and Saturday March 14th & 15th. Kindly note however that my rank is Lieut Colonel not Lieut General as written at top of your letter.

Yours truly
Edward Barry

John Porter Esq,
Ormonde House
Newbury
Berks

21st December 1911.

The Managing Director,
    Newbury Racecourse Co. Ltd.

Sir,

    With reference to your letter of
the 15th instant, I shall be pleased to
allow my name to appear in the list of
Patrons of "The United Services Meeting"
at Newbury in February.

        Yours very truly,

        HG Miles

Jan 18th 1913

Dear Sir

    I shall be very pleased to allow
my name to continue on the list
of Patrons of the United Services Steeple
chases meeting

        Yours Very Truly
        HG Miles

The Managing Director
Newbury Spring & United Services Meet

19th December 1910

Dear Sir,

In reply to your letter of 14th Instant. I shall have much pleasure in becoming a Patron of the Meeting at Newbury on 24th and 25th February

next, in response to your kind invitation.

Yours truly,

Sr John Grix, Col.

Comd 2nd South Midland Mounted Brigade

3rd January 1902

Dear Mr Porter,

In reply to your letter,
I shall have much pleasure in
your including my name
among the list of Patrons
of "The United Services Meeting"

to be held at Newbury
on 23rd and 24th February
this year.

I shall hope to have the
pleasure of seeing you there
again, as last year.

Yours truly,

Sir John Gore

5, HANS PLACE,
S.W.

13th January 1913

Dear Mr Porter,

Yours of 10th Instant.

It is very kind of you to again propose that I should be a Patron at the United Services Meeting in March.

I think however that you are inviting me still as the Brigadier of the 2nd S. Midland Mounted Brigade, and are not aware that I have finished my four years in that appointment.

Lord Longford has been selected to succeed me, and probably you would wish to invite him to be a Patron, ex officio.

In case you wish to do so his address is :—

"The Earl of Longford K.P.
Comd 2nd South Midland Mounted Brigade,
Lonsdale Road
Oxford "

I wish you every success with your well managed & very pleasant Meeting.

Yours sincerely,

Sr John Gore?

352

14/1/13

Dear Sir,

Sir Charles Douglas
wishes me to say that it
will give him great pleasure
to remain a patron of the
United Service Steeplechase
Meeting on March 14 & 15.

Yrs faithfully

H.M.Pryce-Jones Capt. Pte Sec

TELEGRAMS: STAR HOTEL, WORCESTER.
NATIONAL TELEPHONE: No 203. (2 Lines.)

STAR HOTEL,
WORCESTER.

G. E. SPURR,
PROPRIETOR.

WORCESTER QUARTERS—
ROYAL AUTOMOBILE CLUB.   AUTOMOBILE ASSOCIATION.   MOTOR UNION.
ROAD CLUB.   AUTO CYCLE UNION.

MOTOR GARAGE.

Dec 29th

Dear Mr Porter,

Sir Charles Douglas wishes
me to say that it will give him
great pleasure to become a Patron
of the United Services Race Meeting at
Newbury.

I apologize for this paper!

Yours sincerely

H.M.Pryce-Jones
A.D.C.

F.-M. LORD GRENFELL, 43, BRYANSTON SQUARE, W.

Newbury Races

I shall be very
glad to act as
a Patron &
& support the
meeting as
much as possible
Grenfell

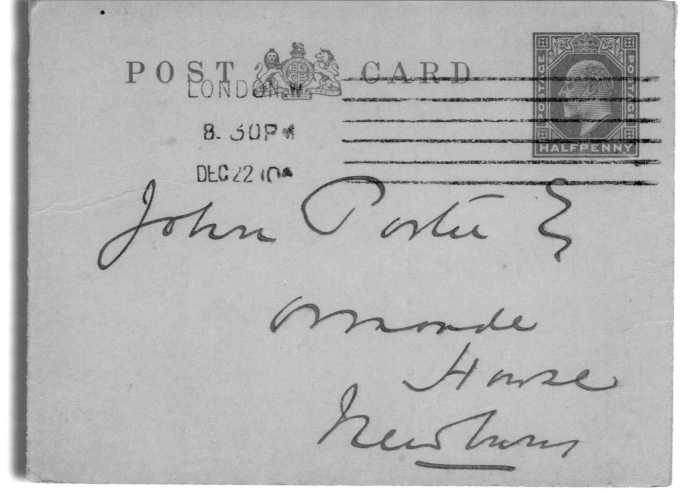

POST CARD

LONDON W

8. 30 PM

DEC 22 10

John Porter Esq

Kingsclere

House

Newbury

The Porter Family

From the archive it has been possible to collate the following detail on the family:-

John Porter was born in Rugeley, Staffordshire. He married twice. His first wife - whom he met and married whilst at Findon, was Emily Jane Moodie, who bore him six children. She died in May 1902, having been ill for some months.

The elder son - John, was unfortunate to lose a leg as a result of a shooting accident whilst they were living at Kingsclere. Apart from one mention of him helping his father transport horses across London prior to the accident, no other mention is made of him.

The younger son - Thomas Barron (Barry) Porter, is mentioned more frequently. He tried to join the Navy, but was clearly unsuccessful. Letters from Admirals Keppel and Stephenson are relevant. He was, however, a sportsman playing football for Ewell and Surrey. He also was a useful cricketer and played in the annual matches arranged between his father and Lloyd H. Baxendale's XI at Kingsclere and Greenham. By trade he became a saddler with his business based in Duke Street, London. In the main he catered for the racing industry. He died aged 76, having suffered for some years with arthritis and heart problems. There is an incomplete letter he wrote to his father from Coburg, dated 21st September 1880, whilst travelling around Germany, Austria and Switzerland which included long walks and some mountaineering.

Alice, the eldest sister, married George Williams, son of Mr George Williams F.R.C.V.S., who was for many years the veterinary surgeon for Queen Victoria and had since 1877 held a similar appointment for H.R.H. Edward, Prince of Wales. George (Jnr) and his younger brother Sidney, continued the practice following their father's death.

Alice and George, who lived in London, always kept very close to Porter on both a family and veterinary level. There are numerous letters in the archive. Alice and George had two daughters – Violet and Kitty. Amongst the archive is a telegram from John Porter at Kingsclere to Kitty on her first birthday. Another letter dated 24th June 1909 refers to Violet enjoying a visit to Olympia to meet the Queen.

Annie was the second daughter and she married Mr G. Gardner Leader – a solicitor. They had a son – Frank, who had a position at the head office of the Great Western Railway in Paddington. This gave John Porter a second line of communication with that company – he already knew Lord Cawdor, who was the Chairman. These connections may well have helped John Porter in getting the Newbury Racecourse Station and the race day trains which he refers to in the chapter on Newbury, that is a reproduction of an article that John Porter wrote for the C.B. Fry magazine, covering the whole of the establishment of Newbury Racecourse.

Nellie was the third daughter. Not much is on record about her, other than she would accompany John Porter to the Newmarket Yearling Sales in June 1909. She stayed with Mrs Jennings – John Porter with Mr Townend.

Mildred was the fourth daughter. She has a mention in a letter from John Porter to George Williams dated 7th July 1893, saying she is "going to a ball at the Bookers' with her sister Nellie".

John Porter and his second wife – Isabel, used to stay with Alice and George and he would call to see them and their daughters when he was in London on other matters.

Letter to George Williams (Jnr) makes reference to George and Alice visiting the stables of Baron Von Hirsch, 2 rue de C. Elysees in July 1893 and John Porter's regret he is not with them.

A letter of 11th June 1913 to Alice saying how busy he is, having taken over the management of Lady James Douglas's Stud, also Mr Waring's stud for Mr Thornycroft, plus his work with Newbury Racecourse, but also saying how he hopes that he and Isabel (2nd wife) will be going to the Grand Prix de Paris and will be staying with the Denmans at St Cloud. The letter is written from Ormonde House, Newbury. From the archive it is obvious that John Porter made regular trips to France and had kept in contact with Robert Denman over the years since they had both departed Rugeley.

A letter of 1st May 1911 from Lugano refers to two days in Paris with Denman and visiting Monsieur Blanc's stud.

John Porter's first wife died at Kingsclere in May 1902, having had considerable ill health for some years. She was buried in Kingsclere church.

John Porter's second wife was Isabel Pilsbury, whom he married in 1903. They had no children. It is clear from many letters in the archive that both wives provided John Porter with great help in welcoming and entertaining both owners and friends. They were both really well liked by all who met them and very supportive with giving lunch to H.R.H. Prince of Wales with his entourage when he visited. The Duke and Duchess of Portland were happy to stay at Kingsclere and reciprocated by having Porter stay with them in Scotland. The Duke and Duchess of Wellington were happy to reciprocate by entertaining them at Strathfield Saye. Both wives were prepared to get involved locally in events that brought Park House and the village of Kingsclere very much together.

The relatively few references to his family in his books and archive letters are indicative of Porter's inclination to separate his private life from his public one. There is however clear evidence of a very close bond within the family. Porter was very much a family man alongside his other diverse interests.

There follows a collection of letters etc., to and from the family. They are not arranged in any particular order but some can be related to the Text above.

OMER COOPER & POVEY,
AUCTIONEERS, SURVEYORS,
VALUERS,
LAND & ESTATE AGENTS.

STEPHEN O. POVEY, P.A.S.I.
C.H. Hickman.

AGENTS TO THE ROYAL INSURANCE COMPANY.

TELEPHONE Nº 430.

ESTABLISHED 1820.

17, BLAGRAVE STREET,

READING......7th.November......19-22

Mrs.John Porter,
    Ormonde House,
      NEWBURY.

Dear Madam,

              re "Dudmore Lodge"

        We thank you for your letter of yesterday's date
and will call upon you to-morrow, Wednesday afternoon at about
3 o'clock which we trust will be convenient to you.

        We are, Dear Madam,

          Yours faithfully,

          Omer Cooper & Povey

---

52 Victoria Rd
Swindon.
24 May.

Dear Nellie,

    I was awfully sorry
to see in the paper the death
of dear Mrs Porter, I was
in hopes she would have
got completely well again.
Please accept my deepest
sympathy in your sad troubles
coming so soon after poor old
John's death too. I trust Mr
Porter is keeping up, please
remember me to him, also to
Mrs Milsom, you must all feel
the loss terribly & I know what
that is; she was always so kind
to everyone it will be a personal
loss to all who knew her.

    I hope Mrs Drake is quite
well, please give her my kind
regards, not forgetting Mr D.

    I am glad at last we have
a glimpse of summer it makes
it quite a treat to be out & gives
one a chance to recover ones
spirits

    With kind regards to all
I remain
Yours sincerely
Oswald Barker

41 Haroldstone Road
Walthamstow
Oct. 7th

Dear Madam,
I have taken the
liberty to write
and tell you I
have removed
from Kingsland Road
to Walthamstow, as
you have been so kind
to think of me —
I hope it will not
make any difference

if you should
have any things
to send
trusting you will
not think it
so liberty

I am Yours Respectfully
M. Moodie

Mother's Aunt or Cousin

Mrs Williams
16 Holbein Place
Sloane Square
S. W. —

358

HOTEL INTERNATIONAL AU LAC LUGANO
Riedweg & Disler, A.G.

Hotel Victoria Luzern   ✤   Hotel Rütli Luzern

Lugano, May 1st 1911

Dear George

We are here after spending
two days in Paris, we spent Sunday with
Denman and saw Le Blanc' stud. he has
a very nice House in Lord Bergquer and some
real good looking two year old colts by Adam
we go back there about the 9th from here
We go to Como then to Luzerno. Stresa.
Montreux. Lausanne. Geneva. Neuchâtel
La Chaux de Fonds. Berne and Paris we hope
to be back in London on the 11th or 12th and
home on the 15th. the scenery is wonderful
everything looking at its best, the fruit trees
are in full bloom and are scattered about

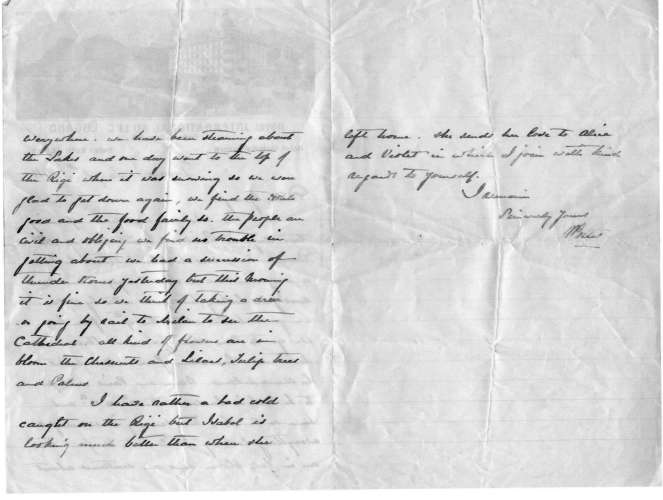

everywhere. we have been steaming about
the Lakes and one day went to the top of
the Rigi when it was snowing so we were
glad to get down again, we find the Hotels
good and the food fairly so. the people are
civil and obliging we find no trouble in
getting about we had a succession of
thunder storms yesterday but this morning
it is fine so we think of taking a drive
or going by rail to Italan to see the
Cathedral all kind of flowers are in
bloom the Chestnuts and Lilacs, Tulip trees
and Palms

    I have rather a bad cold
caught on the Rigi but Isabel is
looking much better than when she

left home. She sends her love to Alice
and Violet in which I join with kind
regards to yourself.

    I remain

    Sincerely Yours

    Walter

Strattons,
Newbury.

Sunday

My dear Aline

Thanks very much for the Plasman Biscuits they are very good I shall take them on with me to Llandrindod when I go on Wednesday, my address there will be.

Ye Wells Hotel

I hope the change may do me good, I have certainly felt better this last day or two, and have fed better.

The Races went off well, I sent you some tickets did you get them?

With love to you all in which Isabel joins

Your aff Father

Porter

Mrs Williams
15 Holbein Place
Sloane Square
London S. W.

Donnington

March 1st 1901.

My dear Grandpa.

I am writing to wish you very happy returns of your birth day, as you told me I was a month too early last time I

From,
Frank Gardner Leader.
X X XX X X X X X X

wrote. I hope you will spend a happy day tomorrow and many many more happy birthdays

I went for a walk on Snelsmore yesterday with Rex, Estie and Jack Clark.

With fond love and kisses to Grandma and yourself.

Emily Alice Porter.

With
Mr. & Mrs. George Harry Williams.
Kind regards.

15. Holbein Place.
Sloane Square.
Chelsea.
London. s.w.   18th Jan.y 1893.

George Harry Williams.

Ada M. East

With
Mr. & Mrs. F. Gardner Leader's
Compliments.

"BELVEDERE."
OTTERFIELD ROAD,
YIEWSLEY.   DECEMBER 1ST, 1928.

Francis Gardner Leader

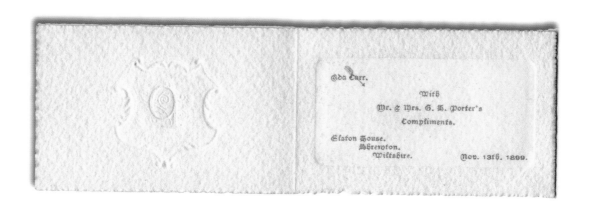

Ada Carr.

With
Mr. & Mrs. G. H. Porter's
Compliments.

Elston House.
Shrewton.
Wiltshire.   Nov. 13th. 1899.

Strattons,
Newbury.

May 30th 1905

Dear George

I shall come up
on Wednesday morning by
the train arriving at Paddington
10.10 I shall then take the
train to Sloane Square Station
we can go down together to
see the Derby.

Love to all
Sincerely Yours
WPorter

Kingsclere
March 20th 1901

Dear George

I am sorry to
hear Alice has again
got a cold, this weather
is enough to kill
any one. Six inches
of snow on the down
this morning, yesterday
a blizzard.

I have nothing for sale
just now that would do
for a Stallion to send
to New Zealand but I
will be on the look out
for you.

"Simon Dale" has sprained
his hind fetlock slipped
up a been cast in his
box, he is very lame
on it.

The Duke & Duchess of
Westminster here yesterday,
this afternoon the
Duke of Portland is coming
to stop the night.

With love to all
I am
Yours Sincerely
WPorter

363

Strattons,
Newbury.
July 31st 1904

Dear Alice

I am sorry to hear that
George is unwell, I am a
little better and leave in the
morning for Ye Wells Hotel
Llandrindod
Wales

Many thanks for the Biscuits
I shall take them with me
With love to all
I remain
Your aff Father
W Porter

Newmarket
Oct 17th 1901

Dear Alice

I have to call
on Mr Faber as I pass
through tomorrow evening
if I have time I shall
call on you also on my
way to the Station.
I remain
Your aff Father
W Porter

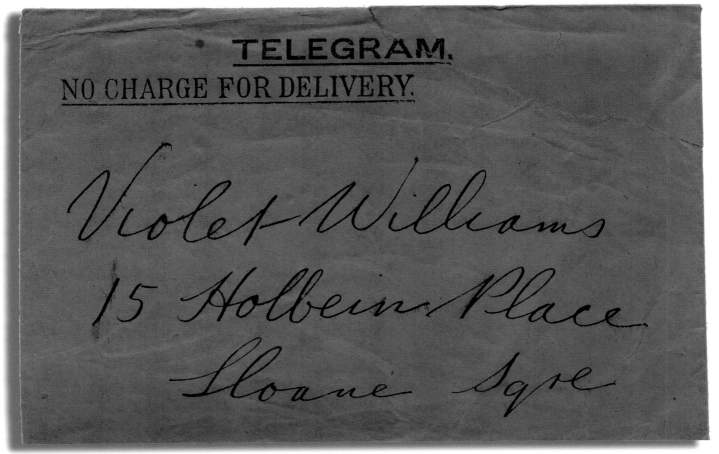

POST OFFICE TELEGRAPHS.

No. of Telegram.....................

Office Stamp.

If the accuracy of an Inland Telegram be doubted, the telegram will be repeated on payment of half the amount originally paid for its transmission, any fraction of 1d. less than ½d. being reckoned as ½d.; and if it be found that there was any inaccuracy, the amount paid for repetition will be refunded. Special conditions are applicable to the repetition of Foreign Telegrams.

EYRE & SPOTTISWOODE, London.

£ s. d.

Charges to pay

Handed in at the *Kings Cross* Office at .M. Received here at 8 46 .M.

TO { *Violet Williams 15 Holbein Place Sloane Sqre Lon*

All wish you many Happy returns of the day Porter

Violet's 1st telegram upon 1st birthday

N.B.—This Form must accompany any inquiry made respecting this Telegram.

TELEGRAM.

NO CHARGE FOR DELIVERY.

*Violet Williams
15 Holbein Place
Sloane Sqre*

365

Paddington
11. 5 Monday

June 24 1909

My dear Alice

I was pleased to receive your letter this morning, I hope you are now quite well. I am not very much better for my visit to Harrogate I still have the severe pains in my shoulder and

arm. I am now going to make a start with electricity to see what that will do. I am sorry to hear Barrie is unwell. I think he ought to go to a specialist with his foot.

We had two good days racing but the weather was bad. cold

and wet.

I go to Newmarket on Monday to see the sales of the yearlings. Nell goes also she will stay with Mrs Jennings I stay with Mr Townsend at Fordham.

Violet would enjoy her visit to Olympia to meet the Queen.

I had a hour and a half with the King on Saturday I went to lunch with Sir Frederick at the Watch and the King came over at 11 – 30 and stayed until 1 o'clock,

Isabel is well and joins with me in love to you all.

I remain
Your aff Father
W Portes

G. Williams Esq[re]
15 Holbein Place
Sloane Square
London. S.W.

NEWBURY
23 DE[C]
17

2.15 PM
27 DEC 17

W. Williams
15 Holbein Place
Sloane Square
London
S.W. 1.

Not Holbein House

Received
Dec 27th

my every way came out first in every
class

Nell joins with me in love and
best wishes to you all and to tell
you she will write another time

Yours Affectionately
Mum

29 Brunnington Square
Dec 21st 1917

Dear Alice

I have been wanting to write
for several days to thank you for kindly
writing to me I do not write much myself but
I got better today, shall be very pleased
if I continue doing so, we so often talk
about you all and the traveller inside &
we hope you will spend as comfortable
& happy quiet Xmas. I do not think I shall

be well enough to go across to Ormside
home if I shall spend a very quiet
day only the maid and self Will and
Charlie will spend it with your father
and Mrs P. What a change from what
it used to be. Aunt Porter is coming
here tomorrow Saturday to stay until
Monday on her way to spend Xmas
with her brother Tom

Mildred tells us that Dolph was likely
to get an appointment at the Electric
Works near you will just called here
yesterday with only Dolly as Marjorie is
not very well and did not return to school last
week, she only stayed a minute or two &
was so clever and told us she was anxious

to get home, Mrs Porter and Eddie Hope
was here to tea yesterday Ted was home
from France for a few days last
week

Annie has been up to see us very
often lately I think her little dog brings her
out more I am very glad to see her
good she did not come yesterday Mrs
P told us he was in bed again with
a chill he had the same last week
your father went to London to a
directors meeting last Monday Mrs P went
with him she went to see Jean and
her sister Mrs James whose children
she tells us were very handsome & her
sister Mrs Hartis boy has improved himself

368

Gordon House
Rugeley
Nov 15/94

My dear little darling

I wish you very many happy
returnes of your birth day and
I trust you will live to see
a great many more. I have
sent you a little dolly but

will if I live to see another
of your birth days to send
you a nicer one God bless
you   from your ever loving
Great grand mama

A Porter

369

Kitty

Kitty

– 6 yrs old.

1891.

Kingsclere
Apr 4ᵗʰ 1900

Dear George

The Bend Or filly
fell down this morning
and has cut her knees
badly. I should like
you to see her.
Love to all
Yours Sincerely
Porter

Windsor Castle.

6 Egramont
Place
Worthing
August 23rd 1879

Dear Alice
    I have received the
sketch and am very pleased
with it and I am much
obliged to you for it. I hope
you are all quite well as it
leaves me at present pretty
well. Worthing is very full
of people but the weather
is very bad So now I must
conclude with kind love
to all and receive the same
yourself from yours truly
    Mary Skinner

Ormonde House,
Newbury.
June 16 1911

Dear Alice
    The King has sent
me two tickets for the Coronation
the Royal Household Stand near
Buckingham Palace, we have
to take our places early in the
morning before any train can
arrive from Newbury could
you put Isabel and I up
for the night, I am afraid
there will be no getting into
an Hotel on Wednesday night

We should come up in the
afternoon of Wednesday
    With love to all
      I remain
    Your aff Father

I am just off to Ascot

371

Kingsclere
Sunday

My dear Alice

Tell George I
can take the Man
or lad whichever he
is. he can come as
soon as he likes, I
hope Mr William has
quite recovered give
my kind regards to
Mr. Mead and

all the rest of the family.

Your nephew grows
and improves wonderfully
thanks to the Country
Air

All are well
and send love.

I rem

Your aff dad
Porter

Miss Alice Porter
77 Warwick Square
London . S. W.

NEWBURY
A
JY 3
92

which my wife joins
I am
Very faithfully Yours
M Lawson

pro James Rose

Melton House,
Exning.

June 19th 1894

Dear Madam,

I am ashamed at
having been so long in
answering your letter, but
I am an invalid and
have been overwhelmed ~~in~~
with correspondence, which
please to accept as my
excuse. I now send you
a piece of Sada's mane
as you requested.

With kind regards and
very best wishes in

373

Mrs Williams
"Park House"
~~15 Holbein Place~~
~~Sloane Square~~
London S.W.

Feby 7th/93

Dear George

I am glad to hear you are enjoying yourselves, am sorry I am unable to be with you in Paris but it is impossible to get away just now. I have to meet Baron Hirsch in London tomorrow Wednesday. mind you go and see his Stables. 2 Rue de l. Elysée they are worth looking at. I expect we shall be in London to meet you on your return, all the presents have been sent up with the exception of the silver and jewelry. Hardman has been up for a week putting things to rights. so I hope you will find all things in order. Nellie and Mildred go to the Barkers tomorrow to a ball. Marion is still here and behaving herself very well,

Ma is laid up with a bilious attack but hope she may be alright in a day or two.

With love from all.

I am
Sincerely your
W Porter

375

Ormonde House,
Newbury.

June 11ᵒ 1913

My dear Alice

I did not go to the
flower show for I have been
so busy lately, I have taken
over the management of
Lady James Douglas's stud
and have now taken Mr Waring's
Stud Farm for Mr Thornycroft
and the management of his
Stud, so with the Race Course

and the race horses of Mr Sutton
I have plenty to do. neither
Mabel or I have been away
but we intend going to Paris
to see the Grand Prix we shall
stay with Mr Denman at
St Cloud. and be away about
a week.

I hope you are all well
has Violet finished with School.
Love to all
I remain
Your aff Father
W Porter

Mrs Williams
15 Holbein Place
Sloane Square
London. S. W

376

Ormonde House,
Newbury.

June 24ᵗʰ 1913

Dear Alice

All being well
Isabel and I leave Victoria
for Paris 11 a.m on Friday
perhaps we may see some
of you at the Station
With love to all
I am
Your aff Father
Worts

PARK HOUSE.
KINGSCLERE.

Nov 11ᵗʰ/99

Dear George

Can you come to
Kingsclere on Tuesday to
examine a Mare for
insurance and afterwards
go on to Mr Swanwick's
at Cirencester he wants
you to see that Colt again.
Bring some of that
cough mixture to put on

---

the horses tongues.
We are off Isa and I
to Leamington this afternoon
to attend the Wedding shall
be home Monday night.
With love to Alice
and Violet. I am
nearly allright again,
Mildred better
Sincerely Yours
Worts

July 17th 1906

My dear Alice

I am afraid there will
be no chance of my getting round
to you to lunch, I have an
appointment with Dr. Goodhart
at 1.30, but I go down
from Paddington by the 5 o'clock
train, I hope to see you there.

I have been a little better
this last two days but am still
off my feed, and have bad dreams

I forgot to say I return on Friday

at night.

It is very nice here and
every one very kind, John Turnocks
House is at the end of the road
where I went to School for
7 years, where his house stands
was the boundary of our old
play ground, so that it makes
one think of old times and old
playfellows now I am sorry to
say all dead and gone,

It is delightful walking on the
Chase the Bilberries are ripe and
the Heather and Fern looking
beautiful.

Mrs Turnock and all the
others send love to you. with
love from self to Violet, George,
and Self.

I remain

Your aff Father
W Orton

378

PARK HOUSE,
KINGSCLERE.

Sunday

Dear George

I enclose cheque
for £50 for Ritchies Cob
send him down by the
11 - 45 train on Tuesday
I will send the little
Bay Mare up by the
11 - 40 from Overton
same day, if you

will send to meet her
at Waterloo. if you
cant sell her for me
Put her in at Tattersalls.

Let me know as
soon as you can what
you decide about Alice
and yourself staying with
us at Ascot,

With love to all.

I am
Sincerely Yours

Porter

Write Pethin or whatever
his name is in Cornwall
and tell him not to
trouble about getting one
for me now I have bought
Ritchies

My dear Father —

We arrived here
this morning at 7 AM —
after having been away
21 days — I received your
letter at Basle and Dr K—
has given me the money,
thanks very much for it;
but it was very late before
we got there so I did not
write from there — I wrote a
letter before I started to Sed
with all the addresses in it
and gave it to a fellow to post
but the fool left it in one of
my draws where I found it
this morning —

We have had a
pretty good tour (plenty of rain)
I am rather disappointed
with Switzerland, I think it
is considerably over rated, However
I don't think I have been to the
best parts — We started on Wednesday
the 1st of Sept and went as far as
Munich stayed there until Saturday
morning. Saw any amount of Churches
and a splendid Palace, very pretty
town — on Saturday railed to
Mernau and walked to Ettal
small place 3 Pubs and a swell
Monastry, with bones of many
Saints in their jewelled cloths
worth no end — slept with my
clothes on and fleas (beds damp)
Sunday walked 5 miles into Ober
ammagau got there at 7 AM fed, went
to the Passion Play house, curtain
was raised at 8 AM. Sun came out
awfully hot nearly got roasted, singing
beautiful — Man that acts Christ lay on
the best is not made up at all, has his
own beard hangs 25 minutes on the
cross — Play lasted until 5 PM, with
an hour to feed most wonderful play
in the world — drove to Garmish had
awful thunderstorm in the mountains—
Mond. drove to Lermoos (in Austrian Tyrol)
and walked through the "Fermer Pass" to
Inst (in the valley of the Inns) 22 miles—
Tues walked all day had some rain slept
at "Umhousen" 13 miles. Weds walked to
Solden bad weather 2 g miles — Thurs mist
rain and mud walked along a pretty
but difficult road on mountain sides
with a glacier stream below about 4000 ft
until 12 oc fed walked with a guide for
5 hours up a mountain to the "Hoch Joch
Glacier" at the commencement of
which we slept the rooms held 3 they
were 5 ft wide 8 long house made wood
awfully cold (8000 ft high) wet through
could not get our clothes dry — had several
mountain torrents that day — Friday
6.30 started to cross the "Hoch Joch Glacier"
one of the highest in Europe (10090 fts)
awfully cold 5 degs below O (French)
found the ice very slipery and steep
K— fell and cut his hand so hung on to the
guide for 1st 5 minutes all fell about like
nine pins soon got on rougher ice and
could travel inclined a sketch of the place
got to — on all in & slept 5 in a room
lost 2 fellows, another fellow and I went
back 4 miles to find them after that walking—
through the valley de la digue — after that
walked saturday, sunday, monday
through the Finaler pass to clothes, tuesday
got to Landquart — through the valley of
the Rhine — Weds took train for Zurich —
got there at 12 — dined — went on the Lake
and enjoyed our selves, left Friday
morning for Basle got your letter —
only stayed there 4 hours — arrived at
Freiburg saturday night stayed sunday
wonderful fort there in the cathedral
bones of saints carried all round the
trondillo with a bit of the small
cross — left Monday morning and
arrived here tuesday at 7 AM
very cold very hungry —

The Sporting Times.
Otherwise known as "THE PINK 'UN."

TELEPHONE:
802 CENTRAL.

97, ~~Fleet Street~~
~~London,~~

110 DEWEY STREET
TOOTING LONDON
Mar 6. 19 5m

Dear John

Herewith the little birthday souvenir I promised you. It is all "home made" and rather rough; the best I could do under the circumstances

With kind regards, and best wishes to you & yours

Very sincerely yours

Arthur Fitzgerald

Some Favourite Kingsclere Colours

A HAPPY
NEW YEAR 1906

With Mr & Mrs Arthur Fitzgerick, Best Wishes for the New Year 1906
6 Hazlebourne Rd, Balham Hill, S.W.

Sources of Information.

Kingsclere by John Porter.

John Porter of Kingsclere by John Porter and Edward Moorhouse.

Men and Horses I Have Known by George Lambton.

Admiral Rous and the English Turf by T.H .Bird.

C.B.Fry's Magazine.

Bertie – A Life of Edward V11 by Jane Ridley.

Edward V11 and His Jewish Court by Anthony Alfrey.

The Archive of Letters and Documents.

Besides the above, information and anecdotes have been gathered from many sources over a period of time.